Merleau-Ponty and the Essence of Nature

New Perspectives in Ontology
Series Editors: Peter Gratton, Southeastern Louisiana University, and Sean J. McGrath, Memorial University of Newfoundland, Canada

Publishes the best new work on the question of being and the history of metaphysics

After the linguistic and structuralist turn of the twentieth century, a renaissance in metaphysics and ontology is occurring. Following in the wake of speculative realism and new materialism, this series aims to build on this renewed interest in perennial metaphysical questions, while opening up avenues of investigation long assumed to be closed. Working within the Continental tradition without being confined by it, the books in this series will move beyond the linguistic turn and rethink the oldest questions in a contemporary context. They will challenge old prejudices while drawing upon the speculative turn in post-Heideggerian ontology, the philosophy of nature and the philosophy of religion.

Editorial Advisory Board
Maurizio Farraris, Paul Franks, Iain Hamilton Grant, Garth Green, Adrian Johnston, Catherine Malabou, Jeff Malpas, Marie-Eve Morin, Jeffrey Reid, Susan Ruddick, Michael Schulz, Hasana Sharp, Alison Stone, Peter Trawny, Uwe Voigt, Jason Wirth, Günter Zöller

Books available
The Political Theology of Schelling, Saitya Brata Das
Continental Realism and its Discontents, edited by Marie-Eve Morin
The Contingency of Necessity: Reason and God as Matters of Fact, Tyler Tritten
The Problem of Nature in Hegel's Final System, Wes Furlotte
Schelling's Naturalism: Motion, Space and the Volition of Thought, Ben Woodard
Thinking Nature: An Essay in Negative Ecology, Sean J. McGrath
Heidegger's Ontology of Events, James Bahoh
The Political Theology of Kierkegaard, Saitya Brata Das
The Schelling–Eschenmayer Controversy, 1801: Nature and Identity, Benjamin Berger and Daniel Whistler
Hölderlin's Philosophy of Nature, edited by Rochelle Tobias
Affect and Attention After Deleuze and Whitehead: Ecological Attunement, Russell J. Duvernoy
The Philosophical Foundations of the Late Schelling: The Turn to the Positive, Sean J. McGrath
Schelling's Ontology of Powers, Charlotte Alderwick
Collected Essays in Speculative Philosophy, by James Bradley and edited by Sean J. McGrath
Merleau-Ponty and Nancy on Sense and Being: At the Limits of Phenomenology, Marie-Eve Morin
Predication and Genesis: Metaphysics as Fundamental Heuristic after Schelling's The Ages of the World, Wolfram Hogrebe, translated and edited by Iain Hamilton Grant and Jason M. Wirth
Merleau-Ponty and the Essence of Nature: A Return to Elemental Symbolism, Taylor Knight

www.edinburghuniversitypress.com/series/epnpio

Merleau-Ponty and the Essence of Nature

A Return to Elemental Symbolism

TAYLOR KNIGHT

Edinburgh University Press is one of the leading university presses in the UK. We publish academic books and journals in our selected subject areas across the humanities and social sciences, combining cutting-edge scholarship with high editorial and production values to produce academic works of lasting importance. For more information visit our website: edinburghuniversitypress.com

© Taylor Knight, 2024, 2026

Edinburgh University Press Ltd
13 Infirmary Street
Edinburgh EH1 1LT

First published in hardback by Edinburgh University Press 2024

Typeset in 11/13 Adobe Garamond
by Cheshire Typesetting Ltd, Cuddington, Cheshire, and
printed and bound by CPI Group (UK) Ltd,
Croydon, CR0 4YY

A CIP record for this book is available from the British Library

ISBN 978 1 3995 2989 1 (hardback)
ISBN 978 1 3995 2990 7 (paperback)
ISBN 978 1 3995 2991 4 (webready PDF)
ISBN 978 1 3995 2992 1 (epub)

The right of Taylor Knight to be identified as the author of this work has been asserted in accordance with the Copyright, Designs and Patents Act 1988, and the Copyright and Related Rights Regulations 2003 (SI No. 2498).

Contents

Foreword　　viii
Acknowledgements　　xi
List of Abbreviations　　xii

Introduction: The Return to the Element　　1
 1. The warp and woof of a moment　　1
 2. From Socrates to Plato and back　　2
 3. Flesh as element: From Sartre to Bachelard　　8
 4. Elemental powers and the remains of nature　　9
 5. The injection of the elemental into phenomenology　　11
 6. 'Germ of the endangered world': The ark of existence　　13
 7. Embodied by forgetting: The other side of the light　　16
 8. Aquatic (non)being in the perceptual cosmogony　　19
 9. A Merleau-Pontian itinerary　　22

1　The Powers of Becoming: Early Greek Thought and Contemporary Biology in Merleau-Ponty's Elemental Ontology　　28
 1. Ionian physis and modern nature　　31
 2. From Gestalt to element　　36
 3. Element as metastable form　　39
 4. Endogenous development as elemental emergence　　41
 5. From Sartre to Heraclitus　　46
 6. The mirror of nature　　50

2　The Correlation of Sensation: From Act to Power　　60
 1. Correlation as act: The soul　　62

		2. Correlation as power: The flesh	65
		3. Finality and flesh: Aristotle in Merleau-Ponty's nature course	70
3	The Elemental Bond: Surpassing Phenomenological Atomism		78
		1. 'Les petits êtres sauvages': The things reconstituted	80
		2. 'Seeing as': Return to the things themselves	82
		3. 'Seeing from': Return to the elements themselves	86
		4. 'Données brutes' and 'être brut': The elemental turn	92
4	Cosmogonic Elementals in Phenomenology: From Husserl and Heidegger to Levinas and Merleau-Ponty		98
		1. Phenomenology and cosmogony	99
		2. The marriage of earth and sky: Heidegger and the horizon of manifestation	103
		3. The nocturns of existence: Levinas and the absence of horizon	107
		4. 'La mer, la mer, toujours recommencée': Merleau-Ponty and the aquatic milieu	110
		5. 'For water to become earth is to die': Ontogenesis as the desiccation of being	113
		6. Primordial depths and the latency of being	116
5	The Savagery of the Symbol: The Barbarian Principle and Elemental Negation		124
		1. Symbol as Naturphilosophie concept	128
		2. Symbolic replication and the birth of the gods	132
		3. Nature against correlation	136
		4. Unmotivated upsurge: The freedom of nature and the primordial negation	140
		5. The interiority of nature: From representation to repetition	146
		6. Symbol and barbarian principle	148
6	Symbolics of the Flesh: From Tautegory to Chiasm		156
		1. Sharing the visible world: Vision as paradigm of chiasm	158
		2. Plunging perception into the elemental past: Time as paradigm of chiasm	160
		3. From collision to sensation: Symbol as chiastic relation	164
		4. The radically incomplete: Symbol and relationship	169
		5. Contaminated by nature: Symbolic repetition and viral replication	172

7 What the Sea Left Behind: The Element as the Unconscious 185
   1. A divergence and a meeting point: Freud and Schelling on the unconscious 186
   2. Year zero: Two new philosophies of consciousness 189
   3. 'Perception is the true unconscious' (1): Unconscious as body memory 192
   4. 'Perception is the true unconscious' (2): Unconscious as perceptual link 195
   5. Symbol as 'most true to perception' 197
   6. Drive and instinct: Symbolism in the human and the animal 200
   7. The meaning of symbol in Merleau-Ponty's analysis of instinct 203
   8. 'Symbol is the true unconscious': The irrational and the ambiguous 206

Conclusion: The Dream of Nature 217

Works Cited 220
Index 228

Foreword

No author can be read in isolation from his or her context. While this is true of every philosopher, it is particularly true of Maurice Merleau-Ponty. The sudden death of the author of *The Phenomenology of Perception* in May 1961 was a trauma not only for phenomenology, but also for philosophy more broadly and for culture in general because 'Merleau', as Jean-Paul Sartre familiarly called him, left behind a body of work 'in motion', suddenly suspended. All we can do is to draw out the consequences, and imagine what would have followed, as Taylor Knight indicates in the opening of *Merleau-Ponty and the Essence of Nature*. An unfinished work at least has the merit of preventing its followers from being trapped in a definitively closed system. This, then, is the task the author sets himself here: opening up passageways through a detailed analysis that makes the late Merleau-Ponty the true precursor of our modernity.

When Taylor Knight's work was first completed (as a doctoral dissertation), I was at once a witness and an astonished spectator. The work was as remarkable in its intention as it was precise in its execution. A 'new face of Maurice Merleau-Ponty' had been brought to light. This was very welcome indeed. Those who make the most noise rarely accomplish the most. The reserved character of the author of this book signals that he is a philosopher who knows how to deepen the work of thought, and who won't give up its rigour simply to express himself or to resolve its complications too easily. After all, there are those who see, and those who don't. Taylor Knight is one of the former, one who lets texts speak to him, just as much as he knows how to make them speak. We can say of him what Hans-Georg Gadamer said of Martin Heidegger, which is not small praise: 'His path through the history of philosophy resembles nothing so much as the wanderings of a prospector with a divining rod: suddenly the rod dips and he makes a find.'[1]

And what, precisely, has Taylor Knight found in acutely and rigorously reading the totality of Maurice Merleau-Ponty's oeuvre? Certainly, a dialogue with the whole history of philosophy that goes far beyond phenomenology (Freud, Schelling, Bachelard, Bataille, etc.), but also a movement of increasing radicalisation that tests the limits of phenomenology itself, not so much to break out of it as to interrogate it in a different way. The 'elemental' of the pre-Socratics – that is, the four roots of Empedocles (water, earth, fire, air) – progressively becomes the model from which we must think. For there is something unspeakable at the heart of phenomenality, and this is what needs to be reached if we are to move beyond mere manifestation (phenomenology) and pure interpretation (hermeneutics). Merleau-Ponty gets to the depths, or seeks to get to the depths, of what we are, that is, the 'element of the flesh' in which we move: 'Just as *the mixture of the flesh* wanders at its extremities', Parmenides has already written, 'so thought manifests in the human being. For the wandering limbs are the same as what thinks in human beings – *the fulfillment of the flesh* both for all together and in each individually. For it is the fullness through which thought is constituted.'[2]

Thus it is necessary to go back to the origin: to the roots of a 'Nature' that we have forgotten, not just to poetise it or even dwell there (Heidegger), but to let the 'common texture' of which we are made emerge. There is no doubt a chaos within the human person, just as there is chaos in the universe. There is certainly a 'barbaric principle' (Schelling) and a 'sphere of the unconscious' (Freud) below all thought. But in this descent into the abyss, the ark of the flesh functions like Noah's ark, leaving neither defeatism nor pessimism the last word on what is to be hoped for. The message is clear, as Taylor Knight has drawn out perfectly. If, for Merleau-Ponty, there is an 'Essence of Nature', it does not consist in an ethereal world, but in our shared rootedness in the earth. In the 'zoo of French phenomenologists', as the author aptly notes, Merleau-Ponty belongs to a forgotten breed that dwells on the frontiers of phenomenality. Perhaps this is precisely what we should be looking for today:

---

[1] Hans-Georg Gadamer and Karen Campbell, 'Heidegger and the History of Philosophy', *The Monist* 64.4 (1981): 440.

[2] Parmenides, *Fragment 16*, used as the epigraph (in Greek) for Didier Franck's *Chair et corps: Essai sur la phénoménologie de Husserl*, Paris: Minuit, 1981. The English here is inspired by Franck's loose but well-defended French translation at p. 137 n17, particularly the 'mélange de la chair' or 'mixture of the flesh' (*krasin meleôn*) and 'épanouissement de la chair' or 'fulfillment of the flesh' (*meleon phusis*).

'This earth is an *ark*: bearer of the possibility of all being above the nothingness, above the flood – the seed of the endangered world from which everything blossoms again.'³

Emmanuel Falque
Paris, 1 November 2023

---

³ M. Merleau-Ponty, 'La philosophie et le problème de la passivité', in *L'institution, la passivité, Notes de cours au Collège de France (1954–1955)* (Paris: Belin, 2003 (édition de poche, 2015)), 223.

Acknowledgements

This book, first written for a doctoral degree at the Institut Catholique de Paris, would not have been possible without the financial support of La fondation catholique anglaise and La fondation catholique écossaise. I would like to thank Emmanuel Falque for directing the thesis, and for the stimulating and challenging comments of Emmanuel de Saint Aubert, Étienne Bimbenet, Paula Lorelle, William Connelly, John Milbank, Leonard Lawlor, as well as the editors who have worked closely with me throughout the publication process, Carol Macdonald, Sarah Foyle and Sean McGrath. I am also grateful for the many others who have accompanied me along the way, colleagues from the Collegium Phaenomenologicum and the International Network in Philosophy of Religion among other philosophical wayfarers who have influenced my thinking in often non-quantifiable ways, not least of which through the ever-unexpected gift of friendship. I would also like to thank my parents (*sine qua non*).

Abbreviations

Maurice Merleau-Ponty – frequently cited texts (with abbreviations)

English pagination follows the French. The absence of English pagination for some of these texts is a consequence of writing an English language book in Paris, where English translations are not always accessible. The translations are generally my own, except in the case of *The Visible and the Invisible*, which has only been very rarely modified from the translation of Alphonso Lingis.

IP — *L'institution – La passivité: Notes de cours au Collège de France (1954–5)*. Paris: Éditions Belin, 2003. [*Institution and Passivity: Course Notes from the Collège de France (1954–1955)*. Foreword by Claude Lefort. Translated by Leonard Lawlor and Heath Massey. Evanston, IL: Northwestern University Press, 2010.]

N — *La Nature: Notes de cours du Collège de France*. Edited with notes by Dominique Séglard. Paris: Seuil, 1995.

NC — *Notes de cours au Collège de France 1958–1959 et 1960–1961*. Edited by Stéphanie Ménasé with a preface by Claude Lefort. Paris: Gallimard, 1996.

OE — *L'oeil et l'esprit*. Paris: Gallimard, 1964.

P2 — *Parcours deux, 1951–1961*. Edited by Jacques Prunair. Lagrasse: Verdier, 2000.

PM — *La prose du monde*. Paris: Gallimard, 1969. [*The Prose of the World*. Edited by Claude Lefort. Translated by John O'Neill. Evanston, IL: Northwestern University Press, 1973.]

PP — *La phénoménologie de la perception.* Paris: Gallimard, 1945. [*Phenomenology of Perception.* Translated by Colin Smith. London: Routledge, 1962.]

S — *Signes.* Paris: Gallimard, 1960. [*Signs.* Translated with an introduction by Richard S. McCleary. Evanston, IL: Northwestern University Press, 1964.]

SC — *La structure du comportement.* Paris: Presses Universitaires de France, 1942. [*The Structure of Behavior.* Translated by Alden L. Fisher. Foreword by John Wild. Boston: Beacon Press, 1963.]

SN — *Sens et non-sens.* 1948. Paris: Gallimard, 1996. [*Sense and Non-Sense.* Translated with a preface by Hubert Dreyfus and Patricia Allen Dreyfus. Evanston, IL: Northwestern University Press, 1964.]

VI — *Le visible et l' invisible.* Followed by working notes. Edited with a foreword and afterword by Claude Lefort. Paris: Gallimard, 1964. [*The Visible and the Invisible, followed by Working Notes.* Edited by Claude Lefort. Translated by Alphonso Lingis. Evanston, IL: Northwestern University Press, 1968.]

Introduction

The Return to the Element

1. The warp and woof of a moment

1961. A field-altering year for philosophy in France. A year that changed the history of phenomenology because of a certain crossing, 'a chiasm', we might call it – an event intersecting with a negation, an addition confronting, but not cancelling, a subtraction. There was the event itself: the defence and publication of Levinas's HDR[1] thesis, *Totality and Infinity*, paving the way for the 'theological turn' in French phenomenology.[2] Already a well-known philosopher, Levinas here introduced into phenomenology the thought of alterity, of excess and of the Wholly Other,[3] whose ripple effect would be magnified in the following generation of French phenomenology. Thematised under the mode of gift, of revelation, of the Word, the Levinasian Other reversed Husserlian intentionality with counter-intentionality, thereby challenging the transcendental limits imposed on phenomenality through its residual Kantianism. Yet as this philosophy of alterity burst onto the scene, another new beginning was fading into oblivion.

On 3 May 1961, Maurice Merleau-Ponty died of cardiac arrest at the age of fifty-three, just a month before he was to serve as a jury member in Levinas's thesis defence. What Merleau-Ponty would have said to Levinas and what dialogue might have ensued is only a small part of the absence that his untimely death has left us to abide within.[4] Two phenomenologists who had up to this point paid scant attention the one to the other, the essential loss is nevertheless not what Merleau-Ponty would have said to Levinas, but what more might he have said to us. In what ways would his late thought, having had the time to ripen to maturity, have echoed in the ensuing development of the phenomenological tradition, a tradition that became very Levinasian, not only on the side of the theological turn, but also through Levinas's enormous influence on Derrida? Although Levinas's thinking of alterity became foundational in its inversion of Husserlian intentionality, Merleau-Ponty was beginning to set another challenge to the limits of phenomenology, a challenge completely different from the one Levinas initiated. But the new ontology that he had only just begun to develop remains a fragment. *The Visible and the Invisible*, our primary source for comprehending this new ontology, is a draft, compiled posthumously. The ever-expanding body of secondary literature has not lessened its fragmentary nature.

The more famous May events seven years later, May 68, created a great deal more hubbub than Merleau-Ponty's quiet passing one evening at his desk as he read Descartes's *Dioptrics*. Yet despite all the clamour, 68 announced nothing new – no new fissures that were not already there in 1961. The events of May 68 simply wrenched open certain fault lines in French culture (and in our case within French philosophy), fault lines that had already begun to widen. Phenomenology began to be conceived as a philosophy of the old guard, while the soixante-huitards took up under the banner of Sartre, Deleuze, Foucault and Derrida who sallied forth in a new direction. As Sartre's influence wanes in the English-speaking reception of French thought, Merleau-Ponty remains the lone French phenomenologist studied by non-religious[5] Continental philosophers, philosophers who are typically drawn to Deleuze, Foucault and Derrida, finding their denunciation of Western metaphysics and European tradition particularly congenial.

This leaves Merleau-Ponty's writings in an unusual position. In its constructive form, phenomenology now develops almost exclusively as phenomenology of religion (to the extent that the only work done today in phenomenology that is not phenomenology of religion takes the position of historical analysis – it has no pretensions towards a constructive project). But within phenomenology of religion – Levinasian in inspiration – Merleau-Ponty has rarely been taken up. And so he is appropriated not within phenomenology in its constructive development (as phenomenology of religion), but instead for the sake of deconstructive philosophy in the lineage of 68. Merleau-Ponty is read *through* Derrida and Deleuze: above all as their forerunner, whose project these later philosophers 'complete', especially insofar as they move away from phenomenology in its pure form.

2. From Socrates to Plato and back

The deconstructive appropriation of Merleau-Ponty isn't entirely off the mark. It does, however, skew interpretation in a certain direction.

It is true that Merleau-Ponty was turning away from a pure phenomenology. But there are many tendencies in Merleau-Ponty that are anti-deconstructive, not least of which: the fundamental structuralism that runs from his first book *The Structure of Behavior* (and its dependency on Gestalt theory) to his late emphasis on symbol and institution.[6] Symbol, chiasm, institution: terms that mediate between form and content, reconfiguring the very relation of the formal to the material. Insofar as these terms make meaning inseparable from its materiality, it leaves little room for the deconstructive and post-structuralist interrogation which depends for its efficacy on a dualism of (manifest) form and (secret, even sinister) content.

My reading of Merleau-Ponty calls for a certain shift in interpretation back towards the irreducibility of structure all the while attending to the 'gap' or 'differentiation' (*écart*) at the heart of existence – a gap to which Merleau-Ponty's perceptual ontology called attention. This *écart* is the essential reason anti-Platonic philosophers have taken up Merleau-Ponty's perceptual ontology. In a certain way, the Merleau-Pontian *écart* is the condition of the possibility of deconstruction. It is the tenuous centre from which to pull forms apart. The irreducibility of forms, however, remains a fundamental constituent of Merleau-Ponty's late ontology even as he zeroes in on the *generation* of form (ontogenesis) and opposes a substantialist idea of eternal forms. He speaks of asymmetrical, open and dynamic forms rather than the harmonious forms of closed systems. I would thus contend that Merleau-Ponty should be read in the tradition that comes from the Ionians and Plato through modern inheritors such as Schelling and Freud, a tradition in which form is productive of meaning and which thus refuses deconstruction's valorisation of content to the detriment of form.[7] If, as David Whistler suggests, 'philosophers tend to read *esoterically*, revealing content at the expense of form',[8] what I want to do is to place Merleau-Ponty in the alternative philosophical tradition that Whistler and Iain Hamilton Grant associate with Schelling against the Kantian and post-Kantian critics of metaphysics. According to these Schellingians, Schelling offers a 'physics of the idea' that valorises form in a way even substantialist metaphysics never could. Schelling is a philosopher of form whose philosophical work repeats and amplifies forms rather than analysing or interpreting them. Can Merleau-Ponty too be understood less as a hermeneut of existence than as one who puts the operations of *physis* on display? After all, Merleau-Ponty's turn away from phenomenology was not done for the same reasons as the ones that motivated the philosophers of the sixties. It was through readings of Whitehead, Freud and Schelling that Merleau-Ponty recognised that phenomenology by itself lacked not only a concept of nature. More importantly, it lacked the dynamic operation of *physis* that, if it is to be *physis* properly speaking, must operate apart from any consciousness or Dasein that stands above it.

With this new interpretation of Merleau-Ponty within a philosophy of form, I am doing nothing more than shifting from one valid mode of philosophising to another. The shift I propose is far from a polemical one. It consists of a deviation – a swerve from Socrates to Plato, or even from Plato's Socrates to Plato himself, that is to say, from Socratic interrogation in its contemporary Derridean guise to a certain Platonic formalism, even a 'physics of the form'[9] derived from Plato's *Timaeus* but which is incompatible with Derrida's reading of the Timaeus and his deployment of *khora* as the tenuous centre from which to pull apart existing things.[10] To better situate this methodological shift, I will reference two books, which, containing a certain parallelism in their titles, illustrate the difference between the American approach to French *philosophy* (which is a Socratic approach) and the French approach to *phenomenology* (which tends towards a Platonic formalism). Exemplary of the Merleau-Ponty/Derrida mélange that we find in America, I refer to Leonard Lawlor's book, *Thinking through French Philosophy: The Being of the Question*.[11] In contrast to Lawlor is Renaud Barbaras's *The Being of the Phenomenon: Merleau-Ponty's Ontology*. Incidentally, this book was translated into English by Ted Toadvine and Lawlor himself, again demonstrating that the differences do not lead to hostility but are often the foundation of philosophical friendship.[12] Barbaras exemplifies a French approach that limits itself to the confines of phenomenology and retains a certain structuralism inherent to phenomenology's focus on the modalities of appearance. Barbaras's structural emphasis contrasts strongly to a general anglophone tendency to see all contemporary French philosophy as deconstructive, especially, but not exclusively, insofar as French philosophy permeates other humanistic disciplines in the anglophone university, as well as the analytic philosophy circles which so despise whatever comes from France.

It goes without saying that within France there is no such thing as 'Continental philosophy'. This claim does not amount to the trivial observation that *Continental* philosophy is a term that 'others' the philosophy of the Continent and displaces it from 'normative' philosophy over the Channel (above all) and (derivatively) over the Atlantic (where we Americans ape the essentially British reference to 'the Continent' as that peculiar group of disorderly Latin peoples and their more pragmatic but all-too-ideological and grandiosely speculative Teutonic neighbours to the north). In practice, the absence of 'Continental philosophy' in France means that philosophical inquiry and scholarship divides along different boundaries than one finds in an American philosophy department – boundaries that are more classical, drawn along subject-based and historical frontiers: phenomenology, political philosophy, history of (ancient, medieval or modern) philosophy. Even though they are all twentieth-century French intellectuals, Foucault, Derrida and Merleau-Ponty would rarely be brought together as a triumvirate in the work of a single French scholar, as they are for American philosophers such as Lawlor.

Even if it often results in what I would argue is a misreading of Merleau-Ponty (particularly of the *écart* as a deconstructive 'tool'), the American approach has its advantages. The American Continental philosopher brings to the table something missing in France. Like a zoologist on safari, he is able to see the lions, the zebras and the giraffes as part of the same ecosystem. The zebras, for their part, are too busy running away from the lions to contemplate their mutual belonging. But the zoologist sees their dependency. Lawlor is able to identify a common questioning among the inhabitants of the French savannah, a common questioning that would be passed over so long as classical disciplinary divisions are heeded. But ultimately, his approach is governed by Derrida, who had been the subject of Lawlor's work long before he took up Merleau-Ponty. American Continental philosophy of this variety is thus characterised by what Richard Kearney calls (in reference to another Derridean) 'a preferential option for [Derridean] *khora*',[13] that is, a decided preference for undecidability and an accompanying antagonism towards philosophies of decision, of determination, hence of form. 'The Being of the Question' (Lawlor's subtitle) becomes the very centre of philosophical inquiry. It expresses a Socratism in its Derridean manifestation (even if it does have some precedent in Merleau-Ponty).[14] While Lawlor calls this collection of essays his 'Merleau-Ponty book', and admits '[w]e do not know the direction that his thinking would have taken',[15] he explicitly chooses to read Merleau-Ponty as forerunner to the philosophy of the sixties, putting him in dialogue with Foucault, Derrida and Deleuze in the various essays that make up the volume. For Lawlor, the late convergence of phenomenology and ontology, of phenomenology and structuralism, and the increasing awareness of the constitutive role of language, tends to make of Merleau-Ponty a particularly eminent precursor to Derrida and Foucault, a thinker 'on the verge' of post-structuralism.[16]

In contrast to Lawlor's, the title of Barbaras's book not only puts Merleau-Ponty squarely in a phenomenological tradition. It even evokes the radiance of the forms – the Platonic idea that being shines forth: *The Being of the Phenomenon*. This shining forth is phenomenalisation itself. The phenomenon is not *mere* appearance, Barbaras suggests, but is a revelation. The phenomenon is the radiance of the forms, bedazzling the philosopher's gaze as he emerges out of Plato's cave in *The Republic*. While Barbaras only references Plato two times in the book, one of these references is on the concluding page, in which he compares Merleau-Ponty's 'patricide in relation to Heidegger' to that of Plato in relation to Parmenides. For Barbaras, Merleau-Ponty platonises Heidegger by thinking Heideggerian being 'from or as the possibility of a phenomenalization and an expression', bringing ontology back towards phenomenality and drawing phenomenality away from idealisation and intuitionism.[17]

Lawlor's work on Merleau-Ponty is subtle and important. While I have learned a great deal from his writings, the limits of an *overly* Derridean approach to Merleau-Ponty (and to philosophical questioning more broadly) will be demonstrated through performing its opposite in this monograph: understanding the work of Merleau-Ponty as a philosophy of form in the tradition of Plato's *Timaeus*, of Schelling's Naturphilosophie and Freud's unconscious – a philosophy that grapples with the emergence of form from a material base while taking as starting point, not a substance, but a taut relation: thinking the solidity of forms within the anti-substantialism of a philosophy of becoming. It is perhaps paradoxical that substantialism so easily falls prey to deconstructive strategies while a genetic philosophy may turn out to be form's true champion. But this remains to be seen.

Viewing Merleau-Ponty as a reincarnated Plato, interested in forms above all, directly contradicts Lawlor's contention that Merleau-Ponty is one of the great contributors to our 'epoch of anti-Platonism'.[18] Lawlor points out that, for the late Merleau-Ponty, the *écart* is at the very centre of phenomenality.[19] This gap is the point of union of the sensing with what it senses, the correlation from which phenomenological method takes its point of departure. But it is all a matter of understanding what this gap is doing, why it is there, what operation it is performing. In the readings which follow, I will emphasise that the *écart* should not be understood as a *failure* to attain coincidence between internal and external object. And if the non-coincidence is not a failure to attain coincidence, then the critical approach is absolutely excluded from the start (even in its deconstructive and hermeneutical guises). This primordial gap is an immediate divergence which speaks equally of an original togetherness. The togetherness of sensing and sensed is not something to be achieved and thus whose achievement could fail. This togetherness is the most primordial reality after which comes separation. Coincidence thus was never a goal of sensation but its starting point. Conceived in this way, the *écart* could never lead towards the destruction of forms through exposing their tenuous nature. For Merleau-Ponty, the *écart* is a source of power in the original togetherness of sensing and sensed. It is a liminal space like that between waking and sleeping – a space of both natural emergence and creative breakthrough. Deploying the non-coincidence of the *écart* against the possibility of any centre or centring, the Derridean concept of the trace, by contrast, 'disenfranchises perception as an origin of sense' by reducing signification to a play of signifiers.[20] The *écart* in Merleau-Ponty maintains the connection between meaning and perception. It is what enables the generation of forms, not their deconstruction. Following Badiou in this case, I would maintain that 'it is not Platonism that has to be overturned, but the anti-Platonism taken as evident throughout the entire twentieth century'.[21] Merleau-Ponty should be situated in this recovery of Platonism rather than within the anti-Platonism where Lawlor situates him.[22] Merleau-Ponty's 'Platonism' will be exemplified in this work, not only through his structuralism and his phenomenological focus on the radiance of forms, but primarily through his engagement with Schelling and Freud, thinkers who both considered themselves the heirs of Plato, and who have at least as much to say about *physis* as they do about form.

Within Continental philosophy, there has already been a certain turn against deconstruction and post-Kantian critique with its fixation on content and signs to the detriment of form and symbols. This turn has been announced in Iain Hamilton Grant's Schellingianism and has often proceeded under the banner of 'speculative realism'.[23] A turn to 'realism' has its limits. But my reading of Merleau-Ponty can go a certain distance with the speculative realist account, particularly that found in Grant's Schelling: Naturphilosophic formal dynamism against Hegel- and Kant-inspired idealism. If we move away from deconstructive critique, however, and remain with Merleau-Ponty, we'd arrive at something quite different from speculative realism, which, at least in Meillassoux's case, includes a radical critique of phenomenology in general and of all forms of 'correlationism' following Kant. Ted Toadvine has already shown that Merleau-Ponty's own challenge to correlationism – the new concept of chiasm – does more justice to a concept of nature than does Quentin Meillassoux's rather odd reversion to a scientific, mathematical concept of 'reality' as a 'truth' radically separate from consciousness and sensation.[24] If a certain notion of a temporality and spatiality *before* consciousness is what is at issue in the critique of correlationism, Meillassoux's mathematically determined concept of 'ancestrality' – the past before humans – can be replaced with a chiastic understanding of the elemental past: the past of the elements themselves, intrinsically sensible elements by which our senses maintain an indelible link to the very origins of the universe, origins that are forever with us in the minerality of our bodies and the unconscious rhythms of our behaviours. In the living body, these sensible primordial elements are unfolded into the power of sensation itself. The body as a closed formal system opens out onto the flesh in which it dwells: the primordial field of the elemental past. In Merleau-Ponty, it is the concept of being-as-element that must be examined to demonstrate his contribution to a Naturphilosophic approach, a 'physics of the form', which will distance us from the readings in which he is understood as a precursor to the philosophy of the sixties. It will enable us to read him within the context of this more recent turn whose primary motivation is to surpass correlationism, but which does not seriously engage the way Merleau-Ponty already had contested both the phenomenological and Kantian correlation. The elemental, in both the enormity of its spatial expanse and its temporal extension into the beginning of time, exceeds the mind's grasp. But this is not to say that the elemental is not always turned towards sensation. In John Sallis's words, the elements are 'of the sensible without being sensible things'.[25] The elemental is the fundamental starting point by which Merleau-Ponty surpasses correlationism without returning to a dualism of objective reality and subjective sensation.

3. Flesh as element: From Sartre to Bachelard

Gaston Bachelard's book, *Water and Dreams*,[26] had a powerful if rarely acknowledged influence on Merleau-Ponty. It is in explicit reference to Bachelard that he began to develop a theory of being as element. In a working note to *The Visible and the Invisible*, he writes not only of his debt to Bachelard but uses it as a way of distancing his thought from that of Sartre:

> Being and the imaginary are for Sartre 'objects', 'entities' –
>
> For me they are 'elements' (in Bachelard's sense), that is, not objects, but fields, subdued being, non-thetic being, being before being ...'[27]

By siding with Bachelard against Sartre we might go so far as to say that Merleau-Ponty uses the concept of the elemental to separate himself from what will become the philosophy of the sixties. This makes the accepted view of Merleau-Ponty particularly problematic.

In his books on the elements, Bachelard's primary aim is to critique the unilateral directionality of meaning from mind to matter, or from forms to materials – in other words, he objects to the thesis that meaning is simply *imposed* on matter and the corollary position that matter is merely the stuff out of which forms take on body. Instead, he proposes an alternative: '[M]atter is form's unconscious.'[28] Ideas are not projected onto materials. Materials give ideas to us. Materials are latent with ideas before the ideas can yet take form. In the concept of an element, the material and the perceptual are eternally bound together. This is the primary reason Merleau-Ponty identifies his primary late concept, the flesh, as itself an element:

> The flesh is not matter, is not mind, is not substance. To designate it, we should need the old term 'element', in the sense it was used to speak of water, air, earth, and fire, that is, in the sense of a *general thing*, midway between the spatio-temporal individual and the idea, a sort of incarnate principle that brings a style of being wherever there is a fragment of being. The flesh is in this sense an 'element' of Being. Not a fact, or a sum of facts, and yet adherent to *location* and to the *now*.[29]

If we bring together this quotation from the completed text of *The Visible and the Invisible* and the previous working note where Merleau-Ponty cites Sartre and Bachelard, we can begin to understand how Merleau-Ponty uses the idea of flesh-as-element to contest Sartre's understanding of the human being as a *nihil* that can reflect being through its own material nihilation. As element, the flesh is a negative principle. It is not identified with the subject. It is partially inside, partially outside the person – the web connecting personality to material world. This in-betweenness prevents the perverse conclusion of Sartrian dialectic where the subject's absolute negation coincides with its spontaneity and absolute power. It never allows such an absolute negation. As we will see later, its negativity is instead a process that leaves its trace in the material.

Merleau-Ponty situates his explicit use of the 'flesh as element' as a means of responding to Sartre's philosophy, particularly Sartre's understanding of nothingness in its relation to being. But this debate with Sartre only provides a certain context. For once we have delineated this concept of the element in Merleau-Ponty's late work, we can begin to see it as a key term and one which helps fill in a philosophical turn that was cut short by his early death. To do this work – which must be at once faithful to Merleau-Ponty and a creative elaboration of his gestures – we will need to go back to his sources, even if his references are often light on citations – even if his references often lack citations entirely. The concept of the element is much more than a bulwark against existentialism and post-structuralism. It has a history that goes back to the earliest philosophy, the Ionian 'prime element' and its operative principle – *physis*. What does it say about the nature of being or the being of nature when we call it element?

4. Elemental powers and the remains of nature

Despite a general disclaimer about the American approach to Merleau-Ponty (see section 2 above), American Continental philosophy is central to the specific theme of this book: the elemental. The elemental has been taken up with much more vigour by Continental philosophers in the

States than in France. Merleau-Ponty is not typically the primary French influence on the American thematisation of the elemental.[30] There are several factors that motivate the American interest in the elemental. No doubt part of it has to do with the turn away from pure phenomenology among thinkers like Lawlor, John Sallis, David Farrell Krell and Ed Casey.[31] But the thematisation of the elemental also has something to do with how the land has shaped American consciousness. Europe, thoroughly cultivated for thousands of years, gives little experience in the raw. But the wild is central to the very idea of America and of its founding myth. This difference between Europe and America has long been reflected in the literature though academic philosophy has not often let itself be drawn by these fixations of the imagination. While European literature has often dealt with the drama of social mores – the individual in her relation to society – American literature puts onto the stage the great struggle of the human being against the elements – from Melville and Cather to Steinbeck and Hemingway. In the nineteenth century, Thoreau considered America to be still in its national myth-forming age, where gods and elemental forces are still writ large on conscious experience.[32] This American myth-making epoch may have passed with the closing of the frontiers, but the struggle for survival in the wild still stirs up the American imagination. This has given the theme of the elemental a particular vitality in the United States.

When we think of the struggles of man[33] against the elements, we imagine massive, indifferent natural forces – forces that could snuff out our paltry lives in an instant. David Caspar Frederick's 'Wanderer above the Sea of Fog' (1818) is a paradigmatic Romantic image: man on a mountain top peering into the great unknown. It can be taken as an image of defiance and of self-reliance. But it also expresses an awed bedazzlement in the face of the sublime. It does not belittle the powers of nature, and yet it still asserts the powers of man. Despite the hostility of nature, this image gives us hope that the human spirit will somehow prevail. And yet we know that when we pass away (and we will pass away), nature will remain. An essential aspect of the definition of nature is always this. Nature is 'what remains'. It was there in the beginning. It will be there at the end.

In the ecological age, we have begun to recognise the fragility of the natural world. Sheltered from its hard indifference, we have begun to grow aware of its tenderness and its reactiveness. At the forefront of the ecological movement, the poet Gerard Manley Hopkins in 1879 compared the fragility of nature to an eye, where 'but a prick will make no eye at all'.[34] The supplement of technology has increased human power to such an extent that we bear the capacity to destroy the very environment on which we depend. And it is no longer a fringe possibility. It seems now as if it could come about accidentally, that is, if we sit around and do nothing.

But can nature really come to an end? Despite this growing awareness of the fragility of nature, nature's hardness remains an essential aspect. It is we – as individuals, as a species, as an ecosystem – who remain in danger. Whatever remains of the universe after everything is left in ruin is still nature. Nature is what remains, even if what remains is only a remainder, a mere rubbish heap of what was.

The second life of the universe, if there is a second life, would be the life of nature. Nature is not only what lives, what is born and what grows. It is what endures. In its tendency towards death, decay and rot, nature is not destroyed, but renews itself again and again. Passing away is not the passing away of nature. Passing away is one of the central operations by which it remains. Merleau-Ponty writes that nature is

> the primordial, that is, the non-constructed, the non-instituted; from which arises the idea of an eternity of Nature (eternal return), of a solidity. Nature is an enigmatic object, an object that is not in fact an object; it is not in fact in front of us. It is our soil, not what is in front of, but that which bears us.[35]

5. The injection of the elemental into phenomenology

When he speaks of nature as a 'soil' in the above quotation, Merleau-Ponty is alluding to Edmund Husserl's understanding of the transcendental Earth. In an unpublished piece entitled, 'The Arch-Original Earth doesn't move', Husserl boldly announced an anti-Copernican revolution.[36] He aimed to show that Copernicus' understanding of the earth as a body that goes around the sun results in a deficient explanation of what the earth really is as Earth. Copernicus had rejected geocentrism because it seemed to be founded on the trivial fact that we happen to live on the earth and that it only *seems to us* that the sun goes around the earth. The question Husserl raises does not put into doubt Copernicus' calculations and the understanding of the gravitational pull of heavenly bodies. It concerns whether we really 'just happen' to live here, and whether this 'living here' is a trivial fact. Could human beings be roving about equally content on Mars or Venus? The answer is obviously no. Our being is deeply related to the earth as 'the experiential ground of all bodies'.[37] We cannot even explain our movement through space and time without relating it to the earth's soil and to the other creatures that soil bears, the bacteria that live in our gut and on our skin, the animals we raise for food, the forests and vast oceans that provide our oxygen, the weather and atmosphere, the mountains and rivers.

According to Copernicus, the earth had been privileged in the medieval cosmology because of its seeming repose from our point of view. Belief in the fixity of the earth resulted from a sort of naïve lack of awareness of the fact that we always perceive from a perspective. But Husserl argues that the new Copernican model of space, a geometrical model of homogenous extension ad infinitum, opened up a different naivety in the science of nature, a naivety rooted directly in Copernicus' belief that the earth had been privileged *only* because we stood on it and that this 'standing on', being extrinsic, could thus be counted a trivial fact: as if we were standing on a pure sphere like any other large sphere. Copernicus supposed that we were standing on a mere body. He did not recognise that we were being borne up by the soil. For Husserl, the earth gives us our very being in the world. The earth gives our bodies intrinsic orienting features, a front and a back, an up and a down, a right and a left – features intrinsically tied, not to a non-oriented grid model of space, but to the gravitational pull of the earth as a centre of existence and as a source of nourishment for the stomach, for the senses, and for the soul.[38]

Before the earth can be perceived as a body careening through space, it must be lived as a soil. We are no less rooted in this soil than is a tree. While Copernicus critiqued the notion of a stable, unmoving earth and put in its place a moving earth (the earth as a body in space), Husserl argues that 'in the primordial shape of its representation, the earth does not move and does not rest; only in relation to it are movement and rest given as having their sense of movement and rest'.[39] The world opens up before us as a world because we stand upon the immovable earth. Even if human beings colonise other planets, they will do so by terraforming them, that is, referring them back to the originary earth, which is our mother, and for which our bodies were constructed. As Merleau-Ponty describes it, she is 'the living stock from which all things are engendered'.[40] This is what it is for the earth to be not merely a body among others but a soil and a necessarily singular term. In Husserl's transcendental sense, there is only one Earth. A terraformed Mars would still be part of the singular soil of Earth as element: as our element. Understood in this way, the earth doesn't have extension through space and is not qualified in the ways that qualify a thing as a body. It does not have a place in space that could move and thereby be said to be either in movement or at rest.[41] The earth is a transcendental origin of existence, of movement and of stasis as well as of behaviour, knowledge and action. While we cannot deny that his model is true in a certain sense, Copernicus' error was to forget the fact that it took an act of imagination on his part to uproot himself from earthly existence and begin to see the earth as a body rather than as the fertile soil of our being. It took an imaginative negation or abstraction by which he was able to forget that human subjectivity and worldly objectivity are both founded upon a coming-from-the-earth which, as an origin and beginning, is immovable. Husserl shows that our relation to the earth is not merely exterior and geometric but has interior dimensions. Living from the Earth is the very source of the possibility of interiority and awareness. If we are to understand existence in all its dimensions, we must understand how the depth of our soul is related to the elemental past of the earth itself.

What Husserl is describing in his account of the Earth as a soil from which the movements of bodies and the structure of spatiality acquire sense is what Merleau-Ponty will describe as a 'sensible generality', not a universal in the classical philosophical sense, but an element, in the old sense of the four elements, and particularly a prime element, from which everything under heaven originates. Instead of the old distinction between intelligible genera and sensible particulars, Husserl begins to introduce a new distinction: the distinction of the elemental from the corporal. Where Copernicus saw the earth as a body, Husserl sees it as an element. From the classical point of view, Merleau-Ponty's term 'sensible generality' would be a paradox or a contradiction, but the element is indeed sensible without containing the determinations of a particular thing. It is general in such a way that it would be impossible for a mind to abstract its formal properties from the sensible experience of it. The elemental, below movement and rest, is neither a body nor an object. It lacks particularity, spatiality and limits. Husserl's distinction of the elemental and the corporal was a distinction novel in modern philosophy, but it is not novel for humanity. It hearkens back to the earliest mythological ways of human thinking. If Parmenides' understanding of the All as a definite sphere came to dominate Western thought, a more ambiguous thought of the All had persisted in the intuitions of the first Greek philosophers, an ambiguous, indefinite All, that had been passed directly from the oldest religious traditions and mythical ways of expressing the origins of the world, traditions on which philosophers like Thales, Anaximander and Heraclitus had been nourished. If such an All is indefinite, it is no less unified and dynamic.

6. 'Germ of the endangered world': The ark of existence

Since Husserl, the deployment of elements in phenomenology has been manifold. At about the same moment in the 1930s, Heidegger too developed a concept of Earth. His later philosophy will implement terms like Earth and Sky, Divinities and Mortals, terms for an originary world that are deployed with the intention of replacing the concept of being with a term that designates something closer to the origin of the world.[42] Emmanuel Levinas will speak of 'the elemental' as an originary 'night' and as the 'bad infinite' which is the indefinite *apeiron*.[43] Merleau-Ponty will call the flesh an 'element' of being in the sense of the Presocratic idea of the elements.⁴⁴ If these concepts are not unitary (and they are not), in what then lies their difference?

The unpublished text in which Husserl thematises the Earth fascinated Merleau-Ponty. Among other references to this text, he comments on it in both his 1954–5 Collège de France lecture course, *The Problem of Passivity*, and the first of his three courses on nature, *The Concept of Nature* (1956–7). In both courses he makes use of a play with the term 'arche' in the French *arche-originelle*. *Arche* comes from the Greek, αρχή, which is the Greek term for beginning. This term has a central place in this history of philosophy. As philosophy first emerges out of a mythological discourse about origins, αρχή is the pivot term that, as Ernst Cassirer notes, marks 'the point of indifference between the mythical concept of the beginning and the philosophical concept of the "principle"'.⁴⁵ From the very moment that Husserl invokes the arch-original earth, we are called back to philosophy's mythological origins in primordial chthonic gods, deities of earth and sky and ocean. This return to the elemental is not a simple result of a search for beginnings. After all, philosophy as such has always searched for beginnings and for origins. There is instead something peculiar about the way phenomenology understands beginnings that calls us back to the Presocratic understanding of the prime element and *physis*. And because this presocratic discourse was still entangled with mythological modes of thought, we have a similar entanglement that emerges in the thought of these twentieth-century thinkers. As soon as its discourse about principles and beginnings crosses Presocratic notions of prime elements and *physis*, a mythological aura begins to halo phenomenology. This is not to conflate phenomenology with mythology, but it does facilitate a radical rethinking of the very relation of philosophy to its site of origin, a rethinking of the very activity of the αρχή in bringing philosophy into existence. If the first principle of phenomenology can no longer be understood as being (the metaphysical principle par excellence), but is instead the arch-original Earth, how can we say any longer that the relationship of philosophy to mythology is that in which an essence is abstracted from behind a sensuous appearance? The element, after all, remains sensuous in its generality. It is not a pure 'is'.

In Husserl, the Earth is at once an a priori principle and a primordial beginning. It is the condition of the possibility of all that exists. In its evocation of a pre-Copernican universe, it is something quasi-mythic. The French word for ark is the same word as the prefix derived from the Greek word for beginning. This enables a wordplay in which Merleau-Ponty compares the arch-original Earth to Noah's ark. 'The Earth is the root of our history', Merleau-Ponty writes in the first Nature course. 'In the same way that Noah's ark carried all that could remain of the living and of the possible, so the Earth could be considered as the bearer of all that is possible.'[46] This notion of 'bearing the possible' makes the Earth much more than an a priori condition of logical possibility. It is positively full of the possible. The possible resides there not in the manner of already extant logical possibilities. It resides there in seminal form. Again alluding to Noah but without naming him directly, Merleau-Ponty gives us an even more evocative description in *The Problem of Passivity*:

> This 'earth' is *arche* – bearer of the possibility of every being above the nothing, above the flood – germ of the endangered world from which everything blossoms again. It is 'nature' in the sense of a perceptual cosmogony, neither in itself, nor for God, but our horizon.[47]

Comparing the ark to a seed from which the whole world springs forth evokes an ancient mythico-philosophical idea: the idea of the world egg. In the West, the world egg is most associated with certain Neoplatonic systems.[48] It is the idea of a seminality before existence, an initially dormant eternity rich with potentiality. As seminal, the world has an eternal principle analogous to the way that a dry seed can endure eternally as a seed. Once a bit of moisture awakens it, however, it is launched into actuality – towards both life and decay at once. The seminal concept of the world contrasts strongly with the modern mechanistic physics, where every possibility is already actual, or logically actual, so that each interaction in space is like pool balls colliding and each true proposition is deduced from an a priori. Merleau-Ponty's image of the seminal ark represents the type of possibility that is not already logically actual. It also adds another dimension: that the water which activates it also threatens it with non-existence.

The phenomenological tradition has had much to say about the primordial earth. To speak of the phenomenological 'horizon' is implicitly to speak of the primordial earth: existence on the earth and under the sky. Phenomenology has said much less about that which is before the primordial ark of the earth. After all, what is this primordial flood that bears up on its back the ark of the possible? What is this reality before the beginning? Can we even begin to speak about this primordial nothing without which the germ of the world would not germinate – this flood that destroyed so many possibilities, and whose receding was signalled with the bringing of an olive branch in the beak of a dove? At the very least, we can say this: the event of the flood and its subsequent receding is the condition of the possibility of an αρχή as such.

The relation of positive 'bearing' to a negative principle, incarnated here as the 'nothing' of 'the flood', is a central theme of Merleau-Ponty's late work. Despite scattered references to a liquid milieu, the connection of the negative to a certain aqueous element remains largely hidden. Merleau-Ponty critiques philosophies like that of Sartre, which has a concept of nothingness, but whose nothingness is perhaps too conceptual, too abstract, too pure and therefore too thin. The Sartrian nothing does not have the thickness of the elemental. It will be one of our primary contentions that the most fundamental element in Merleau-Ponty's late thought is not the Earth, but something akin to primordial water understood as an essential aspect of the structure and dynamism of the origin in its relation to the *arché*. The aquatic element is not the beginning *and* origin. It is only an origin. It is not arch-originary like Husserl's Earth. The beginning comes after it. Its status is negative: a 'nothing' before the beginning. In the text quoted above from *The Problem of Passivity*, Merleau-Ponty had identified nature as the *arché* that, in a 'perceptual cosmogony', is 'our horizon'. The horizon itself, however, which is the very ark of existence, is terrestrial. Although the horizon is absolute with respect to any position after the fact of an earth, it always rises up upon the primordial, originary flood. This primordial flood – not a pure nothingness but an elemental nothingness that puts existence in danger – begins to be revealed in the dynamic fluidity underlying all being. What would this originary flood, this elemental nothingness, mean for a perceptual cosmogony? What does it say about the modality of becoming? These are the central questions of this book.

7. Embodied by forgetting: The other side of the light

Phenomenality has everything to do with light. The Greek verb 'phaino' means to shine or appear, and is related to *phos*, the word for light, and more distantly related to *pyr*, the word for fire. Light has been thematised to such an extent in philosophy that it has attained the status of a concept. Phenomenality is the conceptualisation of light, for light is what makes appear. Nothing that remains dark can be a phenomenon. Phenomenality is that which reveals eternal truth. It is even what coincides with truth. Not only does light reveal the visible. It reveals the intelligible. In the Western tradition, existence itself is almost synonymous with illumination.[49] To understand the place of the flood as a primordial element, we need to understand not only how it precedes the transcendental Earth. We need to grasp its relation to phenomenality as such, that is, its relationship to the light.

Although he was not the first to do so, Heidegger famously translated the Greek word for truth, *aletheia*, as 'unconcealment'.[50] Truth is the exposure of what had been shrouded in darkness. It is a coming into the light. For Plato, the act of knowing the truth is a kind of recollection of what had been absolutely obscured through the passage into existence. In the Platonic myth of pre-existence, to be born into this world somehow coincides with forgetting what had been known in a previous life.[51] To come to know something is simply to remember what had been forgotten in a forgetting so deep that we do not even remember that we have forgotten. More than an act of revealing what had been concealed, *a-letheia* is literally 'un-forgetting'. To come to know is to bring to mind something that has been immemorially forgotten.

In these well-known commentaries on *aletheia* as unconcealment or as un-forgetting, something essential has continually been glossed over: namely the nature of the realm of forgetfulness. While we have conceptualised the light as phenomenon and as unforgetting, we have not fully thematised the elemental analogue of the contrary term, the elemental analogue for forgetting. In the act of knowledge, something is brought to the light. Something is revealed. But this revelation is privative, for un-forgetting or a-letheia is a negative term of which forgetting is the positive. It is a *lack* of forgetfulness. We normally consider darkness as the opposite term for the light. If light corresponds to existence, darkness corresponds to what is not, to non-being. If we look closely at the valences of aletheia, however, we arrive at a different framework, for *letheia*, the positive opposite of privative *aletheia*, has a different elemental reference than that of the dark. The illumination of truth negates *letheia*, but *letheia* nevertheless refers neither to the dark nor to the hidden, but to the forgotten.

Letheia is connected to the River Lethe, the river of forgetfulness which divides the underworld from this world. In the cyclical model of time dominant in ancient societies,[52] the underworld is both the realm of death and the realm of pre-existence. The souls first traverse the Lethe to come into this world, thereby forgetting their past life. They cross the Lethe again when they pass into the oblivion of death. Plotinus, taking up this theme, describes embodiment itself as a form of forgetting.[53] The souls in the underworld must drink of the Lethe, the River of Forgetting, to enter into life. The waters of forgetfulness weigh the soul down with an earthly body. The body is constituted by (literally filled with) forgetting. Plotinus goes so far as to say that the body itself *is* the River of Forgetting: 'the body's nature, moving and flowing, must be a cause of forgetfulness, not of memory: this is why the "river of Lethe" might be understood in this sense'.[54] The forgotten is what slips out of memory's grasp and into body, leaving the soul hanging down into the material realm.[55] Forgetting is thus not a lack, but something positive and weighty. The body's fluidity is what marks the body as a body of forgetting. Memory, by contrast, is something that is retained. It is not heavy and flowing, but stable and fixed, light and ethereal.[56]

Insofar as the Lethe might be interpreted as the body itself in its liquid, untruthful character, the passage from forgetfulness to knowledge is a passage not from darkness to light, but from liquidity to light. We can consider liquidity the opposite of light insofar as the liquid has a power both to reflect light (off its surface) and transmit light (through its depths). Light on the contrary has the power to be reflected and to be transmitted. Water is the other side of the light in the same way that the invisible is the other side of the visible. If it is water, not darkness, that is the contrary of light, we are working with a different kind of contrary. We need to rethink the relation between the phenomenon and the body, which is to say, between the light and the liquid. The opposite of light is not evil darkness. The opposite is not to be overcome and eliminated by the appearance of the light. It is not an opposite where the one 'is' and, through being, excludes the other. It is an opposite more like the front and back of a leaf (to use one of the examples Merleau-Ponty uses to explicate the relation between the visible and the invisible).[57] The opposing terms remain primordially together. Water presents to us the elemental non-being that remains under all being. Even the body, perhaps *especially* the body, is non-being in this elemental sense – on the verge of destroying the light of truth while remaining its sole condition of possibility. Merleau-Ponty participates in this Platonic understanding of primordial forgetting when in the *Phenomenology of Perception* he speaks of a 'past which was never present', an immemorial past which is embedded *in* and *as* the body structure.[58] He echoes not only Maine de Biran and Bergson, but also Plotinus and Plato. He summons a tradition in which embodied existence is considered according to a primordial liquidity. This liquidity is not at all a mere lack of stable structure. It is a power of generation. In a text that Merleau-Ponty likely read, Schelling also links water to both the human being in particular and the bond or copula of all being more broadly.[59]

We might indeed wonder to what extent Merleau-Ponty was inspired by his master's thesis on Plotinus,[60] an early interest in Neoplatonism that seems to be largely erased or at least hidden in his published work. However much he might hide this youthful interest, it takes a certain type of philosopher to be drawn to the Neoplatonic tradition in the first place. The immemorial past is a deeply Platonic concept: the past that cannot be remembered because it was never present, but is nevertheless structured as memory, which is to say, structured as a *past*. Merleau-Ponty, the philosopher of the body par excellence, retains much of the Plotinian understanding of the body – its nature as an irrecoverable past, its liquidity in relation to the truth. An understanding of the body as liquid non-being fits precisely with Merleau-Ponty's ontology. Non-being is not what grounds being in a reciprocal reflexive relation. Non-being is something that is always intertwined with being. Merleau-Ponty would no doubt contest Plotinus' disdain for the body, but this contestation is precisely on the grounds that the liquid body, the body as an irrecoverable past (a never-having-been-present past) is an a priori condition of the possibility of *aletheia* and thus an a priori condition of phenomenality.[61]

8. Aquatic (non)being in the perceptual cosmogony

How much the implicitly aquatic dynamics of Merleau-Ponty's notion of flesh as element owe to Bachelard's *Water and Dreams* is impossible to measure. We do know that the primary aquatic operations that I will identify are already there in Bachelard: the latency of the depth dimension, the mirroring of the surface, and the power to create by self-negation. But there are no doubt other influences. Understanding the living body as elemental non-being – the liquidity that underlies the luminous – puts Merleau-Ponty within a theosophical tradition (understood as Schelling defines it and as Böhme uses it: roughly as 'rational mysticism')[62] that goes back to the writings ascribed to Hermes Trismegistus, a tradition he only rarely cites, and when he does cite, he does so very obliquely yet always with general approbation (he even cites the legendary Hermes himself).[63]

There is a certain sympathy between Merleau-Ponty's thought and theosophic notions, particularly with respect to the way the hierarchy of being is articulated and the way the human being is considered a microcosm of nature. Despite strong flattening tendencies in his work, the human being remains for Merleau-Ponty in some sense the pinnacle of creation, a humanistic position anathema to current trends that seek an erasure of hierarchically organised difference. While Merleau-Ponty is no doubt primarily a thinker of the horizontal, there is also a vertical dimension which is rarely thematised in the secondary literature except to apologise for it.[64] By the vertical I do not refer to what he calls 'vertical being', but rather to a hierarchy that is not pre-ordained and descendent, but which is emergent or ascendent. A key difference from traditional hierarchical systems is that no level is equivalent to a particular being or set of beings but is instead understood as a field of possibilities. *Homo sapiens* would not be at the summit of a chain of being. Being is not a chain going from one level to the next. The flesh is an inward and upward turning 'vortex', whose pinnacle is not species specific but is an open field of possibilities participated by various species.[65] The field at the summit (where matter, animal soul, and intellect are united) would at least include other potential humanoid species, of which *Homo sapiens* is the only currently extant form. The field would also participate other animals, plants or fungi, possessors of certain intelligences that in many ways far outstrip human capacities but which we often have the capacity to tap into.

Primordial water gives us a complex and precise concept by which we can understand the particular elemental attributes of the flesh of the world as an 'element of Being'.[66] Others have noted the connection of the Merleau-Pontian flesh to the element of water.[67] This has been left, however, at the level of a certain metaphorical affinity. No one has really interrogated the aquatic operation at work. If light has attained the status of a concept in Western metaphysics, particularly under the guise of the 'phenomenon', then water, as its primordial opposite, might also attain the status of a concept. At the very least, if there is not enough light within the liquid to be a clear and distinct concept, it can attain the level of the symbol in the fullest sense of the term, the sense that Schelling and the German Romantics develop from Proclus. Primordial liquidity serves many purposes, not least of which is its resistance to the light: a resistance which is not an absolute negation like the absolute opacity of the soil. If the aquatic milieu is a resistance to luminosity without diametrical opposition, it is the symbol of 'what resists phenomenology in us'[68] without entirely eliminating its trace from phenomenality. The liquid and the luminous encroach upon each other without either complete overlap or complete opposition.

If we can say that primordial water can attain the status of a concept, or at least a symbol, it is only because it gives us an even more precise way of designating and describing the structure of the most primordial. At this level, the concept of being is unable to achieve what the liquid can achieve. Thinking the origin as primordially liquid tells us something more specific and yet more rich and dynamic than thinking being purified of elemental symbolics. Being qua being tells us absolutely nothing about the relation between the primordial and what exists temporally and spatially. In its move away from the strict binaries being/non-being, subject/object, form/matter, Merleau-Ponty's 'mixturism',[69] I would contend, does not deconstruct all formalism. The mixture is the elemental itself. The liquid instead challenges the reduction to appearance, not to form, for appearing without the liquid depths below it lacks a concept of nature. Merleau-Ponty aims to hold these two together, for despite a reintroduction of a concept of nature, what remains for Merleau-Ponty is a *perceptual* cosmogony. Perception in Merleau-Ponty becomes ontological, indeed ontogenetic: the structure of the world is, as such, a perceptual structure. Perception no longer signifies a perception of the thing (*Dingwahrnehmung*) from outside of that thing. Perception is a comportment of being that links us to the thing from the very beginning.[70] We are first of all considering the perceptual structure of various sensorial fields from which perception of 'things' arises as one possible manifestation. These sensorial fields that Merleau-Ponty lists include: 'ideological, imaginary, mythic, praxic, symbolic'.[71]

Merleau-Ponty largely keeps silent about the liquid nature of the 'element of Being'. We intend, however, to explore the liquid dynamics at play in his thought through interrogating certain aqueous operations at work. To give a preliminary justification to this thesis, we can provide one clear citation where he identifies liquidity as ontologically central to his 'perceptual cosmogony'. In *The Visible and the Invisible*, he seeks to expose a certain fluidity that comes before what is fixed, terrestrial, or 'striated', to use a Deleuzian term:

> The manner of questioning prescribes a certain kind of response, and to fix it now would be to decide our solution. For example, if we were to say that our problem here is to disengage the essence or the *Eidos* of our life in the different regions upon which it opens, this would be to presume that we will find ideal invariants whose relations will themselves be founded in essence; *it would be to subordinate from the first what there might be that is fluid to what there might be that is fixed in our experience*, to subject it to conditions that perhaps are the conditions not of every possible experience but only of an experience already put into words, and it would be in the end to shut ourselves up in an immanent exploration of the significations of words.[72]

In his insistence on a primordial fluidity, Merleau-Ponty is not only emerging out of the linguistic turn. He is turning from an immanent entrapment in language to a philosophy of nature, a nature that necessarily exceeds and precedes the linguistic in its non-structural, pre-formal liquidity.

The liquidity of the perceptual field leads to a phenomenological ontology insofar as it describes the origin at 'the birth and rebirth of meaning' which requires not only something 'carnally given' to consciousness but also negative aspects which are neither of consciousness nor of the given: 'lacunas, ellipses, allusions, as "gaps" (*écarts*)'.[73] These negative aspects provide the perceptual with its dynamism and its danger – with its possible birth, rebirth and destruction: the meeting point where something truly new can arise, where the generation of things can take place, such that now the perceptual is no longer the mere spectacle of already existing things displayed in front of the one who sees them.

At this point my placement of Merleau-Ponty in the broader development of American and French Continental philosophy overlaps with my thesis concerning his particular contribution to the elemental in phenomenology. It is in contrast to deconstructive readings of the *écart* that I am able to show that the fluidity intrinsic to Merleau-Ponty's ontology is not a deconstructive fluidity. It is not the deconstructed, but the non-constructed. The liquid milieu is the source of form. It is a cosmogonic fluidity: world-creating, primordial liquidity. The *écart* of the flesh thus follows the tradition of mythological creations out of water, the primordial 'abyss', as well as the Thalian proposal that everything is water. For Merleau-Ponty the structured is irrecoverable – an immemorial past. But because this past is manifested as the body itself, the form bears the traces of a primordially withdrawn liquidity: a Lethean body. In this way, we find Merleau-Ponty in the Platonic lineage more than in the anti-Platonic. It is within this context that the argument of the book will unfold.

9. A Merleau-Pontian itinerary

The argument is essentially as follows: Merleau-Ponty's late thought of the elemental offers a more fundamental category to think about reality than does the concept of being because the elemental includes notions of non-being, negative potential and active withdrawal. It is thus more comprehensive and even more descriptive. It says not only *that* the world exists, but it suggests *how* it comes to exist. Through the governing image of primordial waters, Merleau-Ponty's conception of the elemental can be defined as an elemental non-being, articulating something specific about the *how* of existence: the element is a dynamic ground that creates being by negating itself. This aquatic conception of primordial reality is based upon Merleau-Ponty's argument that the bond is more primordial than any separation. Even in the elemental past when there was no conscious being, mind and matter cannot be separated. The world is intrinsically visible and so is primordially linked to vision.

I began writing this book as a study on the elemental in Merleau-Ponty. It quickly became a book on nature. It was not of course surprising that we would need to approach the idea of nature if we are to understand the elemental. As I moved forward with the implications of Merleau-Ponty's understanding of nature, what was most surprising was the increasing centrality of symbolism. Merleau-Ponty's ideas would necessitate an integration of symbolism into the very essence of nature. In his late work, Merleau-Ponty began to speak of a 'natural symbolism'. The dynamic generativity of the symbolic was not the product of a mind apart from nature. Rather, nature itself created symbolically, and human symbols are but a repetition of this natural symbolics. Implied in all this is a symbolic operation at the most basic level: an 'elemental symbolism'. It is not only the case that we cannot understand the world apart from the imagination and from symbols. The world *is* a symbolism par excellence. While we will explicate the characteristics and implications of an 'aquatic' ontology in the early chapters, this will lead to a more general analysis of natural symbolism in the later chapters. Chapter 4 is the hinge linking Merleau-Ponty's aquatic ontology to a theory of natural symbolism.

There are two different types of books that could be written on the elemental in Merleau-Ponty. One is what is presented here. Its goal is to piece together his late thought into a coherent elemental philosophy. Whether it is the philosophy he would have written doesn't really matter. What matters is a faithfulness to the inchoate gestures of his late thinking. The other type of book would be an analysis of the development of the elemental from his first works to his last. This would be an important work, but it would deviate significantly from mine. The unifying thread of my study is the search for the aspects and operations of the elemental as drawn from and in confrontation with Merleau-Ponty's sources. To trace a proper genealogy of the elemental from Merleau-Ponty's early work to his later work would require a different approach, one that focuses on an internal development of the concept up to Merleau-Ponty's final conceptualisation. The link I draw between the late concept of the elemental and the earlier use of Gestalt theory (Chapter 1, section 2) provides a sketch of how such a genealogy would proceed. Beyond scattered references to the *Phenomenology of Perception* and this brief section on Gestalt, the present study starts from the late philosophy and moves forward.

Notes

1. In France, the HDR, or *habilitation à diriger des recherches*, is a work of scholarship more advanced than the doctorate, qualifying one to supervise PhD students. Levinas had already been teaching and publishing since the forties before he formally submitted this work for examination by a jury of his peers in 1961.
2. For a summation of this turn and arguments for and against it, see Dominique Janicaud, ed., *Phenomenology and the 'Theological Turn': The French Debate* (New York: Fordham University Press, 2000). For a less dated contestation of this turn from within the turn itself, see Emmanuel Falque, *The Loving Struggle: Phenomenological and Theological Debates* (London: Rowman & Littlefield, 2018). I deploy the general thrust of Falque's arguments here.
3. Vladimir Jankélévitch also developed a concept of the wholly other, but it is Levinas's that is decisive for the theological turn. For Jankélévitch's influence on Levinas on this concept and their distinction, see Andrew Kelley, 'Jankélévitch and Levinas on the "Wholly Other"', *Levinas Studies* 8.1 (2013): 23–43.
4. On the possibilities of this unrealised confrontation see Emmanuel Falque, 'Principe barbare et il y a', lecture delivered 16 March 2019 at the École Normale Supérieure (ENS, Paris) for the conference 'Levinas – Merleau-Ponty: Résonances'. Due to appear in the *Archives de philosophie* (2021). Despite a lack of references the one to the other, the many allusions to the *il y a* in Merleau-Ponty's manuscript *The Visible and the Invisible* shows a knowledge of Levinas's early work and the section on sensation in Levinas's *Totality and Infinity* demonstrates how Levinas was trying to engage Merleau-Ponty as a member of his jury.

5. My use of this term 'non-religious' excludes reference to atheist philosophers of religion (Thomas Carlson, Jeffrey Kosky, Ryan Coyne) and includes those Continental philosophers who deploy Buddhist thought in conversation with Continental philosophy (Jason Wirth, Brett Davis, Brian Schroeder). This is because of the generally accepted fact that Abrahamic religions deal with a concept of transcendence foreign to Eastern thought structures and that phenomenology of religion continues to interrogate these transcendences even when it takes on an atheistic form. Those who turn to Eastern thought do so precisely to escape 'Western metaphysics', which, both through its Greek and Jewish heritage, is intrinsically tied to these notions of transcendence.
6. For a general account of structuralism, and particularly its use of symbol, see Gilles Deleuze, 'How do we recognize structuralism?', in *Desert Islands and Other Texts* (Los Angeles: Semiotexte, 2004), 170–92.
7. For a more thorough critique of critical philosophy's valorisation of content against form, see Iain Hamilton Grant, *Philosophies of Nature After Schelling* (London: Continuum, 2008), 1–25.
8. David Whistler, 'The New Literalism: Reading After Grant's Schelling', *Symposium* 19.1 (2015): 126.
9. I am following here a trajectory similar to that of Iain Hamilton Grant who proposes that Schelling needs to be lifted out of the Kant- and Hegel-dominated philosophy of the nineteenth and twentieth centuries, which emphasised content, synthesis, the concept and the sign. For Grant, Schelling was a thinker of form, genesis and symbol. Therefore, to read him correctly we cannot read him through a Kantian or Hegelian lens. See Grant, *Philosophies of Nature after Schelling*, 6–19. Much more will be said about Merleau-Ponty's relationship to Schelling in the last three chapters of this book.
10. Jacques Derrida, *Khora* (Paris: Galilée, 1993).
11. Leonard Lawlor, *Thinking through French Philosophy: The Being of the Question* (Bloomington: Indiana University Press, 2003).
12. Renaud Barbaras, *The Being of the Phenomenon: Merleau-Ponty's Ontology* (Bloomington: Indiana University Press, 2004).
13. Richard Kearney, *Strangers, Gods, and Monsters: Interpreting Otherness* (London: Routledge, 2002), 203.
14. In *The Visible and the Invisible*, Merleau-Ponty writes that 'the existing world exists in the interrogative mode' (VI, 137/103). This seems to have little to do with a taking apart of things from outside of the things themselves. It is instead 'an original manner of aiming at something' (VI, 168/129) that implies that being's own curiosity is what causes it to reach out beyond itself. Thus in the *Nature* courses he says: 'It is not a positive being but an interrogative being that defines life' (N, 207). The interrogative mode defines Merleau-Ponty's revisionist teleology and therefore doesn't eliminate a formal starting point but rather reaffirms it.
15. Lawlor, *Thinking through French Philosophy*, 2.
16. Lawlor, *Thinking through French Philosophy*, 2.
17. Barbaras, *The Being of the Phenomenon*, 320.
18. Leonard Lawlor, *The Implications of Immanence* (New York: Fordham University Press, 2006), 145.
19. Lawlor, *The Implications of Immanence*, 70.
20. M. C. Dillon, *Semiological Reductionism: A Critique of the Deconstructionist Movement in Postmodern Thought* (Albany: SUNY Press, 1995), 12.
21. Alain Badiou, *Deleuze; The Clamor of Being* (Minneapolis, University of Minnesota Press, 2000), 101.
22. Jean-Louis Chrétien likewise writes, 'there is certainly something not yet worked out in the proximity to a certain Platonism in attempts to overcome metaphysics, of which Platonism is, moreover, thought to be the foundation'. *The Unforgettable and the Unhoped For* (New York: Fordham University Press, 2012), 30. Another formalistic reading of Merleau-Ponty is in Mariana Larison's thesis, directed by Barbaras and

published as *L'Être en forme: Dialectique et phénoménologie dans la dernière philosophie de Merleau-Ponty* (Sesto S. Giovanni: Éditions Mimesis, 2016).
23. I intend to refer particularly to Quentin Meillassoux's *Après la finitude* (Paris: Éditions de Seuil, 2006); translated by Ray Brassier as *After Finitude: An Essay on the Necessity of Contingency* (London: Continuum, 2008).
24. See Ted Toadvine, 'The Elemental Past', *Research in Phenomenology* 44 (2014): 262–79.
25. John Sallis, *The Return of Nature* (Indianapolis: Indiana University Press, 2016), 77.
26. Gaston Bachelard, *L'eau et les rêves* (Paris : José Corti, 1942).
27. VI, 314/267.
28. Bachelard, *L'eau et les rêves*, 70.
29. VI, 181–2/139–40.
30. Levinas is certainly a significant influence, but Deleuze also speaks of the elemental specifically in 'Michel Tournier and World without others', *Economy and Society* 13.1 (1984): 52–71. No doubt much of his work relates to ideas of the elemental, for instance his concept of flows in *Difference and Repetition*, trans. Paul Patton (New York: Columbia University Press, 1994).
31. For an accessible overview of not only the French and German phenomenologists (up to Merleau-Ponty and Levinas) who speak of the elemental, but also the most significant American thinkers (Sallis, Casey, Alphonso Lingis), see David Macauley, *Elemental Philosophy: Earth, Air, Fire, and Water as Environmental Ideas* (Albany: SUNY Press, 2010).
32. Henry David Thoreau, 'Walking', *The Atlantic Monthly: A Magazine of Literature, Art, and Politics*, IX/LVI (June 1862): 657–74.
33. I'm going to use gendered generic pronouns throughout (both masculine and feminine). Often the gender is not insignificant, as is the case of the use of the term 'man' here. Undoubtedly it is meant inclusively although the masculine valence is also important.
34. 'Binsey Poplars' in Gerard Manley Hopkins, *The Major Works* (Oxford: Oxford University Press, 2009).
35. N, 20.
36. In English, it has been translated with the more monotonous title: 'Foundational Investigations of the Phenomenological Origin of the Spatiality of Nature', trans. Fred Kersten, in Husserl, *Shorter Works*, ed. Peter McCormick and Frederick A. Elliston (South Bend, IN: University of Notre Dame Press, 1981), 222–33. Here I take the more audacious French title, *L'Arche-originaire terre ne se meut pas* (Paris: Les Éditions de minuit, 1989). Husserl's actual text (unpublished in his lifetime) was enclosed in an envelope which read: 'Overthrow of the Copernican theory in usual interpretation of a world view. The original ark, earth, does not move.' For a defence of Husserl's argument and bibliographic reference to other literature on this piece, please refer to Juha Himanka, 'Husserl's Argumentation for the Pre-Copernican View of the Earth', *The Review of Metaphysics* 58.3 (2005): 621–44.
37. N, 118.
38. For a thorough analysis of the primordiality of oriented directions and dimensions drawing primarily from Husserl and Merleau-Ponty and Whitehead's critique of abstract spatialisation, see Edward S. Casey, *Getting Back into Place* (Bloomington: Indiana University Press, 2009), 43–105.
39. Husserl, *L'Arche-originaire terre ne se meut pas*, 12.
40. N, 77.
41. Husserl, *L'Arche-originaire terre ne se meut pas*, 16.
42. We will discuss this aspect of Heidegger's thought in Chapter 4, section 2.
43. Emmanuel Levinas, *Totality and Infinity: An Essay on Exteriority*, trans. Alphonso Lingis (Pittsburgh: Duquesne University Press, 1996), 130–42. References to the *apeiron* at pp. 159 and 163.

44. VI, 181–2/139; N, 118–19.
45. Ernst Cassirer, *Philosophy of Symbolic Forms II: Mythical Thought*, trans. Ralph Manheim (New Haven, CT: Yale University Press, 1955), 1–2.
46. N, 111.
47. IP, 174/131.
48. See W. K. C. Guthrie, *Orpheus and Greek Religion* (London: Methuen & Co. Ltd, 1935), 79, 94, 102. And Luc Brisson, 'Les théogonies Orphiques et le papyrus de Derveni: notes critiques', *Revue de l'Histoire des Religions* 202 (1985): 389–420.
49. Cathryn Vasseleu, *Textures of Light: Vision and Touch in Irigaray, Levinas, and Merleau-Ponty* (London: Routledge, 1998), 3.
50. Jean-Louis Chrétien suggests that Nicolai Hartmann's *Platos Logik des Seins* (1909) is the first place *aletheia* is translated as unconcealment (*Unverborgenheit*). *The Unforgettable and the Unhoped For*, 5n7. For Heidegger on *aletheia* as unconcealment, see for example Martin Heidegger, *Basic Questions of Philosophy* (Bloomington: Indiana University Press, 1994), 84ff. See also Merleau-Ponty's lectures on Heidegger (NC, 99 and 118).
51. The pre-existence of the soul is recounted in the Phaedo, Meno and Phaedrus.
52. One might of course refer to Mircea Eliade's *Le mythe de l'éternel retour* (Paris: Gallimard, 1949), 81–136.
53. For more detail on Plotinus' transformation of the Platonic tradition, see Chrétien, *The Unforgettable and the Unhoped For*, 23–36. Plotinus takes the image of the Lethe from the myth that ends the *Republic* (621c) and expands upon it a great deal.
54. *Ennead* IV, 3, 26. Translation from *Ennead* IV, trans. A. H. Armstrong (Cambridge, MA: Harvard University Press, 1984), 121.
55. Chrétien writes: 'The soul takes forgetting into itself, it satisfies itself there, fills itself; forgetting is not lightening, but weighing oneself down.' *The Unforgettable and the Unhoped For*, 33. Chrétien references *Phaedrus*, 242c: 'If any soul becomes a companion to a god and catches sight of any true thing, it will be unharmed until the next circuit; and if it is able to do this every time, it will always be safe. If, on the other hand, it does not see anything true because it could not keep up, and by some accident takes on a burden of forgetfulness and wrongdoing, then it is weighed down, sheds its wings and falls to earth.' All translations of Plato are from *The Complete Works*, ed. John M. Cooper (Indianapolis: Hackett, 1997).
56. *Ennead* IV, 3, 25
57. VI, 265/312.
58. PP, 289/242.
59. The passage I am alluding is from *On the World Soul* and can be found in Samuel Jankélévitch's collection of Schelling translations, entitled *Essais* (Paris: Aubier, 1946), from which Merleau-Ponty quotes over the course of his *Nature* lectures. See pp.115–20.
60. For his diplôme d'études supérieures under the supervision of Émile Bréhier he wrote a thesis (now lost) entitled 'La Notion du multiple intelligible chez Plotin' (1929).
61. In a working note of April 1960, he again refers to this 'past' that 'belongs to a mythical time, to the time before time, to the prior life', and says that it is 'not compatible with "phenomenology"' because phenomenology 'obliges whatever is not nothing to *present* itself to *consciousness* …' (VI, 292/243).
62. Schelling privileges theosophy insofar as it is 'much ahead of philosophy in depth, fullness and vitality of content in the way that the actual object is ahead of its image and nature is ahead of its presentation. And this difference certainly approaches incomparability if a dead philosophy that seeks the being in forms and concepts is taken as the point of comparison. Hence, the predilection of those with inward dispositions for theosophy is as easy to explain as the predilection for nature as opposed to art. The theosophical systems have the advantage over everything else hitherto current: at least there is in them a power, even if it does not have power over itself, while in the other

systems, in contrast, there is but unnatural and conceited art.' Introduction to *Ages of the World*, trans. Jason Wirth (Albany: SUNY Press, 2000), xxxix.
63. OE, 70.
64. For example, see Louise Westling, *The Logos of the Living World* (New York: Fordham University Press, 2013).
65. VI, 293/244.
66. VI, 182/139.
67. Galen A. Johnson, for instance writes quite explicitly, 'The Flesh is water and the human body as exemplar of Flesh is water', in 'The Problem of Origins: In the Timber Yard, Under the Sea', *Chiasmi International 2: De la nature à l'ontologie* (2000), 253. See also Frank Macke, 'Body, Liquidity and Flesh: Bachelard, Merleau-Ponty, and the Elements of Interpersonal Communication', *Philosophy Today* 51.4 (2007).
68. S, 290/178.
69. Lawlor, *The Implications of Immanence*, 70–86.
70. IP, 174–5/131.
71. IP, 175/131.
72. VI, 208/158–9 (my emphasis).
73. IP, 174/131.

Chapter 1

The Powers of Becoming: Early Greek Thought and Contemporary Biology in Merleau-Ponty's Elemental Ontology

To define Merleau-Ponty's late ontology in relation to Ionian elemental philosophy is to define it against the thought of Parmenides.[1] It thus finds itself in a certain tension with the mainstream philosophical tradition from Plato and Aristotle onwards. We may think that Merleau-Ponty's ontology simply perpetuates the critique of Parmenidean Being launched by Heidegger, but Merleau-Ponty's critique turns out to be much more radical. Barbaras will even identify Heidegger as 'still dependent on Parmenides' in comparison to Merleau-Ponty.[2] When he explicates Merleau-Ponty's 'ontology of the element', Barbaras refers to the work of Gilbert Simondon, one of Merleau-Ponty's more renowned students, to outline the three characteristics of the Ionian element that are manifest in Merleau-Ponty's late thought. Barbaras refers to Simondon rather than directly to Merleau-Ponty because Merleau-Ponty's allusion to, much less analysis of, Presocratic thought is oblique, often tangential, and lacking in detail. Simondon, however, picked up on the consanguinity of Merleau-Ponty's thought to Ionian philosophy. In a lengthy preparatory study to his thesis on individuation, Simondon traces the philosophical history of the notion of individuation beginning with and privileging the earliest concept, that of the Ionian element.[3] Simondon saw that the dual concept of prime element and *physis* was the best way to understand the *process* of individuation because it did not already presuppose individuated being in some form or other. Already Empedocles, Parmenides and the ancient atomists will use some form of individuated being as primordial. They therefore cannot think the generation of individuated being or the process of individuation. The Ionian idea of the element, however, corresponds to Merleau-Ponty's idea of pre-objective being – being that is not yet defined by individuated formation. Simondon will deploy Merleau-Ponty's idea of the pre-objective to develop his notion of the pre-individual. The basic characteristics of the Ionian element that Simondon outlines can then be mapped back on to Merleau-Ponty's 'ontology of the element', whose 'proximity to Ionian cosmology', Barbaras notes, 'is striking'.[4]

* * *

The first characteristic of the Ionian element is that it is anterior to every difference and every differentiation. It is 'the undifferentiated absolute' as much 'before every appearance of heterogeneity as before every fragmentation'.[5] Simondon notes the remarkable identity drawn between 'two aspects that will later be distinguished': in the concept of the element, 'homogeneity is unity and unity is homogeneity'.[6] In the Ionian conception, everything has unity through an original indifference between things. One might imagine this as the primordial soup of being from which arose everything that exists and in which all things retain a relation to everything else. The homogeneity of the liquid connects all things where the heterogeneity of solids keeps them apart. It is for this reason that Thales, the first of the Ionians, considered everything to be born of water. Water signifies first of all this 'state of original indistinction'. The other Ionians, Anaximander and Anaximenes, proposed other 'prime elements'. Anaximander chose the *apeiron* and Anaximenes chose air, but what they all have in common – the gaseous and the liquid – is *unity by homogeneity*.

This liquid view of the principle radically opposes that of Parmenides, for whom being's unity resides in its formal perfection. Entities, in this view, only partially and imperfectly participate in being, whose unity is maintained insofar as it transcends imperfect beings. While the Ionian element *comes into* being – that is, it differentiates itself into different individual beings – Parmenidean Being, perfect in itself, is a stranger to becoming. In elemental philosophy, becoming is the 'link of continuity that attaches particular beings, productions of immanent *physis*, to the element'.[7] The symbol of Parmenidean Being is the sphere. The sphere is a form that is individuated and complete in itself. The symbol of the prime element, by contrast, is water. Even when certain cosmogonies speak of an originary chaos, this chaos does not signify, as we think today, a big mix of entities tossed about at random. It is 'a reality that can be poured'.[8] And the originary chasm (*chasma*) is not a substantial reality, but a milieu, a space that is deprived of completed form but not deprived of all quality. It is a humid order. Sometimes Proteus will be seen as the symbol of this first reality in elemental thought. Proteus, as 'firstborn' (*protogonos*) and shapeshifter, signifies 'the aptitude of this original material to receive many forms … and to become many different elements'.[9]

We will return to the relationship between myth and elemental philosophy in Chapter 4. It suffices here to allude to the many myths in which the world emerges from primordial water or water divinities. The earth forms by solidification of the liquid in such a way that 'matter is not a distinct principle but is a qualification of water'.[10] Strictly speaking, the prime element is not material. It is latent with matter. Matter precipitates from the liquid principle like a silt deposit from a river. While Parmenidean Being, in its purity, perfection and plenitude, requires external nothingness in order to exist,[11] primordial water, as a state anterior to existence, is not a pure nothingness, nor even the gaping opening of Chaos.[12] It is an elemental non-being.

The second aspect of Ionian philosophy that Barbaras connects to Merleau-Ponty is the notion that sensible qualities have cognitive value and therefore enable us to know the real. For most of the history of philosophy, what we perceive with our senses was considered to be untrustworthy and deceptive. Truth was to be sought behind appearance. The split between the sensible and the intelligible is largely absent in Ionian thought, for this division relies on, or at least parallels, Plato's coupling of myth with falsehood. Without doubt, phenomenology as a discipline was developed to counter this rift – to interrogate the logic of sensible experience and not the logic operating behind experiential phantasms. The sensible is not merely subjective experience that hides objective reality: 'experienced states of the flesh reveal an element from which they proceed, and which makes them possible'.[13] The homogeneity of the prime element allows for no absolute distinction between the sensible and the intelligible. The element is intrinsically of the sensible. It is origin of sensibility and of sensation, of intelligibility and of intelligence. The prime element is therefore never on the side of pure exteriority as is the case with many doctrines of matter. It proposes an original unity of subjective experience and exterior nature. Such a theory coincides perfectly with Merleau-Ponty's late ontology, which proposes 'Being-seen' (*Être-vu*) as originary Being.[14] All being is visible even if this visibility always entails an invisible 'side': the side of meaning and of coming towards sense.

This brings us to the third and final aspect of the Ionian element that Barbaras highlights. The element is not matter in the sense of a passive principle or a stuff that fills a container. It is instead dynamic, always in motion. The principle by which it expresses this dynamism is *physis*, which is 'an active producer of heterogeneity'.[15] *Physis* in Ionian thought is a 'dynamism of development, of growth, more universal and more powerful than that which makes plants and animals grow'.[16] While the prime element is more comprehensive than *physis*, *physis* is the immense potency of the undifferentiated origin, the principle by which the element differentiates itself into the things of the world. *Physis* is the prime element's capacity to differentiate being and to create heterogeneity from original homogeneity and unity. The prime element accounts for existence by means of its dynamic nature, able to create forms and transformations from itself. The circular plenitude of Parmenidean Being is a unity without *physis*. It is unable to create because it lacks nothing. What comes from it can only be less than it, mere shadows or emanations. Nothing truly new arises from it. The *physis* of the element, by contrast, enables it to generate what is genuinely novel. Creation is not mere shadows below the perfect unity of being. To paraphrase Schelling, what is first is not necessarily the highest (see Chapter 5, section 2 below). What *physis* creates is above the elemental, which is its origin.

When we look at what Merleau-Ponty writes about being and the flesh in his later texts, we can see the parallels to the Ionian concept of an element:

> ... there is no longer for me a question of origins, nor of limits, nor of series of events moving towards a first cause, *but a single burst of Being, which is forever* [*un seul éclatement d'Être qui est à jamais*].[17]

> All the architecture of the notions of psycho-logy (perception, idea, – affection, pleasure, desire, love, Eros) all this bric-a-brac is suddenly illuminated when we stop thinking of all these terms as *positive* (of the 'spiritual' + or – thick) to think of them not as negatives or negativities (because this brings back the same difficulties), *but as* differentiations *of a single and massive adhesion to Being which is the flesh* [*comme des* différenciations *d'une seule et* massive *adhésion à l'Être qui est la chair*].[18]

These two quotations – working notes from *The Visible and the Invisible* – have a parallel structure. Each describes one of two aspects of the Ionian element we have outlined. The latter describes the homogeneity by which all differentiated being adheres to the element (the 'single and *massive* adhesion to Being'). The former describes the explosion of undifferentiated being by means of *physis*: the 'single burst of Being which is forever', forever differentiating and forever returning to the element's adhesive liquidity. This eternal return is not the return to the Same, the Parmenidean return to Identity, precisely because the element *is* nothing. It is only the persistence of the 'indestructible milieu', a belonging together which is neither formal nor individuated, a belonging together that rests upon element's latent power, not on its completeness.

1. Ionian physis and modern nature

At the beginning of his first of three courses on the subject of nature given at the Collège de France (the 1956–7 course entitled 'Le concept de

Nature'), Merleau-Ponty reminds us that the Greek term *physis* had quite a different meaning than the modern concept of nature. Etymologically, it is linked to the verb *phyo*,[19] which alludes to the vegetal, to growth and to emergence.[20] The Latin word *natura* refers to birth: *nascor* in Latin, which evolves into the French *naître*. Both *physis* and *natura* make reference to the new, to something that bursts forth onto the scene. The dimensions of newness and of emergence are a far cry from our current understanding of nature as necessity and law. How then did we get to this almost complete reversal of the meaning of nature? From something new and emergent, nature has become something fixed and regulated.

In outlining the meaning of the elemental in Merleau-Ponty, we cannot avoid addressing the history of the concept of nature as it transitions from the original dyad of prime element and *physis* to the modern concept of nature. This genealogy of nature will inform our study of the return of *physis* and of elemental philosophy in phenomenology broadly speaking (Husserl, Heidegger and Levinas, especially). In this chapter, we will only tangentially discuss the phenomenological context, focusing on the relationship of the history of Nature to Merleau-Ponty's unique deployment of a philosophy of nature. This will enable us to begin to distinguish Merleau-Ponty's contribution from that of his phenomenological forebears. In the above quotations, we see in sketch how Merleau-Ponty's late thought parallels the first and third characteristic aspects of Ionian thought that we had outlined with Simondon and Barbaras: (1) original indifferentiation (unity by homogeneity) and (3) auto-production (the power of *physis*). It is, however, the second characteristic, the cognitive value of the sensible, that is key to understanding the meaning of the element's auto-production through *physis*.

From the very beginning of philosophy, nature was thematised. Indeed, the first books of philosophy were all named (by later commentators at least) *Paraphyseon – On Nature*. In the second part of the first course on nature, Merleau-Ponty asks what kind of relationship there is between modern science and the philosophical idea of nature.[21] Philosophy originated in this search for a unifying first principle – the belief that there can be a principle which underlies everything and can act as a certain kind of explanation for existence. *Physis* was thus the first philosophical concept. Together with the prime element, it designated first reality. While the concept of 'nature' as we conceive of it today is something quite different from Greek *physis*, it still holds the place of the primordial, i.e., what is 'at the first day'.[22] In this lecture course, Merleau-Ponty suggests that the 'return of a Presocratic idea of Nature' re-emerged via Schelling, Bergson and Husserl as a tool to critique the modern, scientific understanding of nature as radical necessity.[23] In the modern era, Nature tends to be reduced to a system of laws underlying deceptive appearance. If the modern concept of nature is fundamentally different from the old meaning of *physis*, it does still have roots in this original meaning. As a principle of emergence likened to a plant bursting from the soil, the term *physis* held two essential meanings together. It referred to the origin of a thing – to where it came from – and to what a thing is in itself – to its essential being. A thing's appearing – its coming up from the soil into the light of day – was nothing other than its essential being in dynamic movement. The dynamism of its movement was not a stand-in for a stable and static essence. Its dynamism *was its essence*. Its bursting forth was a manifestation of the thing's origin.

The Greek term *physis* is remarkable in this way. No other language had a concept linking origin and essential being together. When they wanted to appropriate Greek philosophy, the Romans had to coin a new word, '*natura*', for they had no pre-existing term that would suitably translate *physis*. One of the most fundamental reasons Greek thought became the foundation of Western philosophy and science was this happy accident of language. As Johannes Zachhuber puts it, 'Greek had a built in tendency to assume that the world contained in itself answers to its fundamental questions insofar as knowledge of its true being or essence somehow also explained its cause and origin.'[24] While these two meanings of *physis* are compatible with understanding it as dynamic principle of elemental emergence, the concept of nature will later prove capable of retaining the dual meaning of essential being and origin even as it is severed from an understanding of emergence and accompanying ideas of birth, newness, differentiation and manifestation. This severance occurs once being comes to be thought as static form and nature as something underneath or behind the deceptive guises of the world of change and motion. When nature becomes a system of laws regulating the universe from behind appearance, it comes to be understood as radical necessity. It becomes the oppositional force that spars with subjectivity and its freedom.

In his study *Le voile d'Isis: Essai sur l'histoire de l'idée de Nature*, Pierre Hadot shows how the transformation of Greek *physis* into modern nature was intimately connected with the history of the interpretation of a certain Heraclitean fragment: *physis kryptesthai philei* (B123). As with the other Ionian philosophers so also for Heraclitus, *physis* was a principle akin to vegetative growth. While the typical English translation of this fragment is 'Nature loves to hide', the connection of *physis* to the vegetal, Hadot argues, shows that the original meaning of this fragment was quite different. For Hadot, better translations include: 'What makes appear tends to make disappear', 'What grows tends to die', 'The form (appearance) tends to disappear', 'What emerges from the earth returns to the earth.'[25] Later interpretations of this fragment would be essential to the reinvention of nature as hidden law, bringing about the increasing separation of nature equally from appearance as from emergence. Moving further and further from elemental thinking, nature came to be personified as a coy goddess who hides behind a flirtatious appearance. Metaphorically construed in this manner, nature can now be linked to something static behind changeable, deceptive appearance. It becomes something that can be rooted out like a resource, something from which the veil must be stripped away. The goddess Nature, Isis or Diana, must be unveiled to find the essential meaning of the universe, the true structure of things hiding behind the appearances. This new gnostical and esoteric conception of nature, most perfectly formulated with Renaissance allegorizing – Nature that hides her secrets – was the essential image, indeed, the central motivating factor in the discovery of modern science. The commitment to the belief in some fixed and stable truth behind the flux of untruth enabled a scientific practice that, while sceptical of what appeared to the naked eye, believed with absolute conviction that measurable and replicable results adequated to this inapparent but eternal truth. But the uncovering of the fixed and replicable covered over the possibilities of novelty and sensibility, of motion and change: the place of the unpredictable and the unmanageable.

Hadot's analysis is useful in several respects. First (1) it brings to the fore Heraclitus, who is the one Presocratic thinker Merleau-Ponty cites with any specificity. I will read Merleau-Ponty's analysis of endogenous emergence as a new interpretation of this Heraclitean fragment *physis kryptesthai philei*, an interpretation that will radically differ from Heidegger's. In this way (2) Hadot helps clarify why Barbaras called Heidegger still too Parmidean in comparison to Merleau-Ponty. Finally (3) Hadot draws attention to the vital place that the transformation of Greek *physis* into modern nature held in the split between the sensible and the intelligible. If phenomenology intervenes as a means of overcoming a dispute between realism and idealism, Hadot enables me to show why phenomenology's advancement of a logic of sensation would be the very reason phenomenology has resourced the Greek concept of *physis* against the modern concept of nature. Just like in the ancient concept of *physis*, phenomenology requires an idea of nature that gives itself in appearance rather than hides itself behind a veil of deception.

Indeed, from Husserl and Heidegger's conceptualisations of the originary Earth starting in the thirties, phenomenology, in its return to sensation is a return to the elemental. From Husserl's initial slogan 'Back to the things themselves', phenomenology makes a turn 'to the elements themselves'. As Merleau-Ponty puts it in a late working note: 'Perception is not a perception of *things*, but a perception of *elements* (water, air . . .) of rays of the world, of things which are dimensions.'²⁶ What makes a new philosophy of nature 'the phenomenological task par excellence',²⁷ is that phenomenology is able to hold the idea and the thing together in the originary correlation of sensation. While Merleau-Ponty sees the turn to *physis* in Schelling and Bergson as a means deployed to overcome the modern idea of nature as necessity, the concept of *physis* pivots with Husserl and then Heidegger into phenomenology where it serves a different purpose. It becomes a means of overcoming the split between subjective experience and objective nature, between the sensible and the intelligible, appearance and reality. For Merleau-Ponty, nature is no longer merely the object we search for behind the flux of perception. Nature is that on which and from which we see.

In this way, it is no longer possible to posit it either as constituted entirely from our subjective experience, nor as something 'real' and inert in which our perception plays no part. 'Being is not before us, but behind us', Merleau-Ponty writes. 'Hence the return to a Presocratic idea of Nature: Nature, Heraclitus says, is a child at play; she makes sense, but in the manner of a child in the middle of playing a game, and this sense is never total.'²⁸ This Heraclitean understanding of nature as a child at play is deployed within the context of Merleau-Ponty's attempt to overcome the dilemma posed by modern nature between mechanistic and finalist explanation: a nature that loses all potency and all wildness when reduced to a system of laws. Heraclitean nature is deployed against both (1) a view that puts too much meaning in nature and (2) one that puts too little meaning there. Both positions end the same way – in a solipsism of nature closed to the human or the human closed to nature. Here Merleau-Ponty cites Bachelard, who says that 'what we call "natural" is often nothing but bad theory'.²⁹ Aiming to overcome a deployment of the term 'natural' as a 'lazy postulate' in opposition to the 'cultural' or the constructed, Merleau-Ponty seeks to use contemporary science as a means of illuminating such an idea of nature, an idea of nature that is at once close to Presocratic *physis* and compatible with the science of Merleau-Ponty's time, a science in which modern nature and its laws were already beginning to break down, not only in physics (with the theory of relativity) but also in biology. Here I turn to an example from the second *Nature* course, which demonstrates perfectly how the Presocratic understanding of *physis* as the power of the prime element is the best conceptual apparatus by which to understand natural systems without falling prey to mechanism or finalism. Mechanism and finalism result from the dualism of appearance split from reality.

2. From Gestalt to element

We can go further into the relation between Merleau-Ponty's late thought and the Ionian concept of an element if we look at his analysis of emergence in biology. This example will lead us back to Heraclitus and the fragment *physis kryptesthai philei*. But first we need to speak of the insights of modern biology that enabled the possibility of such a return to the element and *physis*. The element, I would suggest, becomes a possible framework in which to think emergence in biology at the same time that the classical distinction between stasis and movement is overcome. It is through Gestalt theory that Merleau-Ponty speaks about emergence in his early work. Simondon notes how modern science overcomes substance philosophy and opens a return to the Ionian element. Substance philosophy was reliant on the ancient dichotomy of stasis and movement. The ancients did not have a conception of metastable systems and so their thought vacillated between absolute change and absolute stability. Gestalt is one way of thinking about metastable systems. The influence of Gestalt theory on Merleau-Ponty's early work is central to his later development of an understanding of being as an element. It is through starting within Gestalt theory that he is later able to use the ancient elemental philosophies of becoming to think undifferentiated elemental power at different levels of being.

His first book, *The Structure of Behavior*, had used Gestalt theory to show that behaviour functions according to meaningful structures (Gestalts) that were irreducible to the sum of their parts. In this early work, Merleau-Ponty described Gestalts as hierarchically embedded, such that the logic that governed the physical, the vital and the mental (each their own Gestalt in themselves) were nevertheless independent of each other though in a nested form, one within the other. Although vital systems emerge out of physical systems, they cannot be understood by the logic that governs the physical. As soon as a vital system emerges, every part relates to the others in such a way that the singular parts cannot be understood without this relationship. What matters is an overall pattern rather than accumulation of parts. Merleau-Ponty compares the Gestalt to a melody, in which an A note, for instance, is heard differently based on which notes accompany and surround it. The melody, however, can be transposed into a different key, such that the A note becomes a C and the B becomes an E#. The melody remains recognisably the same, not because the singular notes are the same, but because the relation between the notes remains the same. Commenting on von Uexküll, who writes that 'Every organism is a melody which sings itself', Merleau-Ponty describes the melodic organism as 'a whole which is significant for a consciousness which knows it, not a thing which rests in-itself'.[30] Every system is thus its own origin. The system can be said to be absolute in this sense. Gestalt is what first provides Merleau-Ponty with a way of understanding form that (he will later discover) corresponds closely to the Ionian idea of an element. This may seem contradictory, given that the element is the formless par excellence, but the starting point of their similarity is not in the form as such, but in the kind of internal originating energy that it has – a form-generating energy.

Like a melody, Merleau-Ponty states, 'We will say that there is form whenever the properties of a system are modified by every change brought about in a single one of its parts and, on the contrary, are conserved when they all change while maintaining the same relationship among themselves.'[31] Merleau-Ponty is arguing against mechanical, vitalist and teleological explanations of behaviour. Considered according to Gestalt, an organism responds to its environment by seeking the orientation of its own being towards the equilibrium of its structure. It searches for 'approximate solutions'[32] rather than being moved through automatic responses to stimuli. Just as it is a structural whole, the organism responds to other structures or patterns in the world. It responds to fields of possibility that can lead it out of the tension of desire into a state of equilibrium for its own field of being. In other words, it does not respond to entities but to situations that themselves exhibit larger structures. When an animal or human learns to do something, the skill they learn exceeds the situation in which it is initially contextualised and the precise motion which is learned. Merleau-Ponty cites the example of a cat that has learned to free itself by pulling a string with its paws. The cat can use this new knowledge to pull the string with its teeth, even if it has never used its teeth for pulling before.[33] Even though the act is not the same, the cat uses the knowledge that pulling strings yields freedom to transfer the knowledge of pulling with paws to pulling with teeth. The content of the knowledge is not essentially pulling-with-paws but pulling-in-order-to-free. As Ted Toadvine describes it, for Merleau-Ponty, learning 'is not a matter of mechanically repeating gestures, but rather of developing an adapted response to similar situations, often by different but equivalent means'.[34]

All behaviour operates according to Gestalt fields rather than automatic responses to stimuli. But Gestalts themselves can be divided into different kinds of behaviours. Merleau-Ponty outlines three levels of structure that organise the relationship between the world and the organism: syncretic, a-movable and symbolic structure. In syncretic behaviour, the organism responds instinctively and rigidly to situations.[35] In a-movable behaviour, the organism learns by recognising signals with the situation in front of it.[36]

Recognising patterns and responding to consequences is a-movable in this sense. The third type of behaviour, symbolic, Merleau-Ponty relegates to the domain of the human. This does not, however, imply that humans do not also participate in the lower two. In the symbolic, Merleau-Ponty discusses the transposition from a musical score written on a page that must somehow be converted into the motion of hands, arms and mouth with respect to an instrument. The goal of the symbolic notation of the score is to result in music being played on an instrument. Merleau-Ponty asks the question: what is that through which the score and the actual playing of the music are related to one another? While there is undoubtedly a relation between the score and the playing of the music, there is no common referent that can be identified as the thing to which each refers, not even by analogical predication. The score certainly is not the ideal to which the various instances of playing the music refer, nor is any one recitation an ideal. There is thus no common referent because there is no ideal and the symbolic representation which is the score cannot stand in for that ideal. Despite this lack of common referent, there is a correct and an incorrect way to play a score. Moreover, merely repeating the score correctly does not produce a good recitation of the score because repeating the score mechanically does not produce good music. Further still, the relationship between score and playing is open to improvisation. And, to make things even more complicated, we can even evaluate whether an improvisation remains true to the score or not. The truth of the music is not in the score, however, for the score isn't music at all. If there is no ideal referent, how are we evaluating the truthfulness of a recitation much less of an improvisation?

What Merleau-Ponty says is that each repetition at a particular point in time on a particular instrument and the score itself relate to one another through 'a common participation in certain musical essences'.[37] The musical essence differs from a Platonic form insofar as the variations and the score do not aim towards the essence as an ideal or a perfection. After all, it would be nonsense to say that the score aims towards fulfilment by becoming the musical essence. The score is, after all, never the music itself and the music played does not become better the more identical it becomes to the score. There are many aspects that make a recitation good, but none of them have to do with attaining an ideal. Variations and improvisations often improve the music rather than detracting from it. Instead of an ideal towards which the variations aim, the musical essence is that from which the instantiations burst into being. There is a dynamic *explosion from* a ground rather than *correspondence to* an ideal. Thus, faithfulness to the music is not contradicted by free expression (improvisation). The true and the free emerge together. Not every deviation is true to the music, but every expression is by right a deviation. It is never a correspondence.

From his early deployment of Gestalt to his later turn to the elemental, Merleau-Ponty's ontology is thus 'resolutely anti-substantialist'.[38] What exists at the most basic level – the physical world – is not things or forces, but Gestalt fields: 'In a philosophy which would genuinely renounce the notion of substance, there could be only one universe, which would be the universe of form.'[39] This notion of form as Gestalt or structure is already contrasted to both 'things' and 'ideas' and is instead a 'new category' of reality. But is this category really 'new' or is it one of the most ancient ideas? Already we can see similarities to how he will later characterise the flesh as an element 'midway between the spatio-temporal individual and the idea'.[40] While this early example of musical expression is linked to Gestalt theory, he links the same example of music explicitly with the idea of an element in his late working notes when he describes it as a universal which is not 'above', but 'beneath, ... not before, but *behind* us'. Musical variations, he says, are an expression of 'the philosophy of Being in indivision'.[41] It is no doubt Gestalt that enables Merleau-Ponty to appropriate the concept of an element in new ways within the context of twentieth-century philosophy and science even as he begins to see the ways in which the concept of Gestalt is limited.

In *The Visible and the Invisible*, the concept of Gestalt – a 'whole that does *not* reduce itself to the sum of the parts' – begins to be seen to be part of the thinking 'from above' (*pensée de survol*) that he wishes to overcome. This definition of Gestalt as an irreducible whole is a 'negative, exterior definition'.[42] The concept of the element, however, does not fall prey to this projection of the object outside the subject, for the element is defined as something that encompasses – something of which we do not see the edges and in which we are always already caught up. We are intrinsically caught up in the element because it is neither a whole nor a part of a whole – it is indefinite by definition. He moves away from this definition of the Gestalt as a 'whole' to a redefinition of Gestalt as something that is, like the element, not a spatio-temporal individual nor an idea ('free, intemporal, aspatial') but instead a region 'where it is everywhere present without one ever being able to say: it is here'.[43]

3. Element as metastable form

Simondon made an explicit connection between the modern discovery of metastable systems and the Ionian concept of an element. He appropriates Merleau-Ponty's metaphysics while drawing attention to the way modern biology and its emphasis on energetic structures surpasses ancient metaphysics. The concept of Gestalts surpasses ancient metaphysics precisely because it understands systems as metastable. One of the fundamental incompatibilities between ancient thought and contemporary science is that 'the ancients knew only instability and stability, movement and rest, they did not clearly and objectively know metastability'.[44] Aristotle and Plato made such fundamental advances in thought because they were able to postulate the stability of forms. This contrasted so strongly with previous systems because stability could only be understood to coincide with the eternal. But this advance came at a price. The introduction of the stability of forms produced a hierarchical top-down model of emanation. For ancient thought, the perfection of an entity is towards its form. The form symbolises rest, the accomplishment of an end. Without the scientific insight into the metastability of forms, Merleau-Ponty would not have been able to reverse this logic and to think the form as inaccomplishment with respect to expression and to understand individuation through expression. The action of an individual is not *towards* a form as a perfection, but *from* the form as an energetic structure yet to be realised and only realised in differentiation from itself. Metastability is the stability of a form within a certain environment that enables it to backload energy without collapsing into a lower, less structured state. Gestalt as metastable systems reveals the possibility of a renewal of the Greek concept of the element and its *physis* beyond the impasse created by the ancient binary of stasis and movement.

Metastable systems are at once stable in relation to their environment and irreducible to their parts. The simple example of an animal in its environment suffices to demonstrate this point. A gorilla, for example, has stability as a form because its energies, behaviour and body correspond to its environment. The form of the gorilla as such only has stability in relation to the jungle it roams. As long as it can climb trees, find bananas and find mates, it will continue to thrive. An organism is said to thrive when there is this correspondence, that is, when what it wants to do and what it can do are expressible in the place that it is. If the environment disappears or is altered in a radical way, the form must either transform into another form (adapt) or it will disappear. Adaptation, however, is only possible from the already interior but latent powers of the form itself that nevertheless only become real (and realisable) possibilities when the conditions of life are altered radically. At this point, its stability has come to an end. Its stability is not absolute but relative to the environment. Its relation to the environment, however, is also what makes it sufficient to itself – such that the form of the gorilla is greater than the sum of its parts.

It can thus be said to be absolute, and not relative, in a difference sense. Metastability is stability in motion, a stability that, once achieved, creates an augmentation of power – a power that corresponds to its stability. The most important thing about Gestalts is not that they are irreducible wholes, but that their wholeness results in a backload of energy. The irreducibility to its parts that defines a system also signifies the generation of a new energy that is only possible within that form. The system has a principle of energy and motion intrinsic to itself alone. As the arch of a doorway has a power to hold up a wall that the stones in themselves do not, so the emergence of a Gestalt also creates new powers.

Without metastable systems and structures, all energy would exhaust itself into a state of non-energy. While this strict dichotomy between movement and stasis dominated ancient thought, the Ionian understanding of an element is richer than its historical context would permit it to be comprehended. In our historical epoch it can now be understood more fully within the context of metastable systems. The ideas of metastasis and of potential energy (the energy of a structure) introduce a new relationship between form and matter. In Heraclitus, the elements seem to continually convert one into the other. In Plato and Aristotle, form establishes the persistence of being against the elemental flux where being finds its end in a principle of stasis: the form into which all being flows as into a container. Metastasis gives us a means to think form in such a way that it is no longer the exhaustion of potentiality in actualisation but the creation of a new potency. Each new potency, stable in itself, but rich with possibility, is like another *physis*. In an unpublished note in which Merleau-Ponty cites Simondon, he insists that we avoid understanding 'regulation' of systems mechanically or objectively, and that we should not consider this regulation as the operation of '*the same* Nature'.[45] Form as Gestalt is a way of thinking form as the generation of powers rather than the accomplishment of an act. By becoming a particular Gestalt, an energy is attainted that is not the sum of its parts but is an expression of its form. A power is generated that would not exist were it not for this form and this instantiation. While Simondon articulates the relation to Ionian philosophy much more comprehensively than Merleau-Ponty, we can see that his thought is largely derived from that of his teacher. Indeed, Merleau-Ponty's analysis of emergence within biology can be seen as a way to understand the *physis* of the prime element within the context of metastable structures. It is to such an analysis that we now turn.

4. Endogenous development as elemental emergence

If Heraclitus thinks the power of *physis* according to an analogy to the vegetative, the life forms of aquatic animals are definitive for Merleau-Ponty.

To avoid a theory that is either substantialist (Platonist, Aristotelian) or functional (Merleau-Ponty references Darwin, Lamark and Freud), he uses George E. Coghill's studies on the development of the axolotl, a type of salamander, as a demonstration that animal maturation can be explained as endogenous emergence. Maturation from egg to tadpole to salamander does not require either finalist or mechanistic explanations, i.e. positing causes from without. The animal matures based on an inner potentiality towards something that is not yet present, not even present in the inner life or coded information. How can a potentiality that lacks any kind of presence help explain animal development? How does an animal learn to walk if it does not know that its legs are for walking (teleological explanation) nor does it have a walking gene, as it were, that, once activated like one activates a software, imparts the information its brain needs to operate the leg muscles (mechanical explanation)?

Thinking of animal movement as behaviour takes us out of the choice between the immanence of the whole to its matter (mechanism) and its total transcendence (finalism). Against Darwin's understanding of animal behaviour as an automatic response to the 'ultimatum' of the environment,[46] Merleau-Ponty follows the work of biologists of his time who were arguing that there is an endogenous character to behaviour that grows out of the animal itself. Neither a collection of functions nor a mechanical reaction to the environment, the behaviour 'precedes the functioning' and 'bears a reference to the future'.[47] While the concept of Gestalt is still deployed here, the lack by which an organism develops towards a future state reveals the problem with a thinking that is concerned only with wholes and not with privations, negations and the reference to a future that is not present in any positive form. Merleau-Ponty argues that in Coghill

> the behaviour comes out of the organism fully armed, or at least there is an initiative, an endogenous character of the behaviour that is highlighted: the behaviour is neither a simple architectural effect nor a bundle of functions, it is something that is ahead of its functioning, that has a reference to the future, that is beyond its immediate possibilities and cannot immediately achieve all that it already sketches out. By virtue of its endogenous initiative, the organism traces what its future life will be; it traces its environment (Umwelt); it contains a project in reference to the whole of its life.[48]

Merleau-Ponty uses Coghill's studies on the axolotl to analyse the shift from original indifferentiation in the organism towards an increasingly differentiated being.[49] Undifferentiated being is represented by the undulatory movement of the tadpole form and differentiated being is represented by the salamander learning to walk. It learns to walk through a process by which the leg breaks away from the undifferentiated movement of the whole in its undulatory movement.

The time delay between the maturation of the nervous system and of the muscular system shows how an internal principle of development individuates the parts starting from a generalised movement. From an embryonic twitching back and forth, the tadpole soon learns the undulatory movement of swimming. When the legs first develop on the tadpole, the muscular system is not developed enough for them to function as legs. They are no more than 'branches' of the trunk. Not yet having the proper musculature, they can do nothing more than follow the wave-like movement of the whole organism. Because the nerves are already developed while the musculature is not, 'the nervous system anticipates the development of the organism, the central government sends local representatives to the different parts of the body, before they can yet have an independent existence'.[50] In other words, since the legs aren't generated to walk immediately, they can't be understood to be an automatic response to an environment. They come into being with reference to the whole animal, including its future states. When walking is learned, it is not because the legs automatically 'know' their proper purpose. The salamander learns to walk not by having an innate teleological knowledge (knowing what the legs are *for*) but by the legs resisting, even refusing, the movement of the whole. The body must stop undulating so that the differentiated movement of the parts can take hold. They start to walk by means of restricting the generalised movement of the organism. This restriction enables a new movement. By restricting the wave movement of swimming, the leg learns how to move itself. When the muscular system of the leg develops, it must first negate the undifferentiated movement of the whole body. By this negation of the undifferentiated, the general movement becomes the movement of walking. 'The leg emerges, absolutely subjugated to the trunk', Merleau-Ponty writes, 'and then it fights for its freedom.'[51]

The final knowledge arrived at in maturity, the knowledge of walking, is gained through the previous knowledge of swimming, but it is not something added onto that knowledge by accumulation. It is a radically different movement dependent on the movement of swimming precisely insofar as the axolotl generates the movement of walking by negating the movement in which it previously existed. Likewise, the mind itself is emergent: 'The mind is not what goes down into the body in order to organise it, but what emerges from it.'[52] In this sense, Merleau-Ponty thinks of the lived body itself as an elemental field. Life starts with an undifferentiated power – here manifested as the undifferentiated undulatory movement. The undifferentiated, rich with potentiality, tends towards a differentiation it already contains in virtual form but not as an already existing possibility that merely needs to be activated. The narrative that only speaks of possibility and actuality no longer obtains when the negative operation is mixed with the potency of becoming.

Each present state, the knowledge of swimming, for instance, is not merely a step towards the next state: the knowledge of walking. It was a knowledge and a structure sufficient to itself. There is no deficiency of the system that would lead us to expect a future state. It is for this precise reason that we cannot say that it *exists* as a possibility to be activated, but only becomes real through a negating resistance. The negation lies in a refusal that is launched from within, such that this interior power is not all positivity but has a negative or negating dimension that makes it open towards future states. The negative and negating dimension is together with the resistance by which the potency contained in the whole arrives at a state that is not part of the system or a possibility of it. The emergent structure does not arrive merely as a positive expression of natural energy but has this negative and negating dimension with respect to the entire generalised movement while the generalised movement itself is the negative dimension of the differentiated movement. The negation of the generalised movement is not an erasure pure and simple, for the emergent system depends upon its own resistance to what it negates – even a maintenance of a certain friction, by which it converts the generalised and undifferentiated into the more differentiated movement, in this case, of walking. While the negation is not 'pure', it is, however, absolute. The disappearance of the generalised movement is an absolute disappearance. It is absolute not in the sense of being the opposite of what replaces it, nor in the sense of being annihilated to the point that there is no memory of it. That which takes the place of what disappears depends absolutely on that which has disappeared, for the disappearing remains as the ground of what replaces it. Futurity emerges through refusal, through negation and through resistance.

This example explains in the terms of motor movement how *physis* is an inner dynamic and self-expression. It seeks to avoid using the hylomorphic and mechanical idea of 'function' as an explanatory term. Even higher forms of learning than that of attaining motor skills like walking, also derive from some kind of embryonic indifferentiation and a virtual potency.[53] Merleau-Ponty notes that the ability of higher vertebrate animals to learn comes from the fact that 'nerve tissue is surrounded by a matrix of embryonic tissue' which is 'a repository of growth potential'.[54] 'There is potential in the organism', he concludes. 'The embryo is not simple matter, but matter with reference to the future.'[55]

It is precisely in this context that Merleau-Ponty proposes a formula that I would suggest as an alternative reading of Heraclitus' fragment, *physis kryptesthai philei*, but which for Merleau-Ponty functions as an ontological principle derived from Coghill's analyses of the axolotl:

> On the one hand, there is an expansion of the whole behaviour throughout the body. At the beginning, the animal doesn't inhabit its whole body and it is only little by little that the behaviour develops through the whole body. On the other hand and at the same time that the pattern of the whole spreads through the whole organism, the parts of the organism acquire an existence that is proper to them and this in the very order in which they are invaded by the pattern of the whole. *Life hides itself in the measure that it is realised.* [*La vie se cache dans la mesure même où elle se réalise.*]⁵⁶

Here we glimpse an echo of the Heraclitean fragment which would amount to nothing less than a new interpretation: 'Life hides in the very measure in which it is realised.' That is to say, there is a negative principle in the growth of *physis*. This negative principle, its 'hiding', is the condition of *physis* itself. What begins as a vibratory and undulatory movement is differentiated by suppressing, even killing the undifferentiated vibration of the whole. Only thereby does it convert that very vibration which it killed into an emergence. When the parts realise and differentiate themselves from the total pattern, they must deny the pattern, the total movement of the body, for their own specific movement. The leg, for instance, must inhibit the undulating movement of the whole so that it can move on its own, do the work proper to itself – that is, move like a leg. The leg movement, now differentiated, still refers to the whole. It is still a movement even if no longer a movement of the whole. Now it is the movement of a new whole against the old one and for which the old whole is always precisely that: something old, but not annihilated, a past which is never surpassed even when overcome.⁵⁷ It is a means of locomotion for the animal, not for the leg alone. The legs that were there as 'branches' of the whole (almost vegetative), take on their own vital (and animal) signification when they break with the rhythm of the whole, in this case, the undulating rhythm of swimming and begin to be used as legs to walk.

Merleau-Ponty appropriates what I am identifying as a Heraclitean logic, but it is no doubt in an atypical sense that it would be Heraclitean. It isn't so much that things that grow also die. Nor is it that what appears does so by concealing itself. What Merleau-Ponty's analysis suggests is that there is negativity (disappearance) in growth itself. The negated is even the milieu in which growth takes place. Nature emerges in negating itself, but this negation is not equivalent to the emergence, for it leaves something behind as its past. We can say that Merleau-Ponty describes a Heraclitean elemental transformation within the life system: the death of aquatic movement engenders a means of terrestrial movement. There is not only a resistance, but an elemental transformation from water to earth.

If this can be described as a Merleau-Pontian interpretation of 'Nature loves to hide' (though he does not say so explicitly), it must be contrasted with that of Heidegger, who gives us several variants: 'to self-revealing ... there belongs a self-concealing',[58] 'Hiding is the predilection of Being',[59] 'Being subtracts itself by showing itself in a being as such.'[60] In short: 'Being shows itself by veiling itself.'[61] In Heidegger's identification of *physis* with being, the milieu behind *physis* is forgotten. The nature of *physis* is to be the dynamic principle by which the element emerges into being. It is the principle of self-differentiation. If it is true that, as Alain Renaut says, the late Heidegger no longer thinks of being as a 'dark background' but a 'subtraction' and a 'self-retraction',[62] such a subtraction cannot comprehend the negation that an individual entity performs against the whole, a negation that constitutes its internally constituted individuation. In Merleau-Ponty's description what is endogenous to the individuating entity has a negating action in its positive self-assertion. The field within which it arises also includes this mix of being and non-being. The field however is not 'external' to the entity. Its capacity to be negated is elemental and is not a merely logical opposite. For which reason it remains at the deepest centre of the being that emerges from it. Only a positive entity could be considered external. This elemental milieu is related negatively: it is participated but resisted. To convert *physis* into being or being into *physis*, à la Heidegger, does not leave the possibility of an elemental power behind being, an elemental non-being that is not being's opposite (pure nothingness) but its milieu of emergence.

5. From Sartre to Heraclitus

The analysis of the axolotl has brought to the fore the ontological import of negation in Merleau-Ponty's late thought. While I have read the negation intrinsic to emergence as an implicit interpretation of the Heraclitean fragment *physis kryptesthai philei*, we can also examine this principle with reference to Merleau-Ponty's explicit references to Heraclitus. One of Merleau-Ponty's inspirations for the image of the circular movement that appears frequently in his last writings is Abel Jeannière's book *La pensée d'Héraclite d'Éphèse et la vision présocratique du monde* (1959).[63] Jeannière emphasises the cyclical nature of Heraclitus fire metaphysics. The cycle of oppositions and transitions in Heraclitus was a means of expressing a metaphysics of difference grounded in an elemental bond: 'beings are born one from the other and their opposition is only a mode of bonding [*liaison*]'.[64] Jeannière contrasts Heraclitus' understanding of pure movement with Aristotle's view of movement as entelechy – the movement to a 'proper place', from power to act, where the final goal of all movement is stasis.[65] For Jeannière, Heraclitus surpasses the other Ionians because he invents a logic. His is a logic of contradictories: 'Heraclitus would not have accomplished such an advancement of human thought had he not recognised the value of negation; and thus this value can only be recognised if we give to relative non-being a reality and a metaphysical import.'[66] Unlike Parmenides, Heraclitus asserts the existence of non-being, but it is a relative non-being, manifested in the dynamism of movement.

Heraclitus can ontologise negation through movement. For Heraclitus, contradiction expresses transition. It is not the denial of the principle of non-contradiction. But Aristotelian non-contradiction only obtains for things that are not in movement. It obtains for a static logic. In a static logic, non-contradiction says that if one thing is, its contrary is not. But in Heraclitus' dynamic logic, non-contradiction shows that one thing cannot be except by the non-being of its opposite. The 'existence' of non-being is what makes Heraclitus' logic dynamic. The strict opposition of being and non-being makes logic static through substantialising being and de-substantialising non-being, but in Heraclitus, contradiction expresses the dynamism of pure movement. Contradiction is not simply a matter of insisting that one thing cannot be another at the same time (Aristotelian non-contradiction). It is rather that the being of one thing arises on the death of another. The being of a plant is the non-being of the seed. The transition point is life-death. Death for the seed is life for the plant. In Merleau-Ponty's analysis, as we have seen, the differentiated movement of the leg is dependent upon the negation of the undulatory movement of the whole. The whole in movement is the seminal world which dies in the emergence of beings.

We can now better understand the sole direct reference to Heraclitus in *The Visible and the Invisible* when Merleau-Ponty declares his search for a new dialectical thought

> capable of differentiating and integrating into one sole universe the double or even multiple senses, as Heraclitus has already shown us, the opposite directions coinciding in the circular movement[.] This thought is finally capable of effecting this integration because the circular movement is neither the simple sum of the opposed movements, nor a third movement added to them, but their *common sense*, the two component movements visible as one sole movement, *having become* a totality, that is, a spectacle: thus because the dialectic is the thought of the Being-seen, of a Being that is not simple positivity, In Itself, and not the Being-posed by a thought, but '*Self-manifestation*, unveiling, in the process of forming itself …[67]

Contrary to what Plato says about Heraclitus, Jeannière argues that Heraclitus links the senses with perception of sameness and stability rather than with flux and movement. Habitually, we perceive the sameness of the river, not its difference in movement.[68] This is because our senses have the propensity to stop at the terms of movement, to fix on the being that movement has engendered and to give it an absolute value. It is the task of philosophy to draw attention to this movement that underlies seeming stability. To recognise fundamental movement, we must go through the sensible towards the intelligible *logos*. The *logos* is precisely this pure movement in which all things are bonded. Heraclitean logic sets up the relation of the sensible and the intelligible in an entirely different way than the one that determined the history of metaphysics. In Heraclitus, we move from the sensible to the intelligible by means of a dynamic contradiction: from the perception of the river as substantial and identical to itself, to the insight that the river (which is a way of talking about *logos*) is a site of perpetual differentiation. As Heraclitus says, 'It scatters and again comes together, and approaches and recedes.'[69] Merleau-Ponty's ontology in which a thing is defined through differentiation within the 'one sole and massive adhesion to Being'[70] is in this regard a Heraclitean ontology – an ontology not of identity, but of difference.

This single reference to Heraclitus in *The Visible and the Invisible* is situated within a critique of classical 'philosophies of reflection', exemplified, for Merleau-Ponty, above all in Sartre's dialectic between being and nothingness. Merleau-Ponty's critique of such philosophies comes down to a critique of the modern construal of the motif of the human being as a mirror of nature. Although he is not against the man as mirror thematic as such, the 'philosophies of reflection' that Merleau-Ponty critiques propose a symmetrical reflection between the two terms that thereby places them in absolute opposition. This symmetry enables necessity to be wholly on the side of nature and freedom wholly on the side of the human. Merleau-Ponty's use of Heraclitus by contrast is part of an argument that shows that the mirroring capacity of the human being only takes place within the broader mirroring capacity of the element. The human being has a power of reflection because the power of reflection is already built into nature from the beginning. It is structurally doubled. Such a construal of mirroring nature, which we also find in Bachelard, leads from a symmetrical oppositional mirroring to an asymmetrical dynamic transformation. To understand Heraclitus' place within this argument – and thus the place of the elemental – we must first understand Merleau-Ponty's critique of Sartre particularly and of the problem of the real and the ideal in modern philosophy more broadly.

Merleau-Ponty makes clear he is constructing an argument against Sartre, who defines being as 'surrounded by nothingness'.[71] In Sartre nothingness is a limit concept,[72] the negation of the pure positivity which is being: 'what Being *will be* will remove itself from the ground (*fond*) of what it *is not*'.[73] For Sartre, the 'For Itself' of consciousness is pure nothingness confronted by the absolutely positive being, the 'In Itself'. Sartre's means of overcoming the antagonism between the exterior world and the world of consciousness was to radicalise the distinction to the point that consciousness becomes an absolute nothing. The duality of the real and the ideal, the In Itself and the For Itself, is surpassed only insofar as the ego is an absolute nothing which can thereby fill itself with being. The absolute negativity of consciousness is completed by the absolute positivity of being and it is through their absolute self-negation that human beings can become all things. Merleau-Ponty sees that while this conception 'describes our factual situation with more penetration than had ever been done before', it nevertheless remains deeply problematic as a philosophy that is being performed 'from above' and not within our actual situation in the world.[74] It does not penetrate into what being is in its depth or how consciousness might receive it and be transformed in that reception. In the end, the relation between being and consciousness is static because they are absolute opposites that complete each other without the one transforming, penetrating or affecting the other:

> As soon as the one is negated the other is there, each of them is only the exclusion of the other, and nothing prevents them, in the end, from exchanging their roles: there subsists only the split between them. Reciprocally alternative as they may be, they together compose one whole universe of thought, since each of them is only its retreat before the other. ... Thus, if being and nothingness are absolutely opposed, they are together founded in a sort of Hyper-being, which is mythical, since the force that requires it is their absolute repulsion.[75]

The result of an absolute separation of being and nothingness is thus the complete absorption of nothingness into the pure positivity of being.

The only way for negativity and nothingness to retain a resistance to being is if being and non-being are not absolutely opposed, but mixed.[76] To this end, Merleau-Ponty critiques the philosophy of identity, replacing it with a philosophy of difference. Difference implies position as well as the negation of what came before. It requires both being and non-being. Merleau-Ponty calls for an 'operative non-being' instead of an oppositional non-being that would have 'already decided to think according to identity'.[77] Instead of an absolute nothingness, operative non-being is an elemental nothingness:

> There is a trap inherent in the thought of the negative: if we say that it is, we destroy its negativity; but if we maintain strictly that it is not, we still elevate it to a sort of positivity, we confer upon it a sort of being, since through and

through and absolutely it is *nothing*. The negative becomes a sort of quality precisely because one fixes in its power of refusal and evasion. A negative thought is identical to a positive thought, and in this reversal remains the same in that, whether considering the void of nothingness or the absolute fullness of being, it in every case ignores density, depth, the plurality of planes, the background worlds.[78]

We must keep in mind what Merleau-Ponty implies at the end of this quotation. The authentic thought of non-being, an operative non-being, must start from a thought of depth. Because the operative non-being cannot be strictly what is not, I will call this non-being 'elemental nothingness' – the nothingness signified in a concrete form by primordial water, but which can only be known as dynamic transition.

Since consciousness cannot be understood as pure negation without secretly asserting a hyper-positivity that would encompass all negativity, the human being cannot be understood as a pure nothingness that opposes the absolute positivity of external being. For a philosophy of differentiation and of becoming, both human being and the being of the world would need to be mixtures of being and non-being, of positivity and negativity. Just as we think human being as a participation of the one sole being, so we must think human nothingness within elemental nothingness. Operative non-being can first of all be understood in this way: every form results either from the negation of the indefinite (elemental homogeneity) or from the negation of another form. The second case amounts to the same as the first, for the negation of a realised form arises from the indefinite latent potency within it. The endogenous emergence of the axolotl is one example. But we are now dealing with the place of the human being. When the human being is no longer conceived as a void to be filled by the positivity of being, man too takes up a particular place as a site of dynamic non-being, the jointure between contradictory terms in dynamic movement.

6. The mirror of nature

If, in his critique of philosophies of reflection, Merleau-Ponty has in mind certain traditions in which the subject is thought as a 'mirror of Nature', he nevertheless proposes his own phenomenology of the mirror. The mirror is a metaphor for the negative void of the self. This void is able to reflect nature. While understanding the mind as a mirror seems to imply absolute passivity, it tends to give the subject absolute agency. Being nothing in itself, it can become anything whatsoever. If in order to overcome this problematic conception, we add positive being to the subject, we must also add negativity to nature. The world cannot be merely the sum of all positively existing things and possible things. It must also consist of negativities. Merleau-Ponty's critique of the modern conception of mirroring stands upon an older, non-representationalist tradition that understands the human to be a mirror in a different way than as an absolute and pure reflection. This is a tradition that draws on Heraclitus and the Greeks, and which continues through Neoplatonism, rational mystics like Eckhart, Cusanus and Böhme and continues with Schelling. Bachelard sets up the terms of what is at stake when he writes of the difference between glass mirrors, which are 'too civilised, too compliant, too geometric',[79] and the mirroring effect of water, which, for Bachelard, is a more powerful mirror precisely because it is less exact, and in which the image is 'a little vague, a little faded':

> Glass mirrors, in the clear light of the bedroom, give too stable an image. They will become living and natural again when we can compare them to living and natural water, when the *renaturalised* imagination will be able to receive the *participation* of the spectacles of the spring and of the river.[80]

In the same way that Merleau-Ponty speaks of 'open' sense – meaning in the process of forming itself – Bachelard speaks of the mirror of the fountain as the site of 'an *open imagination*'.[81] He is referring particularly to Narcissus. Popularly believed to concern solipsistic self-reference, the myth of Narcissus cannot in fact be about such a closed self-referential mirroring. Narcissus is not looking in a geometrically exact mirror. He looks instead into the mirroring element. The vagary of the image in the depths of the water lets the imagination run beyond the image, suggesting to the mind an idealisation that is yet to be accomplished: 'Before the water that reflects his image, Narcissus feels that his beauty *continues*, that it is not completed, that he must complete it.' The myth of Narcissus is thus about transformation rather than solipsism. It concludes with Narcissus' transformation into a flower.[82] It gives us a phenomenology of the mirror completely other than solipsistic self-reference.

The Sartrian reflection of being in the nothingness of consciousness results in a symmetrical and therefore static mirroring. Merleau-Ponty detaches reflection from the subject, converting it into a power of nature, as for Bachelard it is a power of water. In this way, reflexivity becomes an asymmetrical dynamic of transformation. Merleau-Ponty shifts agency away from the subject towards being itself, so that it is no longer I who think, but being who thinks through me.[83] It is not the individual existences of nature on the one hand and consciousness on the other that yields the duality by which we could then have a mirroring relation. Mirroring is already intrinsic to nature in itself. Nature is intrinsically doubled in the element's mirroring power. Consciousness receives its reflexivity from the element's own mirroring powers. The sense that arises between the two is not a closed solipsistic loop but an opening towards transformation. In other words, the dehiscence intrinsic to nature is already a mirroring: nature 'at play in the process of forming sense' (see Chapter 1, section 1). This transferal of the centre of power from the subject to being is the basis for speaking about the flesh as what is shared between world and human. The flesh of my body and the flesh of the world reflect each other: 'the culmination of subjectivity and the culmination of materiality' are both in the capacity to be felt and to be seen.

To define both the world and the human body through sensible capacity is to define them with a term that mixes the negativity of passivity with the positivity of being. Further, it endows the human being with a mirroring capacity that is received from the mirroring capacity of nature. In the working notes of *The Visible and the Invisible*, Merleau-Ponty calls the flesh a 'mirror phenomenon'. Here he speaks of the mirror as 'an extension of my relation with my body'.[84] It is precisely this commonality with the world and not its separation from the world that makes my body 'not merely one perceived among others', but a certain mirror of nature. The human body is 'the measurer [mesurant] of all, Nullpunkt [the zero point or vanishing point] of all the dimensions of the world'.[85] The power to be seen is the *sine qua non* marking both the flesh of the world and the flesh of my body as mirrors. This power to be seen is primary. There is no pure positive being precisely insofar as all being is being-seen – being that is inherently visible and curls back on itself. That the visibility is a latency or a power to see its own visibility means that the negativity of being-seen introduces not only the surface of the mirror but the depth dimension as the surface's opposite. It should already be clear that Merleau-Ponty's sense of the mirror here is the dynamic aquatic one that Bachelard linked to Narcissus. In speaking of the explosive nature of the being-seen, Merleau-Ponty explicitly refers to narcissism in a way that echoes Bachelard's use of the myth of Narcissus: 'To touch oneself, to see oneself, accordingly, is not to apprehend oneself as an object, it is to be open to oneself, destined to oneself (narcissism).'[86] The parenthetical is Merleau-Ponty's. Or again:

> To touch oneself, to see oneself, is to obtain such a specular extract of oneself. I.e. fission of appearance and Being – a fission that already takes place in the touch (duality of the touching and the touched and which, with the mirror (Narcissus) is only a more profound adhesion to the Self.[87]

To be destined to oneself is therefore not to 'reach oneself, it is on the contrary to escape oneself ... by divergence [*d'écart*]'.[88] The narcissistic economy results in a transformation beyond oneself which 'does not cease to be hidden or latent' because it continuously plunges back into the depths of mirroring waters. These working notes, especially in their relation to Bachelard, help clarify the dynamic aspect of narcissism which is not spelled out in the reference to narcissism in 'The Intertwining – the Chiasm', a reference which leads directly to the definition of flesh as element of being precisely because the 'more profound sense of narcissism' is

> not to see in the outside, as the others see it, the contour of a body one inhabits, but especially to be seen by the outside, to exist within it, to emigrate into it, to be seduced, captivated, alienated by the phantom, so that the seer and the visible reciprocate one another and we no longer know which sees and which is seen.[89]

This fusional togetherness with the visible world ('caught up in one same "element"'), a 'cohesion' which 'prevails over every momentary discordance', nevertheless, in the 'coiling over of the visible on the visible' possesses a dynamic transformative principle. It is a 'wave [that] arises within me'.[90]

Now, to begin to sum up the import of this chapter: Merleau-Ponty deploys a Heraclitean movement towards an opposite as an instance of the kind of dialectic that overcomes the dialectic exemplified by Sartre. The dialectic he proposes is not centred on the subject and does not lead to synthesis. On the one hand,

> dialectical thought is that which admits that each term is in itself only by proceeding toward the opposed term, becomes what it is through the movement, that it is one and the same thing for each to pass into the other or to become itself, that the centripetal movement and the centrifugal movement are one sole movement.[91]

On the other hand, such a dialectic would necessarily depend upon a non-substantialist ontology such as that of Heraclitus. The point for Merleau-Ponty isn't to thematise movement. That would itself substantialise movement as a positive being and enable the subject to escape from the field of the visible once again. The point instead is to see being as differentiation instead of as identity to itself. It is differentiation that enables the possibility of a 'being in depth'. The dialectic must be 'capable of differentiating and of integrating into one sole universe the double or even multiple meanings, as Heraclitus has already shown us opposite directions coinciding in the circular movement'.[92] Here Merleau-Ponty is appropriating Heraclitus as an example of the unity of recto-verso. The invisible is the reverse side of the visible, the depths beneath the mirroring surface.

It isn't entirely clear to what Heraclitean fragment he is alluding. He may simply be indicating the general theme of the circle highlighted by

Jeannière. Though cyclical patterns are common in many of the fragments, the only one that explicitly mentions a circle is the one in which Heraclitus says that the end and the beginning in a circle's circumference are common. One interpretation of this fragment says that it refers to the cycles of nature – night-day, summer-winter, life-death. Where something begins, another thing ends. This interpretation fits with some of Heraclitus' other fragments.[93] Another interpretation would locate it alongside fragments that concern the coincidence of opposites, such as 'the way up and the way down are the same'.[94] Among these fragments, we might include *physis kryptesthai philei*: what appears tends to disappear. Instead of interpreting it as a temporal succession however – where disappearance follows appearance, and appearance follows disappearance, or death follows life and life follows death – Merleau-Ponty interprets the circular movement as a dynamic structure. Dynamic structure, while intrinsically temporal, must be differentiated from mere succession. Succession lacks a principle of dynamic movement so long as one thing meaninglessly follows another. The past and future must somehow be latent in the present, but not as another possible present. What is present must contain a dynamic tension that launches the past towards what is to come without a simple conversion of the former into the latter.

Merleau-Ponty is also probably alluding to the principle exemplified in fragment B8: 'what opposes unites and the finest attunement stems from things bearing in opposite directions, and that all things come about by strife'.[95] The unity that Merleau-Ponty articulates through expression, which is not a unity of substance, can be described as a centrifugal force. Without the opposite (centripetal) movement the force would collapse completely, either flying off and abandoning its centre or collapsing back into the centre. 'The circular movement', Merleau-Ponty thus writes, 'is neither the simple sum of the opposed movements, nor a third movement added to them, but their common sense [*sens commun*], the two component movements having become one sole movement, having become a totality, that is, a spectacle.'[96] Centrifugal and centripetal forces depend reciprocally on each other, even relying on 'an autodestruction which gives the other'.[97] Since dialectic is the 'thought of the Being-seen' the separation of the In Itself (pure positivity) and the For Itself (pure negativity) is not possible. It is 'self-manifestation, disclosure, in the process of forming itself'.[98]

In other words, in a metaphysics of differentiation, disappearance and appearance come together. They are not successive moments in time but the duality from which time springs. Their mutual belonging is the basis of time itself. It is not at all a matter of 'perspective' as some commentators read Heraclitus. It is not that disappearance from one point of view is appearance from another, that the circle's end from one perspective is its beginning from another. Rather, the centripetal energy and the centrifugal energy are one sole energy, which both negates and makes appear: two necessary components of the same movement of differentiation. Merleau-Ponty's critique of philosophies of reflection is ultimately a critique parallel to Bachelard's critique of geometric mirrors. It is not the rejection of mirroring that overcomes representational metaphysics, but the reconfiguration of mirroring starting from the mirroring element. Everything about *The Visible and the Invisible* depends on an implicit utilisation of the aquatic element as the essential metaphysical starting point of the being-seen. Philosophies of reflection are not wholly replaced. They are altered so that the mirroring gaze emerges within the mirroring element and not in a pure opposition to it. Merleau-Ponty's 'solipsist world' again quietly evokes Narcissus and the depth dimension, or 'preobjective being', required for narcissistic transformation. It is, after all, Heraclitus who takes the next step from Thales: 'For souls it is death to become water' but 'from water soul is born'.[99] The cycle is not symmetrical but has forward momentum.

These analyses now illuminate Merleau-Ponty's descriptions of the flesh as element in 'The Intertwining – the Chiasm':

> [T]he flesh we are speaking of is not matter. It is the coiling over of the visible upon the seeing body, of the tangible upon the touching body, which is attested in particular when the body sees itself, touches itself seeing and touching the things, such that, simultaneously, as tangible it descends among them, as touching it dominates them all and draws this relationship and even this double relationship from itself, by dehiscence or fission of its own mass. This concentration of the visibles about one of them, or this bursting forth of the mass of the body toward the things, ... *these two mirror arrangements* of the seeing and the visible, the touching and the touched, form a close-bound system that I count on, define a vision in general and a constant style of visibility from which I cannot detach myself ...[100]

Thinking *physis* as the negation of the undulatory energy of a Whole makes Merleau-Ponty a Heraclitean. But because he rearticulates the place of the negative (hiding), he is a Heraclitean in a different sense than Heidegger. Each appearance is an individuation by means of the suppression of the oceanic rhythm. It is therefore necessary to think of individuation through resistance to an energetic milieu and to understand appearance within an elemental non-being. This play between positivity and negation is important in a larger context than that of biological endogeny. It completely transforms the metaphysics of reflection. The mirroring power of the human being can only be properly understood within the mirroring of the element. It no longer copies what it sees but transforms it.

* * *

Merleau-Ponty is part of a phenomenological return to *physis*. What makes his concept unique is the passage he takes towards the idea of the flesh as that of which *physis* is the dynamic principle of emergence. He arrives at his late concept of flesh as element through his early interrogations of Gestalt theory. Gestalts are wholes but only retain their intrinsic energy in relation to their environment, thereby no longer counting as closed substances. Such an idea of an energetic whole open towards the outside thereby makes room for elemental operations at different 'levels of being'.[101] The prime element is no longer constrained to pure absolute indifferentiation. It is the undifferentiated possibility at the heart of every energetic structure.

While Lawlor is right to point out the direct influence of Merleau-Ponty on Derrida, Deleuze and Foucault (see Introduction, section 2), the problem with this view, can now be stated with more precision: the split between power and matter implied in Foucault's understanding of the inseparability of power and knowledge (on which Derrida's deconstructive project is also founded) relies on the developments of Empedocles and Parmenides in a way that is foreign to Merleau-Ponty's late understanding of the flesh as element.[102] Empedocles is one of the primary early elemental thinkers, but he was not the earliest. Already he begins to separate the 'roots' (the four elements) from the powers of love and strife which for him are the primordial forces that cause the elements to join and separate. For Empedocles, the elements themselves cannot explain their own movement nor can they explain the generation of form and meaning. They are instead subject to these forces.[103] This distinction of powers from elements opens the way towards Aristotle's concept of matter deprived of its own power of formation. The general thrust of post-structuralism is in this Empedoclean tradition insofar as power is identified with content in a way that trivialises both the emergence of form and its stability. If Merleau-Ponty in a certain way goes back to Ionian elemental philosophy through his understanding of Gestalts, then his philosophy takes another direction than the one taken by the mainstream philosophical tradition from Empedocles and Aristotle onwards.

Notes

1. 'If we could see the source of the ontology of the object in the thought of Parmenides, we find in the Ionians (Thales, Anaximander, Anaximenes) an ontology of which the sense is completely different, and of which the philosophy of the late Merleau-Ponty is the heir.' Renaud Barbaras, *Le tournant de l'expérience. Recherches sur la philosophie de Merleau-Ponty* (Paris: Vrin, 1998), 220.
2. Barbaras, *Le tournant de l'expérience*, 223.

3. See the volume dedicated to the relationship between Merleau-Ponty and Simondon – *Chiasmi International* 7: *Vie et individuation* (2005); and also Jacques Garelli's introduction to Simondon's *L'Individuation à la lumière des notions de forme et d'information* (Grenoble: Millon, 2013).
4. Barbaras, *Le tournant de l'expérience*, 221.
5. Simondon, *L'Individuation à la lumière des notions de forme et d'information*, 358, paraphrased by Barbaras in *Le tournant de l'expérience*, 220.
6. Simondon, *L'Individuation à la lumière des notions de forme et d'information*, 358. Quoted by Barbaras, *Le tournant de l'expérience*, 220.
7. Simondon, *L'Individuation à la lumière des notions de forme et d'information*, 359.
8. Jean Rudhardt, *Le thème de l'eau primordiale dans la mythologie grecque* (Berne: Éditions Franke, 1971), 18–19.
9. Rudhardt, *Le thème de l'eau primordiale*, 22.
10. Rudhardt, *Le thème de l'eau primordiale*, 15.
11. Simondon, *L'Individuation à la lumière des notions de forme et d'information*, 359.
12. Rudhardt, *Le thème de l'eau primordiale*, 16.
13. Barbaras, *Le tournant de l'expérience*, 220.
14. VI, 123/91; 299/250.
15. Barbaras, *Le tournant de l'expérience*, 220.
16. Simondon, *L'Individuation à la lumière des notions de forme et d'information*, 358.
17. VI, 313/265.
18. VI, 318/270 (my emphasis).
19. I follow the old-fashioned habit of transliterating upsilon with a 'y' throughout.
20. N, 19.
21. N, 117–65.
22. N, 76. This phrase is borrowed from Lucien Herr's article 'Hegel' for the *Grande Encyclopedie*, vol. XIX (p. 99), reprinted in *Choix d'écrits*, vol. 2 (Paris: Rieder, 1932), 109–46.
23. N, 118–19.
24. Johannes Zachhuber, 'Nature', in *The Routledge Handbook to Early Christian Philosophy* (2020).
25. See Pierre Hadot, *Le voile d'Isis: Essai sur l'histoire de l'idée de nature* (Paris: Gallimard, 2004), 25–31.
26. VI, 267/218.
27. Ted Toadvine, *Merleau-Ponty's Philosophy of Nature* (Evanston, IL: Northwestern University Press, 2016), 16.
28. N, 119. Merleau-Ponty misconstrues Heraclitus here, who actually says that *time*, not nature, is a child at play.
29. N, 119. See Chapter 1 of Bachelard, *L'activité rationaliste de la physique contemporaine* (Paris: PUF, 1951).
30. SC 172/159.
31. SC 50/47.
32. SC 38/38.
33. SC 106/96.
34. Toadvine, *Merleau-Ponty's Philosophy of Nature*, 28.
35. SC 114/104.
36. SC 118–19/108–9.
37. SC 132/121.
38. Toadvine, *Merleau-Ponty's Philosophy of Nature*, 33.
39. SC 144/133.
40. VI, 182/139.
41. VI, 267/218.
42. VI, 255/204.
43. VI, 255/205.

44. Simondon, *L'individuation*, 26.
45. Notes published in *Chiasmi International 7: Vie et individuation* (2005), 40.
46. N, 201.
47. N, 201–2.
48. N, 201–2.
49. The axolotl has become a recurring figure in Continental thought given its neotenic form potentially helps us understand the human being as a neotenic primate 'born essentially premature and thus destined to an eternal infancy or incompletion'. Thomas Carlson, *The Indiscrete Image: Infinitude and Creation of the Human* (Chicago: Chicago University Press, 2008), 26. For more on this theme refer to the opening chapter of Carlson's book.
50. N, 190.
51. N, 190.
52. N, 188.
53. Even the difference between motor cells and sensory cells is governed by a logic of emergence. The nerve cells are determined according to the intrinsic polarity of the animal. A vegetative or aboral pole, and an animal or oral pole. The difference of the nerve cells depends on the conduction towards the tail (motor) or towards the head (sensory). 'The animal's primary behaviour is therefore organised under pre-neural gradients: the nervous system emerges from pre-neural dynamics' (N, 192).
54. N, 192
55. N, 193.
56. N, 193–4 (my emphasis).
57. I am intentionally echoing Schelling with this phraseology. See Chapter 5, sections 4–6 below.
58. Heidegger, *The Principle of Reason*, trans. R. Lilly (Bloomington: Indiana University Press, 1991), 65.
59. 'Ce qu'est et comment se détermine la *phusis*', trans. F. Fédier, in Martin Heidegger, *Questions*, I and II, trans. Axelos et al. (Paris: Gallimard, 1990), 581.
60. Heidegger, *Gesamtausgabe 6.2 Nietzsche, II (1939–1946)*, Frankfurt: Klostermann, 1997), 359.
61. I am indebted to Pierre Hadot for collecting these Heideggerian references all in one place. He discusses Heidegger's interpretations in *Le voile d'Isis*, 303–7.
62. Alain Renaut, 'La nature aime se cacher', *Revue de métaphysique et de morale* 81.1 (1976): 106–7.
63. Emmanuel de Saint Aubert, *Être et Chair. Du corps au désir. L'habilitation ontologique de la chair* (Paris: Vrin, 2013), 195.
64. Abel Jeannière, *La pensée d'Héraclite d'Éphèse et la vision présocratique du monde* (Paris: Aubier, 1959), 22.
65. *Metaphysics*, θ(8) 1050a.
66. Jeannière, *La pensée d'Héraclite d'Éphèse*, 58.
67. VI, 123–4/91 (translation modified).
68. Fragment B12.
69. B91. Translation from Patricia Curd, ed., *A Presocratic Reader* (Indianapolis: Hackett Publishing, 2011), 45.
70. VI, 318/270.
71. Jean-Paul Sartre, *L'être et le néant* (Paris : Gallimard, 1976), 44, 815.
72. Sartre, *L'être et le néant*, 58: 'the nothingness of Being is only encountered in the limits of Being, and the total disappearance of Being would not be the advent of the reign of non-Being, but to the contrary the concurrent fading of nothingness: *there is no non-being except on the surface of being*' (Sartre's emphasis).
73. Sartre, *L'être et le néant*, 44. (Emphases are those of Sartre).
74. VI, 120/87.
75. VI, 104/74.

76. VI, 77/52.
77. VI, 95/67.
78. VI, 95/67–8.
79. Bachelard, *L'eau et les rêves*, 32.
80. Bachelard, *L'eau et les rêves*, 33.
81. Bachelard, *L'eau et les rêves*, 33.
82. Leon Battista Alberti too picks up on the transformational rather than solipsistic dimension of the myth of Narcissus. See *On Painting* (New Haven, CT: Yale University Press, 1966), II, 26.
83. For more on this theme, see Chapter 4, section 6 below and Toadvine, *Merleau Ponty's Philosophy of Nature*, 84–6.
84. VI, 303/255.
85. VI, 297/248–9.
86. VI, 297/249.
87. VI, 304/256.
88. VI, 297/249.
89. VI, 181/139.
90. VI, 183/140.
91. VI, 122/90–1.
92. VI, 123/91.
93. Particularly B88, B67, B31.
94. B60, also B51, B54.
95. B8. Translation from Heraclitus, *Fragments*, ed. and trans. T. M. Robinson (Toronto: University of Toronto Press, 1987), 15.
96. VI, 123/91.
97. VI, 123/91.
98. VI, 123–4/91.
99. B36.
100. VI, 189–90/146 (my emphasis).
101. VI, 151/114. 'Levels of being' is a phrase used by Merleau-Ponty and cited from Jean Wahl, 'Sein, Wahrheit, Welt', *Revue de métaphysique et de morale* 65.2 (April–June 1960): 187–94.
102. Michel Foucault, *Discipline and Punish*, trans. Alan Sheridan (New York: Pantheon, 1977), 184.
103. See Simondon's brief exposé of Empedocles as part of his history of the notion of the individual: *L'individuation*, 362.

Chapter 2

The Correlation of Sensation: From Act to Power

Emmanuel de Saint Aubert writes that Merleau-Ponty's contemporaries, due to the inevitable incomprehensibility cloaking any truly new way of thinking, tried to situate him in the history of philosophy – variously 'consecrated a Cartesian, an Aristotelian, a sceptic, without, however, ever approaching the central theme of his work, the question of the flesh'.[1] In response to a conference paper Merleau-Ponty gave in Geneva, R. P. Dubarle would comment that the concept of the flesh resembled that of Aristotle's theory of the soul as the 'act of the organised physical body' by which Aristotle was able, like Merleau-Ponty later, to conceive 'an actuality penetrated by the whole corporeal flesh'. Merleau-Ponty replied to this comparison to Aristotle that, although he was not a great scholar of Aristotle, he had 'no reason to refuse this illustrious parentage, if Aristotle thinks what you say'.[2]

Although many have drawn links between Merleau-Ponty's theory of perception and that of Aristotle, Aristotle is curiously absent from *The Phenomenology of Perception*. This absence of reference, however, does not necessarily signify an absence of commonality. That Aristotle's is 'the only great thought of perception that Merleau-Ponty ignores' leads Barbaras to ask whether this absence marks 'a theoretical abyss between these two philosophies or on the contrary ... a forgetting with respect to a reference in reality very present, a forgetting that would be explained then by this very familiarity'.[3] One way Aristotle implicitly operates within Merleau-Ponty's phenomenology is through the Brentanian heritage of the phenomenological doctrine of intentionality. But there are other commonalities. Aristotle's approach to perception depends on act and power in a way that modern mechanistic and geometrical approaches to optics will not. Barbaras sees Merleau-Ponty's connection to Aristotle in precisely this: the renewal of the link between perception and power.[4]

The unity of the sensing and the sensed is a major aspect of Aristotle's theory of perception, just as it is for Merleau-Ponty. But for Aristotle it is also critical for his theory of the soul. The sensing-sensed correlation is not only linked to, but even establishes, Aristotelian substantialism – the hylomorphic body – that Merleau-Ponty will emphatically reject. It is precisely this juncture that we must therefore interrogate. It is their thinking of the location of power, I will argue, that makes the conceptions of the Aristotelian soul and the Merleau-Pontian flesh radically distinct even as the mutual development of a philosophy of perception with a philosophy of power draws Merleau-Ponty back to Aristotle and away from mechanistic modes of accounting for perception. The doctrine of powers is an important aspect of Aristotelian thought. For Aristotle, power (*dynamis*) is always situated in relation to act (*energeia*). While Aristotle sees the correlation of sensation as the accomplishment of an act, Merleau-Ponty will see it as an originary belonging-together outside of any accomplishment. The togetherness of sensing and sensed is thus in the category of a power rather than an act. Already such a conception of the correlation confronts Aristotle's notion of final causality which is linked to act and accomplishment. Thus, in Merleau-Ponty's late works, the *implicit* inversion of the correlation of sensation (from an act to a power) is interwoven with an *explicit* engagement with Aristotle's doctrine of final causality. Here Merleau-Ponty places a positive value on a drastically revised version of Aristotelian final causality in light of his resolutely anti-substantialist ontology. While it may seem like an eclecticism to pick and choose which Aristotelian doctrines to keep, which to reject, and which to transform, I will show that his relation to Aristotle is coherent, indeed systematic, despite the fairly scant appearance of Aristotle's name in Merleau-Ponty's oeuvre. It is a coherent position precisely because the rejection of the one Aristotelian doctrine (substantialism) and the retention of the other (finality) are maintained for the same reason: their relation to the correlation of sensing-sensed. It is precisely because Merleau-Ponty does not think the correlation as act that he does not need the doctrine of substance. And conversely: because he does not start from the supposition of substances, he does not need to think the correlation as act. In other words, this reversal is contained in his move from a metaphysics of identity to a metaphysics of expression and of divergence. In short it is a move from substance to element. Yet to avoid purely meaningless divergence ad infinitum, he still needs to retain a certain type of finality.

1. Correlation as act: The soul

The first task is to unpack Aristotle's understanding of the correlation as an act. In creating the distinction between act (*energeia*) and potency (*dynamis*), Aristotle is trying to describe what is happening when a sensitive being senses something sensible. In thinking through the relation between sensing and the sensed, the one term, *energeia*, is meant to describe their sameness in sensation, while the other, *dynamis*, describes their difference. For Aristotle, a sensitive being has the potency to sense something sensible, but this does not mean that its sensing capacity is always activated. It is possible for a nose to smell nothing. In this case, its olfactory power is not active. However, when something odiferous wafts over to the nose, the olfactory power is activated. In smelling this odour, the nose does what it is meant to do. For Aristotle, this shift from potential to actual brings the sense to its perfection. It enacts its purpose. The sensible object is thus what enables the sense to achieve its end. This is what it is to be in act: to have accomplished its final cause (what it is for). If the nose is for smelling, this end is only accomplished in the presence of something with the capacity to be smelled.

Like the power of sensing, the sensible object has a power that is distinct from its actuality. There are things that are visible, yet unseen. When someone gazes upon them, their visibility (the intrinsic power to be seen) is activated. It is not that the object becomes visible, for its visibility was already there as a power. What happens instead is that its potential visibility becomes an active visibility. In the power to be sensed and the power to sense, we might then presume that we are dealing with two powers that are activated as two actualities. This is not, however, what Aristotle says. Instead, he says: 'The activity of the sensible object and that of the sense is one and the same activity.'[5] Aristotle sees the unity of sensation – the unity of the sensing and the sensed – to be so strong that, in the act of sensation, the two are indistinguishable. Yet while the sensing and the sensible are the same in act, 'the distinction between their being remains'.[6] How does he get to this formulation?

Aristotle sees the way in which the possibility to be sensed precedes the actuality of being sensed. It is only in the mode of possibility that the sensible thing precedes sensation. While the possibility adheres in the thing itself, the actuality must be activated by another – that is, by a being capable of sensing. Similarly, the power of sense cannot activate itself. This inability to activate its own sensibility Aristotle likens to something that is combustible.[7] Even if wood has the power to burn, it only actually burns if an agent ignites it. Thus also with sense: the sense is ignited, as it were, by something sensible. Aristotle uses the example of sound to show in what way the act of sensation is one act that unites the power of the sensible and the power of sensing. Again, the distinction between one who hears and an object that can make a sound lies for Aristotle in their potentiality. A man who can hear is not always hearing. A gong that can sound is not always sounding. The mode of the actuality of the man-who-can-hear is his hearing. The mode of the actuality of the gong that can be heard is its sounding. It is the one sound, however, that is the actuality of both, each in their proper mode: that of sounding and that of hearing. The modality of activity is different, but it is a modality of the same act, the act of audition. It is because it is one act that 'the actual hearing and the actual sounding appear and disappear at one and the same moment ... while as potentialities one of them may exist without the other'.[8] Through the distinction of actual and potential, Aristotle claims to have surpassed earlier thinkers who thought that without sensing there could be no sensible object.[9] Aristotle's introduction of the distinction potency and act helps to clarify an ambiguity in the terms 'sense' and 'sensible object'. While it is true for Aristotle that there is no *actual* sensible object without an actual sense sensing it, it is false to say there is no *potential* sensible object if there is no sense to sense it. Conversely, it is also false to say there is no potential sensing if there is no sensible object.

It is precisely here that we might mark both the similarity and the divergence of Aristotle and Merleau-Ponty. Merleau-Ponty could agree (though he might make certain qualifications) that the potential sensible object can exist without a sense to sense it, but he could not hold that there is a potential sensing if there is nothing to be sensed. What I am suggesting may seem strange at first glance to Merleau-Ponty scholars. I would appear to be putting him on the side of 'realists' who believe that the sun can exist without anyone to see it, a position which he adamantly rejects (see Chapter 6, section 2). What I want to draw out here is the way in which Aristotle's claim about the existence of each term in potentiality without the other term of the relation presupposes his substance ontology. The refusal of the second claim – that there can still be a potential sensing even if there is no sensible object – which I claim Merleau-Ponty does indeed refuse is the way out of Aristotelian substantialism. Such a position is implied in his anti-substantialism. My argument may seem counterintuitive for a further reason. Aristotle associates Presocratic thought with the belief that objects cannot exist outside of something or someone to sense them. I am associating Merleau-Ponty with Presocratic thought, on the one hand, while claiming, on the other hand, that he retains the aspect of Aristotelian potency that seems most against this Presocratic idea by which there is a certain ontological priority of the sensible over sensing and thus of the indefinite over the definite.

It is unclear whether Aristotle believes there is ever a real state of affairs in which a potential sensing exists without any actuality whatsoever (except when the sense is entirely impaired as in blindness). Given his close identification of life with sensation, he probably does not believe that such a state of affairs ever really exists. But even the fact that he makes it a logical distinction is telling. Certainly, within Merleau-Ponty's conception of the body, there is never any state of affairs in which there could be a potential sensing without a sensing of something. This goes back to one of Husserl's founding principles of phenomenology – all consciousness is consciousness of something. If nothing else, the body senses itself. It is always situated within a sensible world, even if that world is itself alone.

The difference of actual and potential is above all a logical distinction deployed to clarify an ambiguity in the terminology of sensation. Actuality and potentiality are thus essentially limit terms. This recourse to act and potency underlines the difficulty, if not impossibility, of thinking the difference of sensible and sense (even of world and mind) outside of their relation. The potentialities are posited to adequately define *what* is in act, but in the act the only difference is in their modality of appearance, not in their quiddity. Quiddity is outside of the act. The distinction between the sensed and the sensing lies, for Aristotle, in an unrealised, unactualised substance, a substance that always remains hidden – an unreal potency that lies behind the act as its condition and limit. Indeed, Aristotle's very theory of perception is grounded in the doctrine of substance. The theory's challenge – how to think the separation of sensing and sense – is resolved through the insertion of a concept, the concept of 'substance', that claims to surpass a logic of appearance by distinguishing the appearing (actual existence) from the merely logically present (potential being, essence). Nevertheless the non-appearing essence is determined through the unity of sensation, which is to say, the problem of apparition as a duality. The self-identity of things beyond the duality in appearance is injected as an unfounded presupposition by which Aristotle avoids thinking the sensing-sensed correlation as originary in the way that he thought his Presocratic foils had. By negating its originary status, he does not thereby avoid making the sensing-sensed correlation determinative. For Aristotle, a potentially sensing being can exist without anything to sense because this being is a substance. It has an identity that obtains before there is anything outside of it to sense.[10] In the case of substance as substantial form (such as the doctrine of the soul) the substance is that which determines and limits a body. The soul is a substance in this sense. It is a limit term, the form that circumscribes the body. This limitation is precisely the power to act. But the limit concept of soul-as-substance is not derived phenomenologically, as from the shock of the perceptible. It is inserted as a presupposition necessary for a philosophy of identity which sees individuated being as something prior to all relation and all becoming.

So while the powers are in the substances, these powers are exhausted in the act that unites them. The being of the sensing and of the sensed is completed and used up in the act of sensation. This unification is the end towards which the sensing being and the sensible being find their mutual fulfilment. If the *telos* of being a sensing thing is to sense something, then its end is entirely accomplished in the act of sensation. Likewise, if a sensible thing finds its end in being sensed, its end is also used up in sensation. For Aristotle, when an existent thing attains its end, its potentiality is converted into actuality. It attains the rest or stasis in which there is no potentiality left over. Thus, we arrive at the paradox by which pure act is that which does not move. In the act of sensation there is no remainder of potentiality in either entity. Aristotle's theory therefore cannot explain the energy that remains after or is generated by the union of sensation (the energy created by a metastable system, for instance).

Potential in Aristotle is as much a logical distinction as a real power. As a logical distinction it is used to distinguish what in the world of actuality is only distinguishable according to modality (sensing-sensed). But it only accomplishes this distinction through splitting each substantial being itself into two possible modalities that become absolute limit terms delineating the substance: act as that which exhausts potency and potency as the basis on which act is possible. The two terms are the same in act because act functions as the finality of each term and erases their potency in completion. The claim that there is a potential sensing without sensible object rests entirely on the presupposition of substance as limit term. We will see that it takes phenomenology some time to free itself from this presupposition.

2. Correlation as power: The flesh

The distinction between act and being is the crux of the matter and will help us distinguish Aristotle and Merleau-Ponty. In Aristotle, the being (*ousia*) of each term is what differentiates the sensing and the sensed. Aristotle describes 'being' as subsistence outside of the relation. In Merleau-Ponty, by contrast, being is the principle of their togetherness. It is their indifferentiation from each other rather than their identity as separated entities. For Merleau-Ponty, it is not the single act but the single potentiality that holds both sensing and sensed within itself. For Aristotle, the differentiated potencies are exhausted in the singularity of the act which unifies them and completes them.

Merleau-Ponty defines the flesh as the unity of the sensing and the sensible, of the seer and the visible, where 'we no longer know which sees and which is seen'.[11] Thus far seemingly close to Aristotle, but with an essential difference: flesh is a ground of being, not the expression of its actualisation. In the correlation of the sensed and the sensing, Merleau-Ponty (and Husserl before him) owe an enormous debt to Aristotle. The concept of intentionality – all consciousness is consciousness *of* something – is but a correlate of the unity of sensation (all sensing is sensation of something sensible). In *The Visible and the Invisible*, Merleau-Ponty moves away from a position that is in the *Phenomenology* much closer to Aristotle, where he states, for instance: 'To see is to see something. Seeing red is to see red existing in act.'[12] The fundamental shift of *The Visible and the Invisible*, however, is to surpass such an Aristotelian formulation in order to move beyond the closure and completeness that the doctrine of act implies. Merleau-Ponty is moving towards an open ontology. The body's self-reflexivity or auto-affection 'is not an act, it is a being towards [*être à*]'.[13] The correlation of sensation describes an openness to oneself, rather than a means of apprehending oneself as an 'ob-ject'. In this same working note, Merleau-Ponty links this openness to the narcissism that we analysed in the previous chapter (section 6). The correlation of sensation operates as a power rather than as an act – a power that is originary, before differentiation into sensing and sensed. It is no longer the result of the union of sensing and sensed accomplished through an act in which the terms find themselves to be united. The indistinction of subject and object is thus the same indistinction as that of the Ionian element, an indifference that comes before and 'bears at its heart the principle of a distinction, that holds in itself the difference it denies, in short, a relationship deeper than the terms it links'.[14] The solipsism of the flesh is grounded in the principle of elemental mirroring, the open mirroring that retains the depth dimension of a primordial liquid milieu.

Understanding sensation as power thus links Merleau-Ponty back to the 'earlier students of Nature' that Aristotle critiques for not recognising the ambiguity of the terms sense and sensible object.[15] More clarity on Merleau-Ponty's relation to the Presocratics can be obtained if we return to the conclusions Aristotle draws. The distinction of actual and potential enables both a potential being-sensed and a potential sensing to exist individually without their correlate while in act they coincide. I had earlier suggested that Merleau-Ponty could accept a potential sensible without sensing while he would reject a sensing existing apart from a sensible milieu. Merleau-Ponty's genetic approach has aimed to show that the sensing capacity is itself part of the sensible world: that seeing emerges within the visible and does not constitute it.

In both Aristotle and Merleau-Ponty, the invisible marks the potency of the visible. But the distinction between the location of each invisibility marks off the gulf between the Merleau-Pontian and Aristotelian notions of power. In Aristotelian substance ontology, the invisible is the intemporal, non-local and non-existent essence, awaiting actualisation, which determines 'from forever and nowhere'.[16] As essence, the invisible is an absolute positivity. By contrast, Merleau-Ponty's concept of the invisible is, in the words of Barbaras, 'a negative dimension, an indetermination, a retreat, or inaccomplishment at the heart of the visible'.[17] Merleau-Ponty argues that 'renouncing the essence that is intemporal and without locality' would enable us to free the thought of the essence from a conception as 'a limit idea that makes it inaccessible'.[18] The invisible no longer lies 'behind' as an unreal potency that functions as an ideal determining limit. Now the invisible is not in one limit or the other – sensible or sensing – but at the heart of sensation itself. It is within the correlation, within appearance as such. What Merleau-Ponty then designates as the 'indecisive milieu' of life[19] can no longer seek its starting point at the limits (of essence or of existence): 'it would be naïve to seek solidity in a heaven of ideas or in a *ground* (*fond*) of meaning – it is neither above nor beneath the appearances, but at their joints: it is the tie (*l'attache*) that secretly connects an experience to its variants'.[20] In other words, sensation is itself the elemental. The element is neither ground nor idea, neither above nor below. It is a middle, a milieu, a bond.

In this way, Merleau-Ponty flips Aristotle's theory inside out. Sensation is no longer defined as act, but rather as potency that extends in both directions from the middle: towards existence and towards essence, towards sensibility and towards sensitivity. As Barbaras notes, the possible is no longer determined as 'a positive being distinct from the real that will be its actualisation: it is an ingredient of the real'.[21] The potency of sensation is the power of being itself. Inherently undefined, this milieu of power is unlimited in a very precise sense. Not the absolute power of the view from nowhere, the correlation is unlimited in the sense that it has no externally imposed limit. Any sensing, however, is nevertheless situated in place and time. This situatedness is not primarily an extended situatedness (from a perspective). Place and time are depth dimensions beyond extended space. It is the weight of a being with history and geography:

> a time and space that exist by piling up, by proliferation, by encroachment, by promiscuity – a perpetual pregnancy, perpetual parturition, generativity and generality, brute essence and brute existence, which are the nodes and antinodes of the same ontological vibration.[22]

Situatedness is not an end in the way that the sensed milieu is an end for sensing in Aristotelian ontology. It is a midpoint and a milieu.

Here we can already note the change that the bond-as-power has brought to the concept of intentionality. This bond is a weight. Without resistance, intentionality remains abstract, something Bachelard saw in his analyses of the elements. Phenomenological intentionality, Bachelard argued, had not taken into account the 'coefficient of adversity' of objects.[23] If in the *Phenomenology of Perception*, as Alloa notes, Merleau-Ponty still has a philosophy of 'towards' (*vers*), it is radicalised under the influence of Bachelard already by his 1948 *Causeries* into a 'phenomenology of contra'.[24] It will appear quite forcefully and fully in his 1951 *L'homme et l'adversité*.[25]

The correlation is not a relation of constitution. To free the correlation entirely from constitution, *The Visible and the Invisible* will see correlation converted into chiasm, but Merleau-Ponty had already been moving in that direction through the idea of institution thematised in the mid-fifties. In this regard, Merleau-Ponty aims to surpass the Husserlian, and even Aristotelian, idea of 'impressional consciousness' and the assumption that its sensations and knowledge arise from 'coincidence' or 'fusion with' the thing. He goes on to associate Husserl and Sartre with this Aristotelian heritage, writing that it is not 'an act or Auffassung, (this Husserl said), nor is it a nihilating (Sartre)'.[26] These are models of perception as a fusion or correspondence with the thing. Perceiving retains a different modality of being – nihilation in the case of Sartre, the intentional act in the case of Husserl – but perception is still fundamentally construed under the fusional Aristotelian model of the act of sensation. The absolute separation of consciousness from the thing, of sensing from the sensible 'presupposes the idea of the "for itself"', which Merleau-Ponty says is 'an incontestable, but derived characteristic: it is the culmination of separation (*écart*) in *differentiation*'.[27] As we have already seen, Merleau-Ponty does not do away with reflection, but radically modifies it. If the flesh starts in indifferentiation, then as soon as there is difference, there is mirroring between the differentiating terms. Apparition yields reflection. In this note, Merleau-Ponty describes the flesh as that which casts a shadow: 'To be conscious = to have a figure on the ground – one cannot go back any further.'[28] We are speaking of the 'mirror phenomenon' once again (see Chapter 1, section 6). The distance of consciousness from what it is conscious *of* can only be understood from this dynamic – an undifferentiated togetherness that results immediately in a doubling in the pre-sensual: the latency of consciousness on the one hand and sensitivity on the other. Power is thus in every sensing not because the sensing is a substance that can be actualised in contact with the sensible world. Power is in the sensing because sensing participates in the sensible from the very origin. In the beginning, sensing recoils from the sensible milieu. This is a direct manifestation of the mirroring nature of the element, which is what enables us to say that the element coincides with sensation as such.

For this reason, Aristotle's other claim fits perfectly with Merleau-Ponty's ontology – there is a power of the sensible without sensing. This is not the pure 'in itself' of realism. It is the power of a world that is sensible all the way down to the lowest levels of being and all the way back to the origin of time. It is the prehistory of a sensing that comes to be in time and place, not a sensing that is eternally opposed to the sensible. Merleau-Ponty goes back to elemental philosophy in order to go beyond it along a different path than the one Aristotle chose. He retains the originary nature of the correlation from the Presocratics and distinguishes sensing and sensed by freeing their unity from an 'actual' coincidence and from the corresponding teleological model. Every perception has a prehistory of perceptual being. That which is perceived is perceived as surpassing my present perception of it. At the very least, we perceive it as existing from before we began to perceive it. This is true of the barest object. Some perceptions, such as landscapes, even seem to be latent with antiquity.[29] Some bear inklings of futures to come. The sensible surpasses the correlation of sensation through the vector of time. Its temporality is linked to spatiality through the dimension of depth/latency. Latency is the pregnancy of space with futurity. In this model, sensing is an expression of the becoming of the sensible. It is no longer a static potency of a substance. Sensing and sensed are now separable along a different axis than Aristotle makes them – not separable by potency, they are separable along the axis of time – for the sensing is always *late* to sense the sensible. Time becomes the milieu of sensation – a potent milieu in which sensing and sensible objects emerge in motion towards a futurity which is their difference. There is a thickness of the world and of the sensing body that is not a thickness of space, and which resists identity within the correlation. The thickness is not the 'thing in itself' or an unchanging substance. The inversion of the correlation from act to potency converts correlation into a chiasm with a thickness that precedes it. Chiasm retains 'being in depth', a being that extends beyond the intentional correlate of the mind and beyond extension in space through its plunging back into the depths of time (see Chapter 6, section 2).

The conversion of the correlation into a potency depends upon the destruction of the dualistic structure in which effective power is confined to form. Now it is the very unity of sensing-sensed that arises in power, and for which reason it is not coincidence, but a non-coinciding contact that explodes into differentiation. It reinstalls power in the elemental milieu, which enacts the mirror phenomenon as primordial (the originary process of differentiation) such that sensing arises from the sensible (and does so, at least in some nascent form, from the very beginning). Sensation as potency fits the concept of a prime element insofar as the originary unity of sensation defines being as the non-identical union of the two terms in a mirroring but upward moving economy: the indeterminate power to become (which is the power of the sensible) and a power to determine (which is the power of sensing). Because sensing is at the heart of the sensible, it is part of the power to become and has the capacity also to determine in a particular way. Sensing draws out certain possibilities of the sensible that had remained latent and could only become manifest through sensing and subsequently through perceiving. In Merleau-Ponty's concept of the flesh as element, not only is the *difference* between sensing and sensed no longer on the order of unreal potency, but the *unity* of sensing and sensed is no longer on the order of act. Where this union had been pure actuality in Aristotle, the flesh of the world becomes the site of all potency. This has everything to do with overcoming the Aristotelian understanding of unity as determination (the fulfilment of an end) and recovering an elemental concept of unity (indeterminate homogeneity).

3. Finality and flesh: Aristotle in Merleau-Ponty's nature course

The phenomenological doctrine of intentionality is a doctrine related not only to Aristotle's theory of perception, but especially to his doctrine of final causality. Insofar as perceiving accomplishes itself in the act of perception, there is a purposefulness of perceiving's reaching out towards the perceived. This accomplishment makes sensation itself teleological. Aristotle uses act (*energeia*) and *entelecheia* interchangeably. His own neologism, *entelecheia*, contains the idea of finality (*telos*) within it. *Entelecheia* is the inner drive of a being towards self-actualisation. Merleau-Ponty, however, wants to think the *telos* outside the logic of actualisation that Aristotle inaugurated. He wants to decouple it from *energeia*. It is through keeping a close eye on intentionality and its transformation in Merleau-Ponty's late works that we may examine the metamorphosis of both the correlation of sensation and the doctrine of finality. His concept of finality, I will show, leads to a paradox. While the end (*telos*) in Aristotle is quite literally an end, in other words, a limit concept, the *telos* in Merleau-Ponty is a middle. It is thought from elemental indetermination and the originary bond. While it is in this way closer to an origin than an end, what distinguishes it from a typical origin is its emplacement with temporality.

Engaging the thought of Descartes in the years after he had claimed to be 'no great Aristotelian', Merleau-Ponty would engage the work of Étienne Gilson, the great Thomistic philosopher. In Gilson, Merleau-Ponty would find a sophisticated critique of Descartes's destruction of the Aristotelian-thomistic doctrine of the analogy of being.[30] In *Eye and Mind*, Merleau-Ponty opines that Descartes turns resemblance into 'the result of perception, not its cause [*son ressort*]', such that 'nothing remains of the oneiric world of analogy'.[31] In his 1956–7 course at the Collège de France, 'Le Concept de Nature', Aristotle will be the first major figure in his account of the history of nature. Aristotle's role here is largely a positive one. And yet in this course, Aristotle is not rehabilitated for his theory of perception or his theory of the soul, but for his theory of final causality. Merleau-Ponty uses final causality particularly as a foil to early modern, anti-Aristotelian theories that understood nature's operations in exclusively mechanistic terms.

The Aristotelian dichotomy of act and power is a useful means to transition from a phenomenology of perception to a perceptual ontology precisely because Merleau-Ponty already recognised the modern distinction of consciousness and world as a modified repetition of Aristotle. 'Hegel already renewed the distinction between power and act', Merleau-Ponty writes, 'by replacing it with the distinction of the in itself and the for itself.'[32] In the *Nature* lectures, Merleau-Ponty insists that we must reject entelechy as the error of understanding a 'positive principle' behind phenomena. Also included among these positive principles is the philosophy of the idea or of the essence, insisting that the difficulty is to 'neither "Platonise" nor "Aristotelianise" (*aristoteliser*)', which is only a matter of 'doubling the reality under our eyes without at all solving the problem'.[33] At the same time, Merleau-Ponty warns against a second error at the other extreme: 'not seeing a regulatory principle at all'. It is to avoid the first extreme that Merleau-Ponty wants to reject teleology, but it is to avoid the second that he wants to retain some form of *telos*. Neither a positive principle nor an absence of principle, he proposes the solution to be a 'principle that is *negative* or is *absence*'.[34]

The negative principle must be at once regulative and generative, holding the two extremes together. To understand it as *telos*, we must first consider why Merleau-Ponty engages Aristotle at all here. Why does he need to rescue Aristotle if he has so modified the notion of finality? What Merleau-Ponty wants to retain of Aristotelian finality is the qualitative aspect of the movement towards an end. In Aristotle's theory, all things seek their ends. The end is the proper place of a thing – not an empty space but a qualitative location. Since, for Aristotle, it is the nature of light bodies to ascend,[35] 'an idea of qualitative destination is attached to Nature'.[36]

For Merleau-Ponty it is not the movement through space that counts as this seeking of proper place. What counts is the link, even the correlation, of the light body with height as a qualitative rather than spatially quantitative region. Here Merleau-Ponty is aiming to think through the implications of the originary belonging together of the two, the body and its place, rather than the temporal movement of the body towards a certain domain. Aristotle's idea of the intrinsic relation of bodies to qualitative places is, for Merleau-Ponty, connected to the stoic idea of a 'sympathy' which, he emphasises, is 'a *liaison*' (and not a connection of causes).[37] The high does not cause light bodies to ascend. Light bodies *are* with respect to the high. For Merleau-Ponty there is an original link between the thing and its final cause. The final cause does not 'produce' the thing in the way we normally conceive causation. The thing is 'in' the final cause from the beginning as things are 'in' place. Even when a thing is not in its proper place spatially, the desire for its proper place expresses a certain interior dimension of the thing that is always already bound to its proper place.

Merleau-Ponty thus understands the movement of things towards their 'proper place' in Aristotle as expressive not of a quantitative but of a fundamentally qualitative aspect of space that is linked to spatial potency – how space is grounded in place. The qualitative dimension is the power that cannot be determined mechanically and is thus before every quantitative extension. It is a movement from a non-existent potentiality to an actualised possibility. In the mechanical view, the entire universe is already fully actualised. There is no seminal potency. 'The high' is the proper place of light bodies only within a description of space in which different parts of space are qualitatively different than others based on the different capacities of the elements proper to those spaces. Our modern conception of space does not leave room for 'the high' and 'the low'. All space is homogeneous precisely because materials are stripped of their indeterminate powers that lie outside of actualisation and beyond quantity. What counts for Merleau-Ponty, however, is not the hierarchical space of the pre-Copernican cosmos by which Aristotle described this 'tendency towards' in both a quantitative and qualitative way (after all, Aristotle did believe that the high was somewhere). What counts for Merleau-Ponty is the originary belonging together of height with what ascends. This originary belonging together is a primordial structure. The qualitative aspect of the tendency towards the proper place makes it structural and reconfigures the temporality of movement into an arch-temporality. The principle of qualitative movement is in the thing itself. The principle of highness within the light body is its tension or in-tension towards the high.

Although the 'end towards which' was indeed conceived as exterior to the thing in the hierarchical view of the cosmos, it was quantitatively conceived only because measurable space was first of all qualitative. The exteriority did not designate a purely quantitative exteriority or absolutely measurable separation. (It would be absurd to say that a mass of air was five feet away from its proper place.) Merleau-Ponty notes that finality isn't immediately abolished in the Renaissance notion of the infinity of the world posited against the hierarchical, finite cosmos of antiquity. Rather, what is abolished is the division of nature into regions that are qualitatively distinct: 'A Nature where Being is everywhere and always homogeneous.'[38] This includes not only the destruction of the Ptolemian cosmos in which things obeyed different laws in the sublunar spheres than in the spheres beyond the moon. It also included the destruction of elemental heterogeneity by which fire was irreducibly different than water and air, not because one could not transform into the other, but because each gave a different spatiality that couldn't be broken down into homogeneous individualities (atoms) which would be the same across elements. Because the underlying structure of the world becomes homogeneous with mathematical theories of space and atomic theories of matter, things can no longer find their proper ends in a natural milieu. In this epoch, any cause that lies within nature must be a mechanical cause, and the *telos* is therefore 'sublimated into God'.[39] Nature becomes 'the exterior realisation of a rationality which is in God'.[40] Merleau-Ponty's is a path not taken by modernity, but which remains a viable alternative. It is indeed possible to retain the qualitative aspect of the pre-Copernican cosmos while rejecting the cumbersome quantitative measurements of the ancient spherical cosmos. As moderns, we are not convinced that the Aristotelian explanation by finality – air ascends *because* it has an affinity with height – has any real explanatory value. Merleau-Ponty however suggests that the important thing is not the temporal movement of an element or body towards a domain that it 'desires'. Instead of focusing on the body as a substance, we need to look at the relation.

One way to retain the qualitative dimension of heterogeneously conceived space (the hierarchical cosmos) is by thinking about elemental or environmental heterogeneity – the fittingness of a fish, for instance, to its aquatic milieu. Different elements, in a certain way, have different laws governing their spaces. Density of solid bodies, for instance, is significant in aquatic environments in a way that it is not in terrestrial environment. Because of the negligible density of air, mass matters much more on land than does density. A giant whale is able to float through water because of its relatively low density in comparison to water, whereas it is utterly useless on land where its extreme weight would give it no chance to survive, even if it had legs to get around on. The qualitative dimension can be retained from the Aristotelian framework without the exteriority of the location. We must start from a togetherness of a body and an environment rather than understanding the environment as something external to the body. The 'proper place' now resides in the internal tension a thing bears with respect to its milieu. This turn from the 'body proper' to the 'edge between' – expressed as a taut edge which is also a centre – implies that the *telos* is not accomplished in the act. The light body does not quantitatively go to the high and find its rest there, as towards a place located on a geometrical grid. Instead, the internal tension between body and milieu is a power that continuously aims towards release, a power directed towards a field of possibility not towards an object at the end of an aim and which could be captured by this aim. The tension of intentionality is recovered because the aim is not towards an a priori object. After all, no force is required to know the a priori. The aim is towards a field latent with potentiality.

This analysis leads directly to one of the most significant problems with Aristotle's understanding of teleology. While Merleau-Ponty sees its value in the way it gives ontological import to temporality in an arch-temporality, Aristotle eliminates temporality by defining movement through rest. The end, for Aristotle, was in the form, outside of time. Descartes already saw this problem in Aristotle. In his reaction against it, he rejected all teleology outside of an end in God.[41] If finality is needed to avoid the complete chaos of becoming without regulatory principle, the end goal of telic directness must maintain – and not eliminate – indetermination. Otherwise, it results in the abolition of time. In Aristotelian finality, Merleau-Ponty finds the key to an idea of nature that is not sheer presence and not sheer flux. The primordial togetherness of a body with its place makes nature itself a future, the destination of the world.[42] This destination risks collapsing into a future presence only so long as destination is tied to the logic of act. Merleau-Ponty retains finality without substantialism through thinking the tension that pre-exists within the undifferentiated perceptual milieu: a tension that is both generative and regulative, a milieu that bears a depth of the past and which 'leans into the future'.[43] Properly understood, the *telos* is 'a force struggling against a certain contingency of things',[44] a force that is bringing things back to order against the forces of chaos. There are thus three major aspects of Merleau-Ponty's new conception of finality: (1) an arch-temporality that retains openness rather than the closure of accomplishment in an act; (2) elemental indifferentiation or seminality (a middle that splits open rather than an end that completes); (3) the originary bond (an origin that is structural and symbolic rather than singular).

These three interlinking aspects make up the 'negative principle' which is not motivated from the 'background' which is form. Arch-temporality is not completed in static atemporality such as pure act because the *telos* is now a structure in tension: the present bears towards the future because of a certain absence of presence at the heart of the present itself. He still has the axolotl in mind when he writes, 'We can say of the animal that every moment of its history is empty of what will follow, a void that will be filled later. Each present moment is leaning into [appuyé sur] the future more than pregnant with [gros de] the future.'[45] Futurity is part of the present phenomenon, not as behind it nor as something present. Instead, it is what makes the present a state of disequilibrium. Further, Merleau-Ponty writes that 'the rupture of equilibrium appears as an operative non-being that blocks the organism from remaining in its anterior phase'.[46] Avoiding an explanation of a phenomenon through reference to its background – cause, form or substance – enables finality to be understood as the tension of the ground itself – the springing towards determination which is even a 'force struggling against a certain contingency of things', a bringing things back to order against the forces of chaos. The modern understanding of nature as a fixed system of laws strips it of the interiority by which finality can be understood as this tension towards order.

Merleau-Ponty's negative principle which is at once regulative and generative is compatible with the Greek understanding of *physis*. In Aristotle, however, this unity of the regulative and the generative is already beginning to sunder. The power once reserved for the (indeterminate) element is in Aristotle reserved for form (determination par excellence). Formal cause and final cause thus merge and materiality has no power of becoming which would be proper to itself. Aristotelian prime matter, stripped of determination of even the most minimal kind, is stripped of all potency to become. It is pure possibility without internal potency. Because elemental indifference still retains the power to be this or that and is not a power to be anything whatsoever, the tension towards determination functions as finality within an elemental metaphysics. It does not require the absolute determination of the substance that we find in Aristotle's metaphysics of the act. So in Merleau-Ponty, finality no longer coincides with formal cause. It no longer circulates around a unity by determination. The directing principle 'neither in front of nor behind' is a phantom or a faded image in the reflecting pool. 'It is not a positive being but an interrogative being that defines life',[47] an interrogation that draws us into the future through its essential indetermination, its essential vagueness.

We have seen how Merleau-Ponty inverts the correlation of sensation by converting it into a power. It no longer relies on originally separated substances. The two terms belong together from the beginning. The one and the other express the two dimensions of the perceptual milieu – perceiving and perceived. This power, however, retains a teleological dimension, but without the Aristotelian indivision of entelechy and *energeia* (act). The teleological dimension is expressed insofar as elemental power is an oriented power despite its fundamental indifferentiation and homogeneity. The elemental power is a structural matrix in tension. Seeing shares in the visible milieu as a dimension and a divergence that doubles back upon its origin. All beings are perceptual because the negative principle leaves behind a sensible matrix in which this doubling back is always already embedded.

I turn now to the experiments with the destruction of the world in Descartes, Husserl and Merleau-Ponty in order to show how the elemental, here understood as *être sauvage*, holds together primordially in Merleau-Ponty's ontology, whereas in the work of Husserl and Descartes their togetherness is posed as a problem. It is the overcoming of both substantialism and perceptual atomism that enables Merleau-Ponty to make perception ontological. For this reason the residue of perceptual atomism in Husserl's phenomenology has an important link to Aristotle's doctrine of the correlation of sensation.

Notes

1. Emmanuel de Saint Aubert, *Vers une ontologie indirecte. Sources et enjeux critiques de l'appel à l'ontologie chez Merleau-Ponty* (Paris: Vrin, 2006), 45.
2. Quotation taken from Saint Aubert, *Vers une ontologie indirecte*, 46n.
3. Barbaras, *Le tournant de l'expérience*, 14–15.
4. Barbaras, *Le tournant de l'expérience*, 15.
5. *De anima*, III, 2 425b27–8. English references to Aristotle are from Aristotle, *The Complete Works*, 2 vols, ed. Jonathan Barnes (Princeton, NJ: Princeton University Press, 1984).
6. *De anima*, III, 2 425b27–8.
7. *De anima*, II, 5, 417a7–10.
8. *De anima*, II, 2, 426a15–19.
9. *De anima*, 426a19–26.
10. See *Metaphysics*, VII, 1029a20–6.
11. VI, 181/139.
12. PP, 433/436.
13. VI, 297/249.
14. Barbaras, *Le tournant de l'expérience*, 13.
15. *De anima*, 426a19–26.
16. VI, 149/112.
17. Barbaras, *Le tournant de l'expérience*, 28.
18. VI, 149/112.
19. VI, 153/115.
20. VI, 153/116.
21. Barbaras, *Le tournant de l'expérience*, 29.
22. VI, 153/115.
23. Gaston Bachelard, *La Terre et les reveries de la volunté* (Paris: Corti, 2003), 53.
24. See Emmanuel Alloa, *La résistance du sensible: Merleau-Ponty critique de la transparence* (Éditions Kimé: Paris, 2008), 17–18.

25. Published in *Signes* (Paris: Gallimard, 1960).
26. VI, 245/191.
27. VI, 242/191.
28. VI, 245/191.
29. VI, 315/267.
30. Saint Aubert, *Être et Chair*, 245–6.
31. OE, 41.
32. N, 209.
33. N, 206.
34. N, 207.
35. *De caelo*, IV, 1, 308a14ff.
36. N, 23.
37. N, 23.
38. N, 25. Here Merleau-Ponty cites Alexandre Koyré. His work *Du monde clos à l'Univers infini* would be published the year of these lectures (1957) but was derived from the Neguchi Lectures, given in 1953. *La Révolution astronomique* would be published several years later (1961).
39. N, 25.
40. N, 27.
41. Merleau-Ponty highlights Descartes's critique of Aristotle at N, 31 and N, 173.
42. N, 117.
43. N, 207.
44. N, 28.
45. N, 207.
46. N, 207.
47. N, 207.

Chapter 3

The Elemental Bond: Surpassing Phenomenological Atomism

Contained in the flipping inside out of the correlation of sensation is the move from perception and sensation as epistemological terms to something more ontological, even a 'perceptual ontology'. It is for this reason that I now engage phenomenology's atomistic heritage, which has similarities to Aristotelianism precisely in the context of power. We will examine atomism through the experiment with the destruction of the world by which Descartes inaugurated modern philosophy and which is repeated by Husserl, and then by Merleau-Ponty. While Aristotle for his part argues against the Greek atomists, he and atomism are bound together to the degree that individuated being is primordial in both the Aristotelian idea of a substance and in the idea of indivisible discrete building blocks known as atoms. For Aristotle it is the substantial forms which designate primordial being. For atomism it is the atoms as tiny individuals. Both are philosophies of identity that posit a primordially individuated entity. The two converge and diverge precisely in a phenomenology of perception. The atomism in question is the perceptual atomism of modern philosophy – the belief that our sensation and perception consists first of all in a perception of tiny individuated particles. The mind, in a secondary action (after an original passive reception), reconstructs these atomic perceptions into the macroscopic entities we believe we see. Both Aristotle and perceptual atomism presuppose an original separation of perceiver and perceived. In the search to overcome the fissure of consciousness from being, however, Aristotle can be part of the solution, for such a solution arrives through thinking the two as primordially together: that the *correlation* of sensation is itself primordial. In his doctrine of intentionality, Husserl saw this much. 'All consciousness is consciousness *of* something' means that perceiving and perceived are primordially together. Merleau-Ponty radicalises the phenomenological turn by thoroughly rejecting the substance ontology still implicit in Husserl. This radicalisation is accomplished precisely through inverting the correlation from an act into a power. The inversion is what makes the correlation ontologically fundamental (a perceptual ontology) rather than the accomplishment of an act between discrete entities (in which it remains epistemological). It is only this inversion then that can take Husserl's phenomenology beyond its atomistic presuppositions back to elemental philosophy.

In *The Visible and the Invisible*, one way Merleau-Ponty argues for his understanding of the elemental is through a hypothesis concerning the possible destruction of the world. This experiment is conducted within a tradition Descartes inaugurated. Descartes used the hypothesis of the destruction of the world to prove that the one indestructible thing was the ego. In the face of the possibility that nothing out there actually exists, at least he, the thinker, would still know that he himself existed. Despite the search for a presuppostionless philosophy, these experiments concerning the destruction of the world are not done in a vacuum. I want to examine them to show in what way the idea of the wild (*brut*, or *sauvage*) preconditions the starting point established through these experiments. What is essentially at stake is the location of the 'wild' and thus the way in which the wild is constructed. Is there a wild in the world outside of us? Should it be eliminated altogether and instead should we posit that everything has sense? These questions will be examined with respect to two very different notions of the wild at play in these destruction-of-the-world experiments: (1) the 'wild being' (*être brut*) that Merleau-Ponty proposes is primordial and (2) the 'raw sense data' (*données brutes*) which are the particles that strike our sense organs in perceptual atomism, a presupposition of seventeenth-century optical theory that founds the possibility of Cartesian doubt. In French, the adjective used in both cases is the same: 'être brut' and 'données brutes'. But the brute in each case is not the same, above all because the substantive it modifies is radically different. Raw sense data is raw because it is not yet constituted into meaningful objects. And yet, it is already constituted into data. *Être brut* is 'brute' as a primordial undifferentiated state, not even differentiated into data (*données*) or particles.

We proceed from Descartes to Merleau-Ponty through the intermediary of Husserl insofar as he founded phenomenology precisely by excluding the possibility of the brute. This move was essential to the phenomenological turn. Phenomenology attacked the idea of raw sense data, thereby introducing the absolute reign of signification. Husserl saw that the problem of raw sense data had led to a faulty conception of the act of constitution itself, based on a dualism of exterior world and interior understanding. What Husserl questions in a novel way is the fact there is anything there to be constituted before constitution: that there could be a world before the constituting-constituted correlation. In other words, he questions that there is a 'world as such' outside of its relation to consciousness. I will summarise some of this foundational phenomenological argument. Ultimately, however, it is not the question of constitution, but the problem of individuation and differentiation that is essential, and enables us to focus on the substantive rather than the adjective in the term 'raw data'. We want to interrogate the idea of data or givens of sensation in order to make sense of the return of the wild within Merleau-Ponty's phenomenology. Wildness returns at the heart of a discourse instituted by a refusal of the wild and an elimination of the meaninglessness of *données brutes*.

1. 'Les petits êtres sauvages': The things reconstituted

The beginning of this story is well rehearsed. During the seventeenth century, the corpuscular theory of light and matter came to determine the course of modern philosophy. It determined what kind of questions philosophers would ask and from which starting points philosophers would ask them. The corpuscular theory held that little particles, called corpuscles, would physically strike perceptual organs, thereby leaving an impression through which our perceptual systems would enable us to see, hear, smell, taste and touch the world around us. The problem for philosophy was that – if what we perceive are little particles – how do we perceive meaningful objects? How do we perceive things as wholes and not as amalgamations of little bits? Are the things we perceive really the things of the world if the mind must reconstruct them into meaningful objects out of a piecemeal of particles? The theory held that these little individuated beings, the corpuscles, came to the mind without signification. They were received as raw sense data. It was up to the mind to reconstruct them and thereby produce meaningful wholes. It is thus that what we perceive with sense organs was absolutely severed from what the mind conceives. We therefore could not know if what the mind experiences is the world as it really is, for the mind must constitute a meaning after the body has received the raw data. The corpuscular theory, a variation of atomism, thereby created the problem that philosophers began to try to solve: how is there a relationship between the world and consciousness when consciousness only has access to raw particles? It is here that Descartes founds his new philosophy.[1] Descartes was able to radically question the existence of the world because the ego only had access to raw particles. Insofar as the correspondence between things and our sensible impressions was put in doubt,[2] Descartes began a thought experiment: 'examining with attention what I was, and seeing that I could pretend I had no body, and that there was no world, nor any place that I was; but that I could not pretend for all this, that I was not in any way'.[3] He could not imagine his complete annihilation since he could not *not* think.[4] Whether it is the experiment of the *Discourse on Method*, or the second meditation where he likewise postulates the absence of world and everything in it, the mind thinking is indestructible, even if it is a deceived mind.[5] Yet the type of mind that can be independent of world, even if only hypothetically, would have no access to the world in the first place, and this absence of access to the world as such is never overcome. Descartes's a priori rationalism is based on the premise that we know represented things and not things in themselves as they give themselves to us. Thus, Descartes's experiment with the destruction of the world: little is destroyed if there is no access to the world in the first place. The ego is retained as indestructible principle because of its immanence to itself, confirmed not only by the fact that it thinks but also by the fact that it feels itself thinking. To feel itself thinking is precisely to be affected by immanent sense data (whether there is a 'world' behind that data or not).

In recounting the rationalist (Cartesian) roots of modern idealisms what has been regularly noted throughout the twentieth century is the falsehood of the supposition that there can be a perception without a conception. What has not been noted, however, is how the division between perception and conception depends not only on the idea of a perception without meaning – the 'raw' data – which everyone acknowledges,[6] but depends also on (1) the individuation of sensation into 'data' at the smallest possible level, and (2) the assumption that the smallest is the most fundamental or primordial level of being. The possibility of this division depends on a primordially individuated being. The 'rawness' of the smallest level is thus a qualification of what is not raw at all. It is only viewed as raw if one considers it from the perspective of the act of conceiving larger entities. The 'smallest' level of being in this case is already broken up into particles. Matter is individuated at the lowest level such that the sensory organ is struck physically by individualised particles. If matter is individuated all the way down, the rawness or wildness of this data is not a wildness that also goes all the way down. 'Raw data', we might say, is a misnomer, even an oxymoron, for each datum has a form. Its very definition *as particle* demonstrates that it is not entirely raw. Corpuscularism presupposes the thesis that matter is divisible into small forms that we actually sense even if we do not see. Our relation to the world, then, is a relation to a world individualised all the way down. We are faced therefore with the same difficulty as Aristotle: how to think the togetherness of perceiving and the formed world out there that perceiving perceives. Microscopic individuation demands that every perception be perception of a (meaningless) something, but the fact of being little somethings already contradicts the claim to meaninglessness, that is, the idea of the 'raw'.

2. 'Seeing as': Return to the things themselves

Husserl's project was an attempt to go beyond the limits that corpuscularism had tacitly imposed on phenomenality.[7] 'Back to the things themselves'[8] is a rallying cry that seeks to eclipse the gap between perception and conception. Kant's response to this gap had resulted in a form of knowledge determined by the a priori structures of the mind. If we only have access to the raw sense data and not to the things as they give themselves to us, we can at least still have knowledge of the a priori – that which corresponds to the mind and which the mind is therefore prepared for. Husserl, however, begins to open an alternative. The reception of the things themselves as opposed to the reception of raw data exclusively would mean that signification is given with things.

Not yet challenging the reduction to the a priori, Husserl opened a dimension of transcendence within the transcendental. Husserl's call 'back to the things themselves' is not the transcendence of the 'real' as opposed to what is merely immanent to mind (the Kantian a priori). The object that transcends the mind, for Husserl, transcends it *as perceived*. The doctrine of intentionality projects the perceived out of the subject without thinking that this 'outside' is a 'reality' that sets itself in opposition to 'mere appearance'. What appears *is* the outside. The outside is what sparkles in the radiance of manifestation. Husserl believed he had overcome the representationalist problem by eliminating the traditional 'thing in itself' defined as a hard core resistant to manifestation. By eliminating the thing-in-itself's opposite term, 'mere appearance',[9] he was able to define a thing-in-itself precisely *as* what appears and not as its contrary. He overcame representationalism by bringing the correlation to its extreme limit: making transcendence itself the manifestation of the correlation. Transcendence becomes a dimension of immanent consciousness. For Husserl, the world in itself is the phenomenal world, ontologically dependent on mind. The world *an sich* is not an external world unknowable to consciousness, but is the perceived world, the world that makes sense, the world that has signification.[10] From now on, this 'marvelous correlation'[11] becomes the central tenet of phenomenology.

Husserl understood the correlation's pre-eminence in the thesis that all consciousness is 'consciousness of'. Heidegger will develop this fundamental phenomenological thesis in §32 of *Being and Time* when he says that every seeing is a 'seeing as' or an 'understanding as': 'The "as" makes up the structure of the explicitness of something that is understood.'[12] In the anglophone world, thinkers influenced by Wittgenstein also tried to show that every perception is perception of something, that every vision is a vision *as*.[13] There is no such thing as perception in the raw. I am arguing, however, that these criticisms assume that the problematic and insidious term is that of the 'raw' (*brute*) rather than that of 'data' (*données*). We can only understand Merleau-Ponty's project if we reorient what phenomenology is doing. It is not a challenge to brute being, but to the atomism of modern philosophy hidden in the concept of 'data'. It is for this reason that we must turn from the question of the wild to the question of individuation.

By presupposing that a return to 'things' is what is to be accomplished, Husserl erases the 'raw' without erasing the presupposition of data immanent to perception. Husserl fails to tackle the founding aporia of modern philosophy: the distance between conscious experience and the world out there, wild and independent of consciousness. Why return to things at all? Why presuppose that the 'out there' must – always and everywhere – be beings that are already individuated? What is presupposed is two individual entities, the thing and consciousness, whose togetherness must be accounted for. In short, Husserl repeats the Aristotelian division of the sensible and the sensing as separated substances that can only be unified in an act. The problem of representation is not only the divide between (raw) perception and (signifying) conception. The problem, I will argue, consists in the fact that the perceived is still individuated (as corpuscles) and that this individuation depends on the absolute immanence of the correlation, which is to say that the correlation is once again, in Husserl, conceived as act, just where Descartes had already noted the insufficiency of this Aristotelian account. The brute meaninglessness from which Husserl was trying to escape was a wildness that was already and always individuated. It was not primordially wild, but only wild *for* consciousness. It was raw for perception, but it was significative for a positivistically described scientific domain, namely, the domain that posited it as corpuscles.

It has already been demonstrated that there is in fact a residue of corpuscularism in Husserl's own thinking.[14] While he aims to overcome the limits of modern thought, he is in fact himself limited by this residue, namely the principle of immanence. The principle of immanence is the supposition that what we perceive is immanent to the mind (even if what we conceive is not).[15] If in Husserl the corpuscles were the immanent content given to sense, he thinks immanence originally precisely by thinking it without the division of perception and conception. The 'things' are now immanent as 'successive adumbrations' (*Abschattungen*).[16] Perceptions are extended neither spatially nor temporally because for Husserl nothing immanent to consciousness can be extended: 'experience is only possible as lived and not as spatial'.[17] A central tenet of Husserlian phenomenology is that everything, even the transcendence of the object, is perceived immanently. It is pressed upon consciousness like a footprint in the sand, albeit in the nonspatial domain of lived experience. For Husserl, the lived experience is immanence as such. He does not remove himself from the idea of impressional consciousness and in this way, he retains the Aristotelian framework of a perceiver originarily opposed to the perceived but impressed by the perceived. In his late work, Merleau-Ponty sees that this is precisely the major mistake of Husserl: 'Husserl's error', he writes, 'is to have described the interlocking starting points from a *Präsensfeld* considered as without thickness, as immanent consciousness'.[18] To open perception back to time beyond successive sketches – a time that is not merely succession of moments – perception must also be a perception *of* depth and a perception *from* depth.

We begin to see what is at stake when we examine Husserl's own Cartesian experiment regarding the destruction of the world (§49 of *Ideen I*), i.e. the possibility of the disappearance of the sketches of perception that constitute the world *an sich*: 'that from its procession all coherent order between adumbrations, apprehensions, appearances disappear – in short, that there is no world'.[19] Like Descartes's experiment before him, this experiment too is intended to test whether the ego can truly function as an absolute principle. What happens when the correlate (the phenomenal world, given in sketches) is abolished? Husserl concludes that, even though consciousness is always consciousness of something, the 'of' does not negate the absolute nature of the ego that Descartes had established: 'In the ruin of the world', he writes, 'I would still be conscious intentionally, but aiming at chaos; in this sense I would no longer be dependent on things and a world.'[20] The ego does not depend on anything. The correlate, the world, depends on it. It differs from Descartes's proof through destruction because of this quasi-Aristotelian thesis – the intentionality of consciousness. But the intentional object does not have to be a thing. The transcendental ego is in the experiment intending chaos. The chaos of sketches is not an originary chaos. It is a chaos for transcendental consciousness. It is chaos as a jumble of sketches. The very structure of all consciousness as consciousness of something depends on the transcendentality of consciousness beyond the 'of'. Each something depends on consciousness in such a way that consciousness is its a priori condition of existence: 'Insofar as their respective senses are concerned, a veritable abyss yawns between consciousness and reality. Here an adumbrated being not capable of ever becoming given absolutely, merely accidental and relative; there, a necessary and absolute being, essentially incapable of becoming given by virtue of adumbration and appearance.'[21] Even if the ego is a lived ego, the pure being of the ego 'must be held to be a self-contained *complex of being*, a complex of absolute being into which nothing can penetrate and out of which nothing can slip, to which nothing is spatiotemporally external …'[22] The intentional flow that establishes the transcendentality of the ego without a spatial or temporal outside is grounded in the theory of perception in immanent sketches. The presupposed immanence of perception that underlies the theory of perception in sketches enables the immanent auto-affection of an ego detached from a meaningful world and confronted instead with chaos. While chaos is the ultimate figure of the radically incomplete, it does not challenge at all the logic of the immanent sketch.

In sum, Husserl begins with the supposition that the perceived must be immanent. This is a supposition he retains from corpuscular physics. To avoid the distinction between perception and conception he insists that the phenomenon as such is immanent to conscious-ness (without an exterior referent) and so not given as 'mere appearance'. It now gives itself in the impression of sketches rather than the impression of corpuscles. Finally, to avoid the pitfalls of classical idealism, he shows that, through the projective theory of consciousness, the phenomenon is transcendent in such a way that it does not abandon its immanence to consciousness. The phenomenon is not identical to the mind because the mind projects the phenomenon from itself at the same time as it perceives it immanently. This is to say precisely that the mind is impressed with the sketch. The immanence of the perceived enables Husserl to ratify the transcendentality of the ego as 'consciousness of' even when the thing of which conscious-ness is conscious *of* is not a thing at all, but the unthing par excellence: chaos. The opposition of the world and consciousness – an opposition that immanence mediates and has always mediated – produces the ego as an a priori condition of experience.

Descartes claims to question everything. He nevertheless arrives at the certainty of the ego. Husserl questions the (intentional) world in order to see if the ego can still be retained as principle and thereby justifies an understanding of the world as phenomenological world. Both Husserl and Descartes use their experiments to demonstrate the indestructibility of the ego in the face of the destruction of the world. And they demonstrate this successfully. But the fact that both succeed despite their philosophical differences reveals how such success is built on a shared premise. If the ego remains indestructible in the face of the destruction the world, it is because the immanence of the perceived guarantees that the perceiver is doubled as a perceiving-perceived. This doubling of the ego as immanently affected indeed goes all the way back to Descartes's *cogito*.[23] The auto-affection of the perceiver is built upon the principle that all experience is immanent to consciousness and is thus affective. The affective ego can thereby exist without another, for it can be its own other, following the Husserlian thesis of Michel Henry.[24] That which enables the theoretical destruction of the world also founds the indestructibility of the ego. The residue of corpuscularism manifests itself in phenomenology as the presupposed immanence of the perceived, which is simply shifted from the immanence of raw data on a microscopic level to the level of phenomena that give themselves perfectly in affect.

3. 'Seeing from': Return to the elements themselves

Precisely inasmuch as he retained the principle of immanence, Husserl did not unambiguously escape the corpuscularist framework. This single premise, the heritage of modern atomism, shows that he did not see the presupposition at the root of classical idealism: that being is individuated from the beginning. Whether as microscopic or substantial forms matters little. Merleau-Ponty's critique of the immanence of consciousness in Husserl opens up two interlinked questions: *Why should the perception-conception distinction be entirely abolished?* (as has been the trend in twentieth-century philosophy as a whole) and *Why should the wild be eliminated for the sake of the absolute reign of signification?* Due to his starting point in a philosophy of difference rather than a philosophy of identity, these distinctions will be interrogated along different lines, not at all dependent on the supposition of an immanent perception, or a perception that completes a potentiality in an act. Significantly, Merleau-Ponty uses colour as a prototypical example of his perceptual ontology, whereas in corpuscular theory colour was seen to be a secondary quality, artificially added onto perceived things.[25] Merleau-Ponty describes the colour red as a 'concretion of visibility, it is not an atom'.[26] Perception starts from the undefined, out of focus, and requires 'a focusing, however brief; it emerges from a less precise, more general redness in which my gaze was caught, into which it sank, before – as we put it so aptly – fixing it'.[27] In other words, we do not first of all see *things*. We see an indiscrete world that must come into focus. 'Perception is not first a perception of *things*', Merleau-Ponty writes in his working notes, 'but a perception of elements (water, air …), of *rays of the world*, of things which are dimensions, which are worlds, I slip on these "elements" and here I am in the world, I slip from the "subjective" to Being.'[28] This slipping is not only a phenomenological description of perception. It is the way in which we can, I will argue, slip out of immanence altogether – the subjective, egological approach – and thereby arrive at a starting point within nature. We are caught up in the perceptual from the very beginning, which makes perception not subjective, but ontological.

When Merleau-Ponty then begins to develop the material nature of the flesh as a principle that replaces the egological principle, he is sure to distinguish it from atomistic materiality: 'The flesh is not matter in the sense of corpuscles of being which would add up or continue on one another to form beings.'[29] And again: 'What we are calling flesh, this interiorly worked-over mass, has no name in any philosophy. As the formative medium of the object and the subject, it is not the atom of being, the hard in-itself that resides in a unique place and moment.'[30] These two instances describing what the flesh is not – that it is not made up of atoms or corpuscles – lead up to the two times in 'The Intertwining, the Chiasm' that Merleau-Ponty defines the flesh as an element 'in the sense of a general thing'[31] or 'as the concrete emblem of a general manner of being'.[32] The flesh as element describes the 'reversibility of the seeing and the visible, of the touching and the touched' that is never in fact accomplished. This inaccomplishment of coincidence has everything to do with coincidence and correlation being a type of infinity. With his analysis of the coincidence of opposites, Nicholas of Cusa showed us that as we approach the infinite there is a quantum leap into another register before ever arriving at infinity as such.[33] Thus, similarly Merleau-Ponty notes that 'the coincidence eclipses at the moment of realisation and one of two things always occurs: either my right hand really passes over into the rank of touched, but then its hold on the world is interrupted; or it retains its hold on the world, but then I do not really touch it.'[34]

It is these propositions that we must keep in mind when we examine Merleau-Ponty's own reiteration of the Cartesian experiment with the destruction of the world. Unlike Descartes, Merleau-Ponty sees error as transitory, not absolute. Error and its correction are within time and are marked by a transition from one perception to another. Merleau-Ponty uses the example of perceiving what seems to be a piece of driftwood from a distance, but which, upon further advance, turns out to be a clayey rock. The first perception does not go away without the second replacing it. It is not known as error except through the truth of the second perception. The destruction of the world must be interrogated within this transition from one perception to another. Manifested in the phenomenon of perceptual break-up, the destruction of the world appears in a break-up of one perception which cannot be separated from its replacement with another perception.[35]

When faced with a perceptual appearance we not only know that it can subsequently 'break up', we also know that it will do so only for having been so well replaced by another that there remains no trace of it, and that we seek in vain in this chalky rock what a moment ago was a piece of wood polished by the sea. Even if a perception can be false, we see its falsity from the perspective of the perception that replaces it:

> And this is why the very fragility of a perception, attested by its breakup and by the substitution of another perception, far from authorizing us to efface the index of 'reality' from them all, obliges us to concede it to all of them, to recognize all of them to be variants of the same world, and finally to consider them not as all false, but as 'all true,' not as repeated failures in the determination of the world, but as progressive approximations.[36]

The correlation's ability to fall apart ends up establishing the radical togetherness of perceiving and perceived, the field of being united as inaccomplishment or potency. No previous perception entirely passes away but is 'crossed out' or 'cancelled' (Husserl) still leaving its trace in the perceiver as a past experience even if it has no part in the perception that replaces it. In this epistemological model, we might say that truth is not established by a measure of the certainty of the current perception, but by the duality of the phenomenon: a new perception appears simultaneously with an old perception disappearing. We think the new perception to be true precisely insofar as the old one disappears. That the old one disappears or un-phenomenalises is the basis for seeing the new phenomenon as true, for if the first one stubbornly persisted (if we continued to see the object as a piece of wood), we could not see the truth of the second (that it is in fact a rock). The destruction of the world is not found in the absence of any and every perception so that the ego would remain alone above all this destruction. What remains resides with what is destroyed. It resides in the gap between a false perception and the perception that replaces it. The destruction which is of both ego and world is also the remainder of both. It is the transition that temporally crosses the perceiving-perceived relationship. It is found in the depth manifested in the movement from pastness to futurity.

Since there is something sensible between the false perception and the one that replaces it – both 'variants of the same world' – Merleau-Ponty's experiment with the destruction of the world maintains that the link between the perceiver and the perceived (1) is 'indestructible'[37] (against the Cartesian doubt which destroys every attachment and thereby establishes an absolute being (the ego)) and (2) is not reducible to the signifier (the 'seeing as' or 'consciousness of') which would dominate the sensible (thus always reduced to something sensed). What is indestructible, following Merleau-Ponty's experiment, is not an absolute being but a relative being – indeed a relation – thereby leaving us with a paradox: the indestructible bond. If the bond between perceiving-perceived is indestructible, neither the one nor the other is indestructible by itself. Only the relation itself remains, even in the face of the destruction of the terms of the relation. This is to describe precisely an absolute relation or a relative absolute. The absolute is, of course, defined as that which is free of relation, that which is not relative. Yet the relation here is precisely what breaks free of all relation and thus attains the status of the absolute, its contrary. The bond is what is left behind when everything else is swept away, when even the terms which are said to be related are no longer there. It is the germ of togetherness before anything is. There is thus a doubleness and a structure of the principle itself. The bond between sensed and sensing is not dependent on anything. The world depends on it. It is this new analysis of the destruction of the world that requires the transformation from a philosophy of ideality to a philosophy of difference, from sensation as act to sensation as power, from individuated being to individuating being – a togetherness that is the absolute principle of being.

The transition from one signification to another manifests the irreducible bond of sensation and the wild ground of being. The historicity of intentionality and its correlate, the depth dimension of the perceived and intentionality's ability to slip from one defined perception to another without destroying the unity of perception – shows that the (intending) ego no longer guarantees its own indestructibility as it does for Descartes and Husserl. Thinking the destruction of the world across time rather than from a static position shows that what is indestructible is not one term or the other, but the bond itself, the bond which is nothing less than the wild, undifferentiated milieu. The indestructibility of the bond, however, is no guarantee of meaning. In the late Merleau-Ponty, there is no longer an affirmation of the Husserlian thesis 'all consciousness is consciousness of something'. Merleau-Ponty interrogates the passage from the consciousness of one thing to the consciousness of another in the perception of the same object. He does not propose the destruction of the world on the assumption that the disappearance of the world would be the destruction of the seen object (intentional world). The originary bond does not coincide with the 'of' between consciousness and object, which is atemporal and immanent. The elemental bond is depth dimension and primordial temporality. This shows precisely that Merleau-Ponty is no longer dependent on the principle of immanence which places the bond *in* consciousness as the impression of the thing *on* consciousness. As primordial temporality, the bond is before both consciousness and the thing. It is radically free of the economy of impression. The perceived chaos (following either Descartes or Husserl) has nothing to do with this pre-objective and preconscious layer of which Merleau-Ponty speaks. Any chaos that is perceived is still an object of consciousness and therefore depends on the fact that the one who perceives such chaos also precedes that chaos. Merleau-Ponty, to the contrary, shows the way in which the link between consciousness and thing precedes them both and therefore precedes any chaos possibly present to a mind.

Merleau-Ponty critiques Husserl's theory of time for being 'dependent on the convention that one can represent the series of nows by points on a line'.[38] Merleau-Ponty's experiment with the destruction of the world does not go back to a static ego. It retains originary temporality precisely because it retains the bond as originary. In the face of the destruction of the world, what remains is a transition, the passage from one perception to another. Neither the perceived itself (realism) nor the perceiver (idealism) remains indestructible. What remains is the bond and its transitive power. The origin is a passage because the bond tends towards being – towards both the subjective perceiving dimension and the objective perceived dimension – both dimensions being an expression of the depth of the bond. The temporality of the originary bond implies the impossibility of punctual, impressional existence, for its temporality includes both appearance and disappearance rather than successive immanent sketches. Perception in time never adequates to the truth. With Merleau-Ponty the destruction of the world can no longer consist in a destruction of the visible to the benefit of the seer. Consciousness is placed in a position just as derived as that of the seen world. Consciousness is not a principle but depends upon its indefinite bond to the perceived world which enables it to transition from one perception to another. Each appearance is built upon a ground of disappearance, for what disappears is not entirely negated but remains part of the same world, an aspect of the depth of the past contained in, but not immanent to, the current perception. For Descartes, the deceptive nature of appearance was a veritable crisis for philosophical knowledge. Merleau-Ponty reconfigures it so that it is never an absolute deception, but instead is always the break-up of a *particular perception*. What enables us to recognise the possibility of deception is the introduction of another perceived.

Unlike Descartes, Merleau-Ponty keeps his eye on the very phenomenon of perceptual break-up. Perceptual break-up is not a crisis for perception and for knowledge as such. Instead, perceptual break-up is the very condition of the possibility of knowledge in the first place. There is always and everywhere perception, but for the ascent of knowledge, one perception must be able to break up in order that a new perception might replace it. Consciousness of the thing comes from the break-up of their original belonging. It is not a belonging of act but the primordial bond – the accomplishment of a union of what had been separate – but the belonging of the consciousness with what it had always been a part of – the perceptual milieu, the visible world. Without the principle of immanence, the perceived is no longer impression and act. It is expression and power. And this is the reason Merleau-Ponty gives in explaining why he is not a 'finalist' in the traditional teleological sense. The relation of the interior impression and the exterior world is 'not something *made, fabricated*'.[39] The interior and exterior object are like two sides of one piece of paper [*feuillet*]. Their togetherness does not have to be accomplished. Both the perceiver and the perceived are expressions of the originary bond. Barbaras defines the Merleau-Pontian element precisely as a milieu from which seeing takes place, which I have tried to show is dependent on the original togetherness of seeing-seen or perceiving-perceived – a togetherness that goes out into difference instead of a coinciding that is the solution to an original separation: 'The element is not subjective, nor is it *what* is perceived. It is the dimension *according to which* the perception takes place.'[40]

This experiment shows how we can deploy Merleau-Ponty against Husserl in order to surpass the principle of immanence – now understanding correlation as divergence and as power. With his turn from correlation to chiasm, he contests at once 'the naïve idea of being in itself' (realism) and 'the correlative idea of a being of representation' (idealism). If it is no longer a question of the existence of the world but of 'knowing the meaning of the being of the world', it is because Merleau-Ponty prolongs the phenomenological project that Husserl began, pushing the immanence of sensation to the infinite in order to destroy it as act and thus to destroy its status as principle. In 'La philosophe et son ombre' Merleau-Ponty expresses this double attitude towards the founder of phenomenology, contesting Husserl's reduction through what resists phenomenology: 'It is therefore not the unreflected that contests reflection. The reflection contests itself, because by definition its effort of recuperation, possession, internalization or immanence has meaning only with regard to a term already given, and which withdraws into its transcendence under the very gaze that looks for it there.'[41] And a few pages later: 'There is unquestionably something between transcendent Nature, the in itself of naturalism, and the immanence of the mind, of its acts and its noemas. It is in this in-between that we must try to move forward.'[42]

Regarding the possibility of the destruction of the world, Merleau-Ponty will reject the Cartesian assumption that the existence of the world can be radically doubted. He retains the phenomenological approach in which consciousness cannot be ripped from consciousness of something. Only the assumption that the attachment to the world is secondary – mediated by corpuscles – enables Descartes to question the world's very existence and thereby to establish the pure, separated being of the ego.

Descartes was of course motivated by the real possibility of a deceptive appearance. We know that things are not always as they seem. Philosophy has always looked for a truth that isn't apparent to the masses, a truth hidden from the senses. But it is the corpuscular theory of radical separation from worldly appearance that enables Descartes to question the world as such. Merleau-Ponty also starts from the possibility of a false perception, but he arrives at an entirely different, quite unexpected principle: neither pure being nor pure consciousness, but the 'in-between' which is the link of the world to consciousness. Merleau-Ponty's view then proposes a different place for the wild. *Être brut* is an indeterminate region rather than the '*petits êtres bruts*' or '*données brutes*' of corpuscularism. He does not need to negate all wildness as Husserl had done precisely because *être brut* lies outside of all immanence in the depth dimension of being. Merleau-Ponty's perceptual ontology challenges the reduction of perception to immanence, instead thinking the correlation of perceiving and perceived as primordially together and never coinciding. Only what is limited can be fully immanent, for even the unlimited below (the *apeiron*) and not just the unlimited above (divine infinitude) transcends conscious perception. The depth of the element is a power, and its power is inexhaustible.

4. 'Données brutes' and 'être brut': The elemental turn

In sum, Merleau-Ponty's understanding of the 'wild' ground of the perceptual milieu is radically different than that of Descartes and the subsequent metaphysical tradition. The modern tradition put chaos as something 'out there' and in front of consciousness. Merleau-Ponty places *être sauvage* as that from which both perceiving and perceived emerge together: a fundamentally visible, perceptual milieu. If the problem of the real world derives from the postulate that minuscule particles leave impressions on the sense organs, thereby obscuring direct access to the world, wild being for Merleau-Ponty does not rest on a theoretical postulate at all. Rather it is derived from two phenomenological observations: (1) that sensory organs take a moment to focus, and therefore require a temporal movement from a general, indiscrete perception to a more distinct perception; and (2) that the transition from a false perception to a more accurate perception of the same object implies that this indistinct perception is primary, indeed that the indistinction of perceiver and perceived is part of this indistinction, the blurry vision of the child still attached by the umbilical cord to the warm liquid of the sensuous womb. The link between perceived and perceiving is more originary than what comes into view and more originary than the view that looks at it. The doubling structure of perception is already in being before there is perception of anything. Merleau-Ponty returns to the brute or wild without the individuation of microscopic particles. In corpuscularism, the raw particles are at once the individuated building blocks of materiality and are the postulate that makes possible the absolute division of consciousness and being. We may go so far as to say that corpuscularism is what makes possible Sartre's understanding of consciousness as Nothingness: the dichotomy of the external being and the internal *nihil*.

This entire construction of the interior-exterior division does not fit with an ontology in which the bond is originary. As a linkage between matter and consciousness, the bond cannot be either exterior materiality or interior consciousness. The bond comes before the distinction between the external world and the interiority of the subject, that is, before the individuation into subject and world. The division between world and sensing creatures is not as strict in Aristotle as it becomes in the modern division between being and consciousness. It is nevertheless structured as a division which is overcome through an 'end' (sensation) rather than an indivision whose primordial tension results in a division. The ontology of the bond needs another term to describe the originary – a term that is neither within the realm of consciousness nor within the material realm. For this, Merleau-Ponty chose the term flesh, but it was also why he chose to describe the flesh as an element. The following chapters will explore in more detail why the element is the proper term to describe the perceptual milieu.

It is perhaps incidental to our argument that elemental theory was the primary opponent of atomistic philosophy in Presocratic Greece. The return to a theory of the elemental that has taken place in phenomenology from the beginning was not essentially articulated against atomism. But the genealogy I have traced suggests that precisely what Merleau-Ponty contested in Husserl's philosophy was the residue of modern perceptual atomism. Non-meaning, for Husserl, would remain a product of the gap between consciousness and exteriority. The principle of immanence, this residue of corpuscularism, limits Husserl's possible response. To think correlation and signification all the way down is his solution to the problem of corpuscularism and the immanence of perception. He is unable to think the wild as ontologically basic because the principle of immanence prohibits him from making perception ontological. When the principle of immanence is retained, we cannot observe that the visible also gives the seer, and does so in such a way that the seer is ontologically dependent on the visible because the visible is itself no longer an 'objective world' to be seen but is the primordial bond of all that has the power to show itself. Chaos in Husserl is a perceived chaos – the jumble of adumbrations. It is not an ontological principle. The perception of chaos never risks annihilating the ego. The destruction of the world never puts the ego in danger. This is because the principle of immanence yields the auto-affection of the ego as an automatic output. And for this reason Husserl could only question the 'wild' of 'raw data' and not the individuation of the data.

The return of the brute without individuation into particles is not only a return to an underlying, meaningless level. *Être sauvage* is a means of thinking the bond as originary, before individuated being of any sort – before corpuscles or atoms and before every substance. The Merleau-Pontian principle cannot be a foundation pure and simple. It is between the background of forms and the foreground of individuals. To say that to see visible objects one must be visible oneself means that one sees from the middle: from the point of view of being as it emerges into individuals on one side and forms on the other. Seeing is the immediate self-reflection of this middle term. What we see *from* is not a transcendental ego closed in on itself and its conditions of experience. What we see from is a field of perception whose indistinction is what the power of perceiving originally cuts through, like the Schellingian primordial negation (see Chapter 5, section 4). This field is not a field perceived before our eyes. It is the field in which our eyes physically exist and from which our eyes see. It is a field in which we are caught and in which we 'slip' from one perception to another, which is also to slip 'from consciousness to Being'. If perception is no longer derived from raw data but from raw being, the thing in itself is no longer a world contrary to the ideal (Kant) nor the correlate of intentional consciousness (Husserl). The divisions seeing-seen and exterior-interior are not primordial. *Être brut* is the indeterminate depth behind the correlation seeing-seen, perceiving-perceived. If that which is below meaning is not itself individuated (whether as corpuscles or as a thing in itself), the problem of the external world does not arise. One can maintain – even insist upon – a wild being which is not a correlate of consciousness. This is because the relation between consciousness and matter, between what is interior and exterior is entirely reconfigured, along the lines of the elemental: a belonging together that is not identity or coincidence. That the link of correlation is what is itself indestructible implies that this link itself is the indeterminate milieu repeated such that the elementally indeterminate is primordially together with perception.

In corpuscularism, what we perceive in perception are *les petits êtres sauvages*. They are part of our field of vision. Indeed, they are our only means of contact with the world. In Merleau-Ponty's ontology we see *from* unindividuated *être sauvage* – the non-coinciding belonging together of perceiving and perceived: being as intrinsically perceptual. One final point leads us into the next chapter. The overcoming of the principle of immanence returns us directly to a parallelism with the mythological cosmogony from which elemental philosophy first arose and therefore to an explication of what Merleau-Ponty meant by 'perceptual cosmogony' (see Introduction, section 6). With respect to a theory of immanent perceptions, Cassirer already makes this point although he did not take it to its end: 'myth, as an original mode of *configuration*, raises a certain barrier against the world of passive sense impressions; it, too, like art and cognition, arises in a process of separation from immediate reality; i.e. that which is simply given'.[43] The first philosophers converted the unity of thing and signification which underlies mythological thinking into the unity of the element, with all the symbolic valences of myth retained. These originary unities are configurations that are both concrete and system at once. They exclude the immanence of sensation while not at all escaping into the realm of the pure idea. It is for this reason that phenomenology, to the degree that it overcomes its original Cartesianism, turns to cosmogonic imaginaries: to the originary earth and sky, to the darkness of the primordial night, and the surging of the primal ocean. It is within this context – overcoming the immanence of sense impression – that we turn now to explicate Merleau-Ponty's valorisation of myth and symbol in his late thought.

Notes

1. On Descartes's corpuscular mechanics, please refer to Peter Galison, 'Descartes' Comparisons: From the Invisible to the Visible', *Isis* 17.2 (1984): 311–26, and to references therein.
2. René Descartes, *Discours sur la méthode*, 4e partie, in René Descartes, *Œuvres philosophiques, Tome I: 1618–1637*, ed. Ferdinand Alquié (Paris: Éditions Garnier: 1988), 602.
3. Descartes, *Discours sur la méthode*, 4e partie, 603.
4. Descartes, *Discours sur la méthode*, 4e partie, 604.
5. Descartes, *Les méditations*, 'Méditation seconde', in René Descartes, *Œuvres philosophiques, Tome II: 1638–1642*, ed. Ferdinand Alquié (Paris: Éditions Garnier: 1988), 415–16.
6. See Chapter 3, sections 2 and 3 below.
7. For an account of the relation between Husserl and corpuscular physics, see, Herman Philipse, 'Transcendental Idealism', in *The Cambridge Companion to Husserl*, ed. Barry Smith and David W. Smith (Cambridge: Cambridge University Press, 1995), 239–322. See also, Ronald McIntyre, 'Husserl and the Representational Theory of Mind', *Topoi* 5 (1986): 101–13.
8. Edmund Husserl, *Logical Investigations*, ed. Dermot Moran (London: Routledge: 2001), 168.
9. Edmund Husserl, *Ideas Pertaining to a Pure Phenomenology and to a Phenomenological Philosophy – First Book: General Introduction to a Pure Phenomenology*, trans. F. Kersten (The Hague: Kluwer Academic Publishers Group, 1983), §24, 44–5. Hereafter: *Ideen I*.
10. *Ideen I*, §§49–55, pp. 109–30. See Philipse, pp. 249–52: '[T]ranscendental idealism does not deny that the mental in the psychological sense depends on the physical. What it claims is that the whole natural world, including minds which depend on bodies, is nothing but an intentional correlate of transcendental consciousness' (251).

11. Husserl, *The Idea of Phenomenology*, trans. William P. Alston and George Nakhnikian (Dordrecht: Kluwer Academic Publishers, 1964), 10.
12. Martin Heidegger, *Being and Time*, trans. John Macquarrie and Edward Robinson (San Francisco: Harper, 1962), §32.
13. Stephen Mulhall, *On Being in the World: Wittgenstein and Heidegger on Seeing Aspects* (London: Routledge, 1990). Richard Rorty, *Philosophy and the Mirror of Nature* (Oxford: Blackwell, 1980).
14. Philipse, 'Transcendental Idealism', 292–7.
15. *Ideen I*, §24, 44–5.
16. See Philipse, 'Transcendental Idealism', 257–8.
17. *Ideen I*, §41, 88 (trans. mod.).
18. VI, 224/173.
19. *Ideen I*, §49, 109.
20. *Ideen I*, §49, 110.
21. *Ideen I*, §49, 111.
22. *Ideen I*, §49, 112. Cf. *Cartesian Meditations*, §33.
23. Jean-Luc Marion, 'The Originary Otherness of the Ego: A Rereading of Descartes' Second Meditation', in *On the Ego and On God: Further Cartesian Questions* (New York: Fordham University Press, 2007). Marion provides extensive references to his forerunners, such as Michel Henry's reading of the *cogito* as proved through self-affect and Jaakko Hintikka's reading of the *cogito* as a performative.
24. See, Michel Henry, *Phénoménologie matérielle* (Paris: PUF, 1990), particularly pp. 16–17 where he defines his notion of 'matter' in contradistinction to Husserl's notion of 'hyle' but definitively places it within a notion of 'impression': 'Matter designates first of all the essence of the impression or of what is originally and in itself identical, sensation.'
25. See Philipse, 'Transcendental Idealism', 295–6.
26. VI, 172/132.
27. VI, 172/131.
28. VI, 271/218.
29. VI, 181/139.
30. VI, 191/147.
31. VI, 181/139.
32. VI, 191/147.
33. See *De docta ignorantia* especially, and my article, 'In a Mirror and an Enigma: Nicholas of Cusa's *De visione Dei* and the Milieu of Vision', *Sophia* 59 (2020). While Merleau-Ponty never, to my knowledge, cites Cusa, there is at least an affinity insofar as Merleau-Ponty draws on the theosophic tradition (Boehme and Schelling: see Chapter 5). Merleau-Ponty would have had at least been aware of Cusa when he was writing on coincidence, as there was a short piece on Cusa written by Maurice de Gandillac that was included in the book Merleau-Ponty edited on the history of philosophy, *Les philosophes célèbres* (Paris: Éditions Mazenod, 1956). A new edition, revised and expanded by Jean-François Balaudé now passes under the title *Les philosophes de l'Antiquité au XXe siècle* (Paris: Librairie générale française, 2006). Gandillac writes of Cusa's use of the infinite sphere that it makes man the new centre of the universe, and therefore the only true 'second god' in contrast to the Neoplatonist demiurge. Prefiguring Leibniz and Hegel, Cusa's use of the coincidence of opposites 'takes on a dialectical aspect, for it makes room for negativity and synthesis. The opposites must collide in order to be surpassed' (*Les philosophes de l'Antiquité au XXe siècle*, 411).
34. VI, 191/148.
35. VI, 63/41.
36. VI, 63–4/41.
37. VI, 159/121.
38. VI, 245/195; see also PP, 477/483.

39. VI, 312/265.
40. Barbaras, *Le tournant de l'expérience*, 222.
41. S, 263.
42. S, 270.
43. Cassirer, *The Philosophy of Symbolic Forms II: Mythical Thought*, 24.

Chapter 4

Cosmogonic Elementals in Phenomenology: From Husserl and Heidegger to Levinas and Merleau-Ponty

Philosophy and mythology most profoundly intersect in their common preoccupation with origins, with beginnings, with foundations and founding acts. Mythology expresses this preoccupation in cosmogonies and theogonies and creation accounts, in stories of the founders of cities and the institutors of religions: accounts, in short, of how the world came to be what it is. Philosophy expresses it in the search for first principles. While Neoplatonist and Stoic philosophies in late antiquity would draw directly from the ancient cosmogonies of Orpheus and Hesiod, the link to these mythologists, whom Aristotle called 'theologians',[1] has existed from philosophy's very beginning. The first philosophers aimed to lay out what was, for their day, a sober and scientific explanation of the origin of things against the wild imaginings of the theologians. It is clear however that, for better or for worse, they did not surpass the mythological structure of thought current in sixth-century Greece.

Thales, considered to be the first philosopher, is known for his scientific outlook, famously predicting a solar eclipse. His fundamental metaphysical proposition was that everything derives from primordial waters. It is no secret this idea is connected to mythologies in which water gods were considered the progenitors of all that exists, or even to the biblical idea that in the beginning, 'the Spirit of God was hovering over the face of the waters' (Gen. 1: 2). This is not only a vague connection of terminology. A precise structural parallel can be drawn between the Orphic cosmogony in which all is derived from a primordial Night and the philosophical system of Anaximander, a student of Thales, who considered a sort of material infinite, the *Apeiron*, as the first principle. The Ionian philosophers all proposed a prime element from which the world derives its unity and the power to become what it is. Whether understood as water, *apeiron* or air, the idea of a prime element reproduces the cosmogonic structure of primordial chthonic deities and their generative power, evacuated only of the divine personalities of the primordial gods but retaining their elemental meaning and the material dynamism of the prime element.

When Merleau-Ponty speaks of a 'perceptual cosmogony' he seems to challenge the usual configuration of the relation between philosophy and mythology, particularly the way in which we have looked back at philosophy's origin and have understood the way in which mythological discourse about beginnings was transformed into philosophical first principles. If being is perceptual all the way down, even when it is invisible, then the traditional conception of philosophy's origin cannot be tenable, that is, the emancipative narrative in which philosophy emerges from an archaic milieu by throwing off the mythical superstructure. It is of course true that myth imbues all conceptions of being with a halo of the imaginary, but it is not necessarily the case that the imaginary functions as a veil. In Merleau-Ponty's conception, being itself is oneiric. Merleau-Ponty was able to come to this conception because phenomenology, for its part, had already begun to reintroduce cosmogonic imaginaries. This reintroduction of the cosmogonic was necessary insofar as phenomenology tried to bring a logic of appearance back into philosophy. This logic necessarily opposes philosophy's old story about its own emergence and its belief that it had discovered a logic that operated behind a veil of mystifying appearances. For phenomenology, philosophy is no longer searching for a truth behind 'mere appearance' but seeks to interrogate the truth of appearance itself. Not only do we now go back to *physis* as a principle of appearing, we must also examine anew the relation of philosophical *physis* to the dynamic emergence articulated in the cosmogonies which philosophical *physis* mirrored.

1. Phenomenology and cosmogony

From the very beginning, philosophy has strategically distanced itself from mythology by linking myth with superstition and falsehood. It is perhaps possible, philosophy told us, to mine myth for a kernel of rational truth, but the mythological gods and heroes, the narrative and its allure, are nothing more than rhetorical trappings that at best point the audience to a meaning that lies behind what actually appears to our senses and at worst seduce the audience with a blatant falsehood. In philosophies that viewed mythology positively, this understanding of what myth is resulted in allegorising readings: that myth really meant something other than what it said. Certain philosophers, most notably Schelling, have contested an allegorising interpretation of myth, and undoubtably the study of myth has become more complicated after the rise of anthropology, ethnography and postcolonial studies.

For the most part, phenomenology hasn't directly reflected on myth, even if, as I am arguing, it implies a radical rethinking of philosophy's relation to its origin in mythology. We aren't dealing with a phenomenology *of* mythology. We are concerned with the operative cosmogonic imagination: the way in which first principles, linked back to something like the Presocratic notion of a prime element, continue to bear certain characteristics of particular cosmogonies, of the primordial water divinities, the goddess Night, or the original couple of Earth and Sky (Gaia and Ouranos). Classically, philosophers have spoken of the ground in terms of being. The way in which phenomenology differs from classical ontology is to occupy itself primarily with the 'how' of being, that is, its modality, the way in which being is articulated in its relation to how it shows up. Classical metaphysics is concerned primarily with *why* questions: *What causes being? Why is there something rather than nothing?* It is also concerned with *what* questions. *What is the nature of being and of beings?* The kind of question posed preconditions the possible responses. Attending to how the origin manifests itself would thus articulate something about the origin that could not be articulated if the origin is posed as an answer to a *what* question. In other words, phenomenology suggests a turn from *What is the origin of existence?* to *What is the origin like? How does it manifest?* The originary in phenomenology is an originary *how*, an originary dynamic structure that lies between a consciousness that experiences and a world that is experienced.

Now mythology, like phenomenology, never tends to ask *why?* The gods, notoriously irrational and fickle, are not posed as a causal explanation of the universe. The gods are just there. It has become a commonplace to assume that the gods of mythology were deployed whenever a people confronted a physical phenomenon that they did not understand. Now that we have scientific explanations, we no longer need gods. So the argument goes. This interpretation, however, misses the mixture of physical and metaphysical that chthonic gods present to us. Mythology has much more to do with a *how* that cannot be converted into a scientific causal explanation of things, even when reduced to a rational 'core' in mythological dressing. Because it does not even try to explain through causation, there may be a particular correspondence between phenomenology and mythology, a correspondence between the philosophical and the cosmogonic that was impossible during the epoch when metaphysics was dominated by formal and efficient causal explanation. Despite the fact that they are perpetually going back to origins, both phenomenology and myth have a surprising disregard for the question 'Why is there something rather than nothing?'

If there is a correlation between mythological cosmogonies and phenomenological accounts of the originary, it is nevertheless not a matter of phenomenology 'psychologising' mythical content. It is true that mythologies describe origins as something 'out there' – the drama of procreating and warring gods. And phenomenology describes the originary starting from our self-reflexive experience. For the phenomenologist we discover and participate in the origin not by going outside ourselves. We discover it on the disappearing edge between our self-experience and the *what* that is experienced. For mythological thinking, the positing of creative deities seems to be an answer to a *what*.

That it is particular *kinds* of deities poses an answer to a *how*. The primordial couple of an earth goddess and a sky god suggests a different kind of *how* than that proposed by primordial water divinities. And yet it seems that many cosmogonic narratives take little heed of the *how*. If we look at Hesiod's *Theogony*, for example, we will see how little Hesiod is concerned with ascribing meaning to the fact that Earth and Sky are the proto-gods in his account. It does not change the modality of existence. It just is the case. Phenomenology differs by focusing in more detail on the *how* and putting aside any pure *what*. Phenomenology, when it speaks of origins, is speaking of philosophical first principles. But in phenomenology first principles become an arch-experience rather than a purely logical principle. Inseparable from a logic of the sensible and of the perceptual, these originary aspects that ground phenomenality as such cannot but contain dream content. In this way, the origins of experience correspond in some manner to what myths were trying to get at with their descriptions of the origins of the world. Reciprocally, it would imply that mythological accounts of origins are in some way speaking about principles. Indeed, to get at the full meaning of the principles from which we see and know the world, we would need to retain the figurative content and this precisely for the sake of philosophical precision and not against it: what would replace the precision of abstraction with the precision of completeness. Abstraction can only be so precise because it eliminates the temporal, transformative aspect so essential to the way an origin operates as a principle of becoming. Myth retains modal precision insofar as it is the answer to a *how*.

Merleau-Ponty for one would agree. He understood that being itself, like perception, is never separated from dreaming. In his development of a post-representational understanding of perception, meaning and truth are no longer reducible to something 'out there' in front of us. They participate with us in a field of existence that cannot be grasped entirely by consciousness since consciousness is mixed with what it is trying to grasp.

It shares the same being. Consciousness, in Merleau-Ponty's account, is something within the self-organising field of the meaningful. If meaning is never entirely separable from mind, mind nevertheless isn't the source of meaning, imposing signification on an inert material world. Mind itself emerges with and at the same time as meaning. Citing Valéry, he says that 'language is everything, since it is the voice of no one, since it is the very voice of the things, the waves and the forests'.[2] Meaning emerges from an operation of the elemental – from the operation of *physis*. We must continually remind ourselves, lest it seize the place of the real, that the abstract is abstracted, something taken out of the real. It is not the real itself. The 'full meaning' of any perception, Merleau-Ponty argues, is a figurative meaning, which has phantastic dimensions, at one point calling the unconscious 'the pre-objective, oneiric background of all perception'.[3]

The idea of a prime element is, perhaps surprisingly, what connects the phenomenological thought of Heidegger, Levinas and Merleau-Ponty to Greek cosmogonies. It is Merleau-Ponty's reference to nature as a soil of our existence which could serve as the first concept through which we might make this connection: a soil that is 'not what is in front of, but that which bears us'.[4] If Husserl's late phenomenology opens a way of thinking the origin as an element (see Introduction, section 5), the link to cosmogonies and the Presocratic understanding of a prime element introduces a new question: Why *this* element? Why Earth and not Fire, or Water, or Air? Each of these elements has been, after all, proposed as the prime element by the likes of Thales, Anaximander and Heraclitus. This question is the central question of this chapter. Couldn't the phenomenological originary be thought according to the model of different elements? Although much of Husserl's argument against Copernicus is convincing, the return to an elemental ground leaves so much more to be explored. What is certain, however, is that the thought of the element becomes a theme in phenomenology, starting in the 1930s, not only in the work of Husserl, but also that of Heidegger. It is Levinas, however, who first explicitly coins the concept as the 'elemental'. While it is thematised under this title in *Totality and Infinity* (1961), it is already there in his earlier work *De l'existence à l'existant* (1947). It is his concept of the *il y a*, the 'there is', which he talks about as an absolute Night, a night without the trace of light, that is, without the trace of things that could possibly appear.

Just as the cosmogonic systems of Greek religion put one chthonic power first, but did not agree which was first, so the phenomenological accounts of the originary have proven equally diverse. These accounts are diverse not because they propose a different 'what' at the beginning. Instead, it is because they understand the operation of the origin differently – a different 'how'. It is not insignificant that the analyses of

Levinas and Heidegger correspond not only precisely but explicitly to two of the three primary cosmogonies of ancient Greece, namely the Orphic system in which the world derives from an original Night and Hesiod's cosmogony in which the union of the goddess Gaia and the god Ouranos (Earth and Sky) are the progenitors of all creation. It is in this phenomenological context that Merleau-Ponty is able to speak of a perceptual cosmogony. While Merleau-Ponty gives us less explicit material to go by, I will argue that, if Heidegger matches Hesiod's cosmogony and Levinas a certain Orphic tradition, Merleau-Ponty can be identified with Homer insofar as I have already begun to argue that his understanding of the elemental will ultimately fit into the third cosmogony: the idea of the primordial waters. The following analyses are intended not only to demonstrate that these three philosophers match these three cosmogonies. They are meant to show just what each of these cosmogonic imaginaries express about the modality of the originary, thus about the operation of nature and what it says about existence in the world.

In associating certain phenomenologists with certain cosmogonic systems, my interpretation may seem at first glance to be a kind of allegorising. It differs from allegorising, however, in the most important aspect. Allegory assumes that the signified is behind or beyond the signifying term (the allegorical myth). Such an interpretation assumes that the signified is *something* – that it is a solid 'what' beyond the vaporous myth. Because my phenomenological reading of cosmogonic imaginaries shows that they reveal something about the 'how' of the origin (that the 'content' of the myth is verbal rather than nominative), it avoids this semiotic or allegorical interpretation and uncovers instead a symbolic operation. It is not that the origin 'is' water (as a substantive), but that it operates like water. Again, this 'likeness' is not to be taken as saying that it is similar to water, but that the operation that it enacts is one that is identical to what water does. Thus also for the other elements.

2. The marriage of earth and sky: Heidegger and the horizon of manifestation

Those familiar with Heidegger's late thought – a thinking where early Greek philosophy becomes increasingly central – will see the connection between Hesiod's *Theogony* and the way Heidegger grounds the being of things in the interplay of earth and sky. Hesiod begins his *Theogony* with the earth goddess Gaia emerging out of the Chasm, taking her first offspring, the sky god Ouranos as her husband and engendering with him the Titans from whom in turn are begat the Olympians.[5] Beginning in the early thirties, Heidegger introduces a concept of earth that he starts to develop in the lecture 'The Origin of the Work of Art'. Earth is understood in dialectical tension with world. While earth is 'that which comes forth and shelters',[6] world is what brings the thing 'into the Open'.[7] The essential point of this sometimes-esoteric discourse about world and earth is this: the interplay of world and earth expresses a dynamic of revealing and concealing, of advance into the open and withdrawal into the darkness of the earth. One can easily imagine the world as opening (we have a world that opens before us) and the earth as ground on which something is opened (we must stand on the earth for the world's vistas to be visible). However, the relation of world to earth is not one on top of the other. The earth is not merely the opacity of the soil which the light cannot penetrate. Earth is the very opening of world *as* closure of the soil, a revealing which *is* a concealing.[8] The earth is the shimmer and shine of things, their texture and qualities. Light must indeed strike something opaque for it to reveal something to begin with. And in this sense, revealing is dependent on the unrevealable, on the opaque, on the darkness and coolness of the earth. If everything were translucent, there would be nothing to see. In the same way that a seed must go into the earth's darkness to come forth as a plant, so showing forth depends on burying. Heidegger explicitly identifies earth with *physis* through Heraclitus' fragment: '*physis kryptesthai philei*'. In identifying this fragment with 'the essence of the earth' Heidegger translates it here as 'what emerges has the urge to keep itself closed'.[9]

In many of the ancient myths of creation, earth and sky are in such a tight embrace that there is no room for a world to appear. It takes a hero to come shove the two apart, or slash them apart with a mighty sword, creating a fissure, a space between them where humanity can finally stretch its legs and mill about.[10] This heroic deed corresponds precisely to the place Heidegger gives to the work of art, which he says 'moves the earth itself into the Open of a world and keeps it there. *The work lets the earth be an earth.*'[11] The horizon, that edge where earth and sky meet and which opens up our field of vision, is realised in the artwork insofar as art creates a new world. It makes a new way of seeing possible. It lets a new manifestation emerge. In emerging, it opens new horizons. Through his or her artwork it is the artist who becomes this hero. It is the artist who makes a world not only possible, but livable.

This master concept 'horizon' is what ultimately makes a world-earth tension problematic and Heidegger is not blind to this problem. World is in a certain way synonymous with horizon insofar as it is understood as opening, while earth is understood as closing. But a horizon is made by a conjoining of earth and sky. It is not only the literal horizon that we speak of – that line in the distance where heaven and earth seem to meet.

The Heideggerian concept of horizon concerns how earth and sky function within a thing as it appears in the world. The horizon is a limit, but it is not 'that at which something stops, but ... that from which something begins its presencing'.[12] With respect to the conjunction of earth and sky in a thing, the earth expresses itself as sensible textures and qualities, not yet tied to any determined form: 'the massiveness and heaviness of stone ... the firmness and pliancy of wood ... the hardness and lustre of metal ... the lighting and darkening of colour ... the clang of tone'.[13] Such qualities are not accidents of a substance, but energies of the earth from which a thing might take on identity. Earth is said to be the ground, not as something solid standing on its own. It is a 'groundless ground', which simply means that it is grounded in the thing it grounds. Because it has qualities (firmness, pliancy, lustre) even when it is not a thing, it only appears as earth through the appearance of things, just as, for example, a storm only appears as a storm through raindrops, wind, lightning and thunder. The earth appears as earth when a thing takes on earthly qualities as its own, that is, when a thing emerges into the light of day.

Into the light of day: that is to say, existence under the sky. It is not only the light of day that constitutes the sky. The sky is the theatre of change and of movement: clear blue skies, clouds, tempests and fogs, the rhythm of the seasons, of life and death, of waking and sleeping. The thing manifests the sky not only by showing up in the light, but by being subject to change and transformation. Sky and earth are manifested together in the thing insofar as it is the earthly qualities and powers that not only show up, but also fade, are subject to change and weather conditioning. Heidegger uses the example of a mountain spring where the stone in which 'dwells the dark slumber of the earth' is also that which catches the transient waters, 'the rain and dew of the sky'.[14]

> In the water of the spring dwells the marriage of sky and earth. It stays in the wine given by the fruit of the vine, the fruit in which the earth's nourishment and the sky's sun are betrothed to one another. In the gift of water, in the gift of wine, sky and earth dwell.[15]

The togetherness of the earth with the thing is what Heidegger calls the 'bearing' of earth. In this way it is indeed analogous to a mother goddess without which nothing would emerge, but it is only the sky through which the manifestation is given vigour, life and temporality.

What the marriage of earth and sky finally means for Heidegger is the encompassing of being by the horizon, for the horizon as 'that from which something begins its presencing' is precisely the most encompassing of all.[16] All being arises into the light. All beings are encompassed by this manifestation. Even the concealed is manifested. It is manifested as concealed. Indeed, the concealing of earth is part and parcel of that which is manifested under the sky. In linking the originary to this marriage of heaven and earth, Heidegger determines the originary within a logic of appearance. One might accuse him of being too irenic on this point.[17] In Heidegger, everything moves out into the Open. All is light. All is manifestation. Everything is beautiful, has a meaning, makes sense. There is a sort of soft antique glow that wafts over his later writings. And yet he perceives with absolute clarity the difficulty of a philosophical principle outside the order of appearance. He knows that what is concealed must announce its concealing. Like the child who says, 'I'm going to hide, you come find me', the hidden becomes immediately present once its hiddenness is recognised. If it weren't for this pronouncement of hiding, we wouldn't know there was anything to find. Concealing must show itself or it would disappear into oblivion. We could not know that it existed and not only could not talk about it but could not know that we could not talk about it because we would not know there was anything to not talk about.

In the thirties, Heidegger wanted to put earth in tension with world precisely because he interprets earth as the concealing aspect of manifestation. The concealment of the earth is nothing other than a mode of revealing. In his later thought he realises that world operates on a different plane than earth. It is not an element that could be in tension with earth, or in marriage with it. Earth forms a horizon from which things presence only in the earth's elemental conjoining with sky. But the world does not vanish in the concept of the fourfold. On the contrary, world fades into the background as the all-encompassing principle.[18] Earth, sky, divinities and mortals form the substance from which world is made, in which things come to be. Earth is subjugated to world precisely as far as earth's thickness is nothing other than a concealing, a way of making the horizon manifest. Ultimately, because of his rigorous holding to a logic of manifestation and the impossibility of a concealment that is not a revealing, Heidegger reduces the elements to players within the world, almost like the four elements of Aristotle, which each have their 'proper place' within the cosmos, but lack the generative power of the prime element, which is, properly speaking, outside the world. A dynamic of revealing and concealing cannot in the end comprehend generation and development. Perhaps this is precisely what the originary nature of earth and sky would signify. All reality plays out on the plane of manifestation.

Heidegger ultimately identifies several terms with the Greek understanding of being as an event of self-disclosure: being as *physis* as *aletheia* as *kosmos*.[19] For Heidegger, *mythos* or 'the gods' are an aspect of this self-disclosure which is being, for the advent of the gods is a way in which being manifests itself.[20] Both myth and thus 'theology' (discourses about the gods) risk missing being's self-disclosure however, as soon as we focus on the 'what' (the gods themselves) rather than the 'how' of disclosing. What's a bit odd here about the dismissal of the 'what' is that the 'what' of elemental deities does say something about the 'how' of manifestation, particularly when we look at the way various cosmogonies propose different primordial deities. Heidegger never really interrogates the nature of the self-disclosing of *physis* 'as such', but always already thinks *physis* within the framework of an 'Earth-Sky' cosmogony.

Scholars seem to agree that Hesiod's cosmogony is a corruption of an older tradition.[21] Because he makes the couple Gaia and Ouranos the primordial couple, Hesiod rather oddly includes Oceanos among the Titans, as one of the offspring of earth and sky. Oceanos is not the god of what we call the ocean. He is the great river that flows around the whole world. In the older account, held by Homer, it is Oceanos, the water god, and Tethys, a water goddess, his sister-wife, who hold the role of the primordial couple, first progenitors of the gods. When the Titans are banished to Tartarus, in Hesiod's account, Oceanos nevertheless still flows around the outer limits of the world. This contradiction – counting Oceanos among the Titans and yet free of their fate – suggests that the Oceanos-Tethys parentage is older than the lineage from Gaia and Ouranos. The hypothesis of a river that is beyond the world – encompassing it – suggests a possible challenge to the Heideggerian limits of the horizon, the constitution of being through the union of earth-sky. But there is also another contestation of the world-earth origin: the Orphic system in which all is derived from a primordial night. It is the black night that Levinas uses to contest Heidegger's horizon. Both these ideas, the primordial night and a certain liquid understanding of being, set a challenge to the Heideggerian dialectic of manifestation and its concealment.

3. The nocturns of existence: Levinas and the absence of horizon

In 'The Origin of the Work of Art', Heidegger had said that the artwork makes the world a world. While the young Levinas was probably at this lecture in Freiburg, he will write quite the opposite just over a decade later. Art does not make a world, Levinas posits. It uproots things from the world.[22] Photography is an example he uses to demonstrate this uprooting. The photograph 'interposes between us and the thing an image of the thing that has the effect of tearing the thing from a perspective on the world'.[23] Levinas goes on to argue that the turn in modern art which values 'rupture of continuity' and bears a 'disdain for perspective and "real" proportions of things, announces a revolt against the continuity of the curve'[24] and draws to the fore the sheer materiality of things. This notion of the material is not at all that of classical materialism, 'opposed to mind and thought' and defined by mechanical laws. It is instead 'the thick, the coarse, the massive, the destitute. What has consistence, weight, absurdity, brute but unsurpassable presence; but also lowliness, nudity, ugliness.'[25] This notion of matter 'behind the luminosity of forms' is a sheer shapeless teeming. It is what Levinas calls the *il y a* or 'there is' – what he will later term no longer 'matter' but 'the elemental'.[26]

The elemental in Levinas is much more than matter as such. Levinas understands the elemental as being without beings, existence without entities. Levinas will challenge both the relational aspect – earth-sky coming together in the thing – and the reduction of the elemental to the logic of manifestation. It is not surprising then that Levinas's concept of the origin corresponds to the cosmogony which has a singular principle at the beginning rather than a divine couple. Levinas emphasises not the generative power of the originary, but its neutrality. The Orphic cosmogony described by Eudemos has Night, a female deity, alone at the beginning, who will produce the world by a wind egg, that is, an act of generation that does not require a male partner.[27] In the chapter following the aforementioned chapter on art, Levinas speaks of the *il y a* as the primordial night. In *Totality and Infinity* he will link this night directly to Anaximander's *apeiron*,[28] and to 'faceless gods, impersonal gods to whom one does not speak'.[29]

Simply put, by invoking the elemental as a primordial night, Levinas is speaking of what doesn't have sense, what doesn't have form but nevertheless *is*. In itself, the elemental entirely lacks light: 'Sense is permeability to the mind, a permeability that already characterises sensation, or if one prefers, it is luminosity.'[30] Further on, Levinas writes, 'It is by the light that objects are a world, that is to say, are ours [à nous].'[31] And this Levinas directly associates with the phenomenological concept of a horizon:

> The lighted space is entirely gathered around a mind that possesses it ... In all its dimensions it is accessible, explorable ... The relation of the object to the subject is given at the same time as the object itself. Already a horizon is opened up.[32]

Following Heidegger here, Levinas recognises that in the very appearance of a thing, there is already the appearance of a horizon, and thus of light. It is for this reason that in the primal experience of darkness, the correlation of mind to thing is radically stripped away.

The horizon expresses the encompassing nature of living on the earth and under the sky. But there are other elements that do not give a horizon.

These elements could thus provide a model for thinking the way that the originary exceeds the horizon of manifestation. Dante describes such an experience perfectly at the beginning of the Comedy:

> Midway along the journey of our life
> I woke to find myself in a dark wood
> for I had wandered off from the straight path.[33]

The forest is a dizzying loss of horizon. It is a place of disorientation precisely because we lose horizonal coordinates – the path of the sun, the stars, a point on the horizon towards which to aim. This elemental impossibility of a horizon is a more primordial feature of human dwelling than dwelling under the sun, for to be human is to not know the way, perhaps to have no fixed nature. Unlike other animals, we receive very little knowledge by instinct. The way must be passed down to us from our parents and ancestors or learned by trial and error. This includes not only the moral code. It is true all the way down to the most basic aspects of survival: knowing what is edible and what is not. The horizon in this sense is a means by which we make the world safe, not what constitutes human dwelling in the primordial fears of its obscure depths. While the Heideggerian fourfold articulates the 'groundless ground' – the way in which the thing and its ground are inextricably bound together – Levinas's idea of the Night comes into focus beyond groundlessness. It is not merely the absence of light but the complete absence of horizon, a complete absence of relation between things. And in this way, paradoxically, Levinas's night has something more substantial about it. It remains a pure positivity, a 'there is' without anything there: the thick, the coarse, a shapeless mass.

Writing as a Jew in the wake of the Holocaust it is unsurprising that Levinas is searching for a way to articulate the sheer horror of presence in the face of an absolute loss of meaning, of continuing to exist despite the fact that all sense-making possibilities have been stripped away. Levinas expresses this elimination of the possibility of a horizon as Hamlet's dread: to be, but without the orienting features of a horizon, to dwell at the frontier of the night. Even though it lacks beings and light, the nocturnal is not absence of space. The nocturnal has its own space. It is not an empty space that finds its contrary in the plentitude of things occupying lighted space. It is not like an empty room. The contrasts with lighted space must be comprehended through the understanding of lighted space as space configured according to a horizon, where things make sense. Nocturnal space lacks the transparency that 'at once lets us distinguish things and to get at them'.[34] It is a realm of undecidability because of an overwhelming presence, a presence that lacks meaning – undecidable like Hamlet's question before such a shapeless presence: 'To be or not to be?' Within a horizontal space there are points that refer one to the other so that one can get around, see and choose. In nocturnal space there are points, but the points 'don't refer to one another, as in a lighted space'.[35] It reflects a total absence of association between data, a total absence of meaning, as in trauma where two points of meaning no longer connect. As Levinas puts it, 'It is a teeming over of points.'[36] Here we have a radical critique of the possibility of an originary horizon. The Levinasian origin is without things. It is the night of the *apeiron*, a teeming over of points, a shapeless mass, an 'opaque density without origin'.[37] Levinas aims to overcome the thinking of the horizon as an originary experience by talking of the sheer 'there is', an existence without horizon and without origin.

4. 'La mer, la mer, toujours recommencée':[38] Merleau-Ponty and the aquatic milieu

Perhaps the most widespread creation myth is a creation out of primordial waters. The Babylonian account begins with Apsu, the male fresh water, mingling with Tiamat the female bitter water.[39] From their union 'silt precipitated', the earth was born. The account of Genesis too suggests there was a primordial deep (*Tehom*) over which the spirit of God hovered before he created the world. A couple of verses later, the creation of the world has something to do with a mysterious separation of an upper water from a lower water. The earth comes to be from the residue of receding waters. Earth is what is left behind after the spring floods have subsided, a rich earth for a new harvest. In both these cases the emergence of a world is understood as a drying out. It is not only the ancient river cultures like Babylon and Egypt that have these water cosmogonies. If river silt is essential to the Babylonian cosmogony, the Greeks nevertheless had an equivalent water cosmogony. Oceanos has a cosmic presence not linked to the sea. He is the great river, deep and potent, that flows around the circumference of the world. His main attribute is not his flowing. It is his immense generative power. He procreates thousands of children with his wife Tethys, the Greek equivalent to the Babylonian female bitter water, Tiamat, and the Hebrew 'deep' (*Tehom*). It is not just the first generation of gods that they engender. It is also the nymphs of smaller bodies of water and other minor deities. Jean Rudhardt writes that with Oceanos 'fluidity symbolises here not only what is without form and without precise limits. It also implies agitation, movement. It is rich with dynamism.'[40] Rudhardt suggests that Homer holds to this aquatic theogony contra Hesiod who holds Earth and Sky as the primordial couple. In Book 14 of the *Iliad*, Hypnos calls Oceanos the one that 'establishes the genesis of all things'.[41] And Hera calls him 'the father of the gods'.[42]

I want to conclude this chapter by developing further why Merleau-Ponty's 'perceptual cosmogony' ought to be conceived as a water cosmogony, and why such a cosmogony surpasses the limits that Heidegger imposed – the limits of the horizon. Understanding Merleau-Ponty's thought as aquatic is less apparent than Heidegger with Earth-Sky or Levinas with the primordial Night, but we might draw a first justification from Plato, who already saw that those who believe that 'perception is knowledge' are those who also say that all is motion and flux. Plato goes so far as to connect this belief in perception explicitly to the figure of Oceanos.[43] But while the author of the *Phenomenology of Perception* will indeed retain this privileged place for perception in knowledge, it may be argued that it is this very aquatic understanding of being that enables him to surpass, in his later work, the Heideggerian limit of the horizon, thereby making perception not only epistemological but ontological.

Contra Plato on this point, phenomenology has tried to show that reduction to perception is not reduction to a pure flux. Indeed, we might say that for philosophers for whom flux is a theme, flux can never be a solution. It must remain an aporetic starting point: as it was for Plato and for Descartes. Without retaining the aporia of flux we can no longer be said to be doing philosophy, for philosophy is a search for truth, however difficult or impossible the task appears. Heidegger tries to get beyond mere groundless flux with the idea of the fourfold; Husserl with his idea of the arch-original earth; Levinas with the sheer presence of the 'there is'. While all try to pose a solution to the problem of grounding knowledge in the flux of perception, nevertheless none try to solve it by escaping perception and sensation *tout court*. None resort to the realm of pure intelligibility, the eternal forms. The return to the element is not a return to the 'on high' – the always already individuated perfect forms. It is a return to the below, the pre-individual realm of primordial chthonic powers.

Levinas's critique of Heidegger was primarily a critique of meaning as light. It opened up a space for disorientation, for the non-meaningful, for the pure massive heap of the material. While Merleau-Ponty deals with similar questions concerning the non-phenomenal and non-significative, he does not take Levinas's direction with the *il y a*, which remains a pure positivity, a 'teeming of points'. The heaviness of Levinas's conception of the night, the apeiron as 'bad infinite', means that it cannot account for ontogenesis. It is a pure weight. In contrast to Levinas, Merleau-Ponty is committed to seeing meaning everywhere. He does not theorise the absolute negation of meaning and of manifestation, as does Levinas. For Merleau-Ponty negation cannot be absolute but is mixed with positivity. He aims to conceive a negative operation that brings about meaning and differentiation, an operation that runs like a seam through being as its always present obverse, a lining of invisibility that has a cosmogonic function insofar as it accounts for the creation of beings, a creation that is taking place all the time. While a thought of the elemental seems to be the site where Merleau-Ponty and Levinas are the closest, it is the ostensibly slight variance between Levinas's *il y a* and Merleau-Ponty's *être sauvage* that acts as a fissure of difference that becomes the chasm between the followers of Merleau-Ponty and those who took the theological turn after Levinas. Indeed, it is Levinas's night of the *il y a* that makes room for radical alterity, while Merleau-Ponty's *être sauvage* declares a primordial belonging together and thinks difference not as something that comes from without, heterogeneously, but as the explosion of this originary togetherness.

There are two dyads of concepts that Bachelard examines in the imaginary of water that I want to suggest are operative in Merleau-Ponty's thought in the mid to late fifties. The first is the connection between water's bonding power and the process of drying out. The second is the concepts of depth and latency. We have already begun to see these two dyads have a central cosmogonic role in the idea of the face of the deep, and the idea of creation as a silt left behind by the ebbing of the primordial waters. These ideas, however, can be analysed with more philosophical precision. Further, what I would contend is that an analysis of the Merleau-Pontian reading of the fragment, *physis kryptesthai philei*, exemplifies the cosmogonic operation of primordial waters – the dynamic of bonding by drying, which is a means of creating by the type of negation an elemental non-being accomplishes: 'Life hides itself in the very measure that it is realised.'[44]

In order to understand the import of this sentence as not only an interpretation of 'Nature loves to hide', but as exemplary of the operation of cosmogonic waters, we will not only return to the analysis of the axolotl in which this sentence is embedded, but we want to look at it additionally outside of its immediate context in animal maturation. Exemplary of this will be Merleau-Ponty's analysis of art in his last publication before his death: *Eye and Mind*. If the first example, that of endogenous animal maturation, illustrates the first principle of the aquatic cosmogony – a principle of creating through drying out – the second example illustrates the second principle – primordial waters as the elemental depth of being. It is through the Heraclitean notion of 'hiding' that we can understand how the depth and drying out hold together.

5. 'For water to become earth is to die':[45] Ontogenesis as the desiccation of being

One of the essential ontological features of water is its ability to combine things and hold them together. Bachelard says that 'it is above all with the mixing of water and earth that we can understand the principles of the psychology of the material cause'.[46] Further on he says that dough (*pâte*) 'is one of the fundamental schemas of materialism', remarking also how strange it is 'that philosophy would have neglected the study of it'.[47] Whether dough, paste, mud, clay or silt, what is essential is that wet earth is needed before things can take form. Aristotle's hylomorphic model of beings as a combination of form and matter, forgets not only the materiality of the form and the formality of the material,[48] but first of all that the material must be wet to take form and then must dry out (or cool down in the case of liquid states of rock or metal). In the process of bonding and drying out, liquidity exemplifies precisely the 'negative' aspect of ontogenesis – the elemental non-being – that Merleau-Ponty outlines in his late philosophy. It is impossible to have relation without wetness. The primordial bonding capacity of undifferentiated being enables the undifferentiated to be 'common' or shared being. The dryness of dust, by contrast, is the representation of death. While dust is another representation of indifferentiation – it is different than the liquid because the liquid is shareable, bonding things together, whereas dust is unshareable. It blows away. While wetness must be in the beginning, it must also be negated before form can emerge. It is impossible for form to emerge without the process of drying out, negating the common for the differentiated and individuated. At first there is undifferentiated being, a silt precipitating from water. This liquid earth takes on differentiated form as the water recedes.

This is one of the essential insights of water cosmogonies. They understand that ontogenesis, the creation of beings, depends on a drying out like the silt precipitating out of water. But Merleau-Ponty's theory, bolstered by modern science, is much more sophisticated in its analyses. There is, I am suggesting, a process of drying out that underlies his understanding of ontogenesis. It is of course not a literal drying out. It is the process by which being is differentiated from an initially undifferentiated mass of being. At the beginning, being's indifferentiation is signified by a vibratory energy that all being shares. It is in this context that we should understand the 'hiding' in the fragment, 'Nature loves to hide', to be a drying out: a receding of the oceanic rhythm. Drying out expresses the way primordial waters must negate themselves in order for being to emerge. Drying is not a concealing in the Heideggerian sense of the withdrawal of being, which is part of the earth-sky dynamic of the horizon. Aquatic withdrawal is a negative principle, a principle that disappears in the drying process just as water evaporates from a clay figure. What remains (the dry figure) is entirely dependent for its being on what passes away (the water that made the figure mouldable and adhering to itself in the first place). Heideggerian concealing (and thus Heideggerian *physis*) is grounded in the fact that the darkness of the Earth is necessary for something to be revealed. Without the Earth keeping itself closed, the light could not manifest something there. Merleau-Pontian negation, by contrast to Heideggerian concealing, makes appearance dependent on a more radical disappearance. No longer appearing *as* concealing, the aquatic principle that negates itself is a dynamic movement out of appearance into the absolute past. The primordial waters must *have been* for a form to emerge, but they must *no longer be* for the form to remain.

The example of the axolotl (see Chapter 1, section 4) shows what the aquatic cosmogony means as an expression of the 'how' of the operation of the origin. Even though it is being used in a somewhat metaphorical fashion, the aquatic cosmogony can be useful at a fairly high level of ontogenesis, namely the individuation of complex life forms. Water functions as an adhesive, a milieu in which all being is participated. But it also must recede from beings. It is a milieu which is only present in its absence, as sculpted clay lets us know that water was once there without any actual liquid presence. What a water cosmogony articulates is a principle that is negatively present, present in its absolute pastness, elemental non-being understood along the lines of Heraclitean dynamism. In Merleau-Ponty's account, being isn't 'gathered' as the Heideggerian horizon is 'gathered'. The aquatic principle is a power of formation that forms by subtracting itself so that the oceanic rhythm of the whole diversifies into beings with their own cadences.

What is particular to the case of *living* forms is that the subtraction of the element is performed by the living being resisting the elemental unity, by 'fighting for its liberty'.[49] This resistance is not a direct opposition. We can return to the example of a variation on a musical theme (see Chapter 1, section 2). The variation is not the theme itself but is dependent on that very theme that must remain absent in order to be present in the variation. The theme gives a mode of being to the variation. It is not something towards which the variation aims, but that from which the variation begins. Here we come into a direct confrontation with Heidegger's definition of a horizon: 'that from which something begins its presencing'.[50] The way the primordial waters differ from the horizon as something 'from which' beings become present is that the form they leave behind is not a wet form, in the way that a thing, for Heidegger, gathers the elements of earth and sky. The oceanic, its non-existence in what it leaves behind, is an image of what is more primordial than that which is gathered. The oceanic must first recede before any horizon can gather. It is pre-horizonal. Liquid withdrawal is not the dynamism of 'Being as *physis* as *aletheia* as *kosmos*' beyond which is the abyss of nothingness. Instead, it is a dynamic non-being, an elemental nothingness, at the heart of existence. Each appearance is an individuation by means of the suppression of and resistance to the rhythmic whole. It is therefore necessary to think of individuation arising through a productive resistance to an energetic milieu and to understand appearance starting from a cosmogonic subtraction. The fragment 'Nature loves to hide' translated as 'Life hides itself in the measure that it is realised' is not cyclical transformation of life into death, nor is it the fact that every appearance is also a veiling, as Heidegger describes the play of earth and sky. It is instead a developmental process from undifferentiated to differentiated being. It is the process of ontogenesis. The fluidity is ontogenetic and cosmogenic. Liquid withdrawal is not the withdrawal of being, which for Heidegger constitutes the horizon as such. Liquid withdrawal expresses a dynamic non-being, an elemental nothingness, at the heart of existence.

Thus we can define both the limit and the *écart* more precisely in this context. The *écart* is nothing other than this elemental non-being which lies at being's heart. The conceptualisation of the limit can help us clarify this difference. The limit with regards to Merleau-Pontian aquatic ontogenesis is not the limit that the horizon of being proposes. It is not the limit of a 'world'. It is not a spatial limit, but is a limit of place, the flow of time sedimented in a landscape. In what sense, Merleau-Ponty asks, is

> the visible landscape under my eyes not exterior to, and bound synthetically to . . . other moments of time and the past, but has them really *behind itself* in simultaneity, inside itself and not it and they side by side 'in' time[?][51]

Undoubtedly this question bears upon the 'indestructible tie between us and hours and places'.[52] The elemental, in Merleau-Ponty, withdraws not in the way a horizon recedes in order to show the thing in space. It withdraws in such a way that time precipitates out of it and settles 'in' place. If we were to be more precise, we must say that it precipitates out *as* place, for the place of which we are speaking is not a containing but is the very being which the negation of the elemental leaves behind. It is thus that the negativity of the element understood as 'desiccation' of being leads directly to the second aspect of cosmogonic water, namely the depth dimension that we can already begin to glimpse with the notion that a landscape might be deep with antiquity – a depth that is not spatial, but temporal and of place.

6. Primordial depths and the latency of being

The cosmogonic power of formation goes with the negative aspect of primordial water: the dynamic emergence of being through a process of drying out. The second aspect of water cosmogonies is the depth dimension which expresses the latency of being – its emergent capacity for form. In Merleau-Ponty's account of animal maturation, depth is accounted for as the instability of the present. The present is unstable because it is latent with futurity. It possesses a yearning towards what is to come. But what this latency has to do with the hydric becomes much more apparent if we look at Merleau-Ponty's work on perception, particularly his analysis of Cézanne and Paul Klee in *L'Œil et l'esprit*. Here he insists that depth is not a 'third dimension', but is

> the experience of the reversibility of dimensions, of a global 'locality' where all is at once, from which height, width, distance are abstracted, of a voluminosity that we express in a word by saying that something is there. When Cézanne looks for depth, it is this explosion of Being that he is looking for, and this explosion is in every mode of space, in form as well.[53]

Depth in this sense is the concentration of being, the intrinsic energy that is ready to explode into form.

There has been increasing emphasis on materiality in art since the end of the nineteenth century. No matter how much materiality has always been involved, traditional figurative art focuses on form. But with challenges to figuration, artists began exploring the intrinsic properties of the material as such – the radiance and depth of colour, the way it shines out at us and knocks us backwards, the way we might plunge into it to the point of drowning. This sense of drowning in materiality seems to be intrinsic to the perception of the artist – what she is trying to see and what she is trying to express:

> In a forest, I have felt many times over that it was not I who looked at the forest. Some days I felt that the trees were looking at me, were speaking to me and I was there, listening ... I think the painter must be penetrated by the universe and not want to penetrate it ... I expect to be inwardly submerged, buried. Perhaps I paint to break out.

This quotation from André Marchand, cited by Merleau-Ponty in *Eye and Mind*,[54] expresses much of what Merleau-Ponty expects that the artistic experience of materiality can bring to the philosophical conception of matter. In the much earlier essay, *La doute de Cézanne*, he cites Cézanne who says of his process of painting: 'The landscape thinks itself in me, and I am its consciousness.'[55] There is a depersonalisation of the creative process, a self-emptying of the artist for the sake of being filled by a now subjectified nature. Commenting on the Cézanne citation, Merleau-Ponty says 'nothing is further from naturalism than this intuitive science. Art is neither an imitation nor a fabrication following the wishes of instinct or of good taste.'[56] The artist, who sees rather than thinks, or thinks through seeing but without translating into discursive thought, is able to go beyond the confines of rational philosophy, able to avoid its errors or to surpass its limits in such a way that rational thought must sometimes take its cue from art in order to reorient itself – to get a new hold on the real. In this case, what artists like Cézanne are trying to do, is not to reach forms that are already there hidden in the material, but instead to 'depict matter as it takes on form',[57] to paint the world as it was at the beginning of time, to reach the primordial layer of existence. Matter is not something dead or passive that must be chiselled away as something superfluous to form. It is the living source.

The artist's experience of matter is closer to the concept of the element than it is to the philosophical concept of matter since art deals with matter as something of the sensible – something tangible and invisible that engulfs us – rather than as something that persists through change, as Aristotle defines matter, and which remains definitive for every definition of matter as substratum and 'objective reality' outside of consciousness and underneath appearance (given *with*, but not *as* sensation).[58] The element, by contrast, is the sensuous surface itself, the surface that the artist confronts. But it is not only surface. While science and philosophy have maintained a radical split between appearance and reality, the artist knows nothing of this split. The other dimension of the sensuous surface is a depth dimension. The depth dimension, as we have already seen, is the way primordial temporality is manifested: the way the present bears the depth of the past and is latent with futurity (see Chapter 2, section 3). A definition of the elemental as temporal against the definition of matter as substratum turns to a different metaphor which signals a different way the originary operates: the liquid depth rather than the geological underlayer. It is the liquidity of the magma that first allowed the rock strata to form, it also signifies the liquid essence of our bodies and of our eyes, the condition of the possibility not only of formation, but of sensation.

The only way to access this depth, however, is to draw it up, to convert the latent into a manifestation. What this means is that the depths are only known through an act of creation rather than through an access to meaning. If the traditional problematic of realism and idealism had to do with the possibility of access to signification (which is nothing other than the problem of the relation of matter to meaning), the artistic experience of the elements, by contrast, tells us that our access to matter is through making, but not from the point of view of the 'spontaneous subject'. It is the landscape that 'thinks itself in me'. The artist's experience thus confirms Merleau-Ponty's thesis that consciousness and world emerge together. The elemental only appears through making (*physis*) which draws meaning into being from a latent possibility always in formation, and thus always temporal, in contrast to the philosophical concept of matter, which is pure possibility, spatialised but completely lacking temporality.

A central reason ancient peoples thought of water as the substance before creation is the idea of latency inherent to water: the watery depths seem to be heavy with something to come. The earth precipitates out of the waters as a concretion of their latency. In speaking of the revelatory power of art – its power to draw up from the depth, to make latency explode into existence – Merleau-Ponty cites, of all people, Hermes Trismegistus, who speaks of an 'inarticulate cry' which 'seemed to be the voice of light'.[59] It is undoubtedly surprising to find Merleau-Ponty, eminent professor of the Collège de France, citing the legendary Egyptian father of the esoteric tradition.[60] So as not to become bogged down in mystical obfuscation, he quickly turns to a very ordinary experience to illustrate his point: the experience of gazing into a swimming pool. After all, this 'voice of light' is not something to be found only in the extraordinary. It is the very awakening of 'powers dormant in ordinary vision'. These powers are 'a secret of pre-existence',[61] which is to say, they are linked to what comes before sense, the realm of the 'inarticulate cry'. Merleau-Ponty's banal example of the swimming pool runs as follows:

> When through water's thickness I see the tiling at the bottom of the pool, I do not see it despite the water and the reflections, I see it exactly through the water and its reflections. I see it by means of them. If there were not these distortions, these streaks of sunlight, if I was seeing the geometry of the tiles without this flesh, it is then that I would cease to see it as it is, where it is, that is: further than any identical place. The water itself, the aquatic power, the syrupy and mirroring element, I cannot say that it *is* in space: it is not elsewhere, but it is not in the pool. It dwells, it materialises there, it is not contained there, and if I raise my eyes toward the line of cypresses where the network of reflections plays, I cannot dispute that the water visits them too, or at least sends its active and living essence there. It is this internal animation, this radiation of the visible that the painter looks for under the names of depth, space, and colour.[62]

I have cited this passage at length in order to bring out certain parallels to the Hermetic text to which Merleau-Ponty cryptically alludes. Although Merleau-Ponty does not quote any more of Hermes, nor hint that he is even familiar with the context from which this brief quotation was pulled, it is useful to look at the full passage. What 'secret of pre-existence' does the 'inarticulate cry' reveal? At the beginning of the *Poimandres*, Hermes recounts a vision, first seeing a 'downward tending darkness, terrible and grim' that 'changed into a watery substance which was unspeakably tossed about and gave forth smoke as from fire. I heard it making an indescribable sound of lamentation', he continues, 'for there was sent forth from it an inarticulate cry. But from the Light there came forth a holy Word, which took its stand upon the watery substance; and I thought this Word was the voice of the Light.'[63] There are many similarities to other ancient texts. If the dating of this text to the early centuries after Christ is correct, then we might assume that it draws both from the beginning of the book of Genesis and John's prologue – the Spirit of God hovering over the face of the waters as well as 'In the beginning was the Logos'. In any case, what we have for certain is a water cosmogony. From the latency of this primordial water emerges first an inarticulate cry and then a Logos. Even though Merleau-Ponty employs the example of the swimming pool, such a banality is nevertheless not without reference to the larger context of this opening passage of the *Poimandres*. In the swimming pool the medium of water remains that which functions as an analogy for the depth of pre-existence – a depth that art makes explode into being.

Water in this case is a three-dimensional symbol of what Merleau-Ponty will reduce to a one-dimensional symbol: the 'latent line'.[64] He speaks of the latent line with reference to the way painters use lines in a painting. Painters paint lines to delineate forms or masses in the painting. But these lines are not there in the real world. And yet the placement of fictious lines is not particular to painting. Naked perception too sees lines that are not there in the three-dimensional perceptual field. These non-existent lines are in fact essential to all visual perception. They make it possible to see a thing and delineate it from other things. In other words, it is not simply a tool the artist uses to transpose a three-dimensional perception into a two-dimensional space. It is constitutive of all seeing. Merleau-Ponty speaks of the goal of painting as 'freeing the line' from a dead geometry, revivifying its constituting power. The line is not 'there', but is emergent. The emergence of the line constitutes the painting as something seen rather than something represented. The line is therefore not 'in' the space of the painting just as it is not in the three-dimensional space of naked perception. It is instead constitutive of the relationship between the visible and vision itself. It is the latency of the visible – its power to be seen. The line is not essentially on the surface, but is latent in the visible, waiting and ready for the eye to draw it out.

In his *Treatise on Painting*, Leonardo da Vinci wrote (and Merleau-Ponty cites) that 'The secret of the art of drawing is to discover in each object the particular manner in which a certain flexuous line which is its generating axis, is directed through its whole extent.'[65] Merleau-Ponty says that 'The line is no longer, as in classical geometry, the apparition of a being on an empty background; it is, as in modern geometries, restriction, segregation, modulation of a preliminary spatiality.'[66] This preliminary spatiality was already exemplified in the perception of the pool. The latency of the line is the same 'aquatic power' which is the 'internal animation' of the visible. Just as the latency of the line suggests that the line exists beyond mere two-dimensional extension, so the aquatic nature of space suggests that it has a depth which is not on a three-dimensional axis. In other words, objects are not merely juxtaposed with the line marking their absolute distinction. The line is an edge, a membrane, a site of relation, a power that generates difference through togetherness. This site of relation is materiality itself, a materiality we name the element and which is not to be confused with matter as substratum. Just as one colour's existence in a painting changes all the other colours, so the line is where appearance vibrates with life. It is 'the cradle of things'. 'This means in the end that what is proper to the visible is to have a lining of the invisible in the strict sense, that it makes present as a certain absence.'[67] What is absent is the latency which lacks the differentiation characteristic of existence. The latent coincides with the withdrawal of the waters by which existence 'dries out' or emerges from pre-existence. Cosmogonic drying out, which is to become a distinct form, is also latent possibility becoming an actual reality.

* * *

While Cathryn Vasseleu is right to draw attention to the important place of images of light in Merleau-Ponty's analysis of the visible (see Introduction, section 7), the counterweight of light, I would argue, needs to be understood as primordial water rather than as the Heideggerian 'darkness of the earth'. Even if he uses examples, often rather banal, in which water features metaphorically, this aquatic operation is never thematised in Merleau-Ponty in the way that Heidegger thematises elementals. This obscure reference to the Hermetic text, for example, though he hides the context of a water cosmogony in which the Hermetica places it, is relocated next to Merleau-Ponty's analysis of the water of a swimming pool, which acts as the flesh of space itself, its 'active and living essence'.[68] Water as a cosmogonic principle better articulates the dynamic operation between sense and non-sense in Merleau-Ponty's philosophy and radically distinguishes it from Heidegger. It is the primordial flood on which floats the 'ark of existence' which is the arch-original Earth. As 'germ of the endangered world', the flood, the latent line, both creates this Earth and threatens its existence (see Introduction, section 6).

We can thus sum up the two aspects of water cosmogony that I have shown to be operative in Merleau-Ponty's ontology. The aspect of drying expresses a cosmogonic principle that doesn't operate according to the withdrawal of the horizon, which is always in front of us, as with Heidegger. It is a dynamic principle under us, manifest in the struggle for liberty as a negative rather than positive milieu – a dynamic principle that we live as always already past. Its pastness has everything to do with our identity as individuated beings, whose individuation depends on this elemental non-being, a non-being that has washed through us from all eternity and is therefore 'hidden' in our deepest parts.

Notes

1. *Metaphysics*, 1071b27, where he speaks of the 'theologoi' who derive everything from Night. Cf. 1091b4.
2. VI, 201/155.
3. IP, 244/187.
4. N, 20.
5. Hesiod's *Theogony*, lines 116–20, 126–38: 'In truth, first of all Chasm came to be, and then broad-breasted earth, the every immovable seat of all the immortals who possess snowy Olympus' peak and murky Tartarus, and Eros, who is the most beautiful among the immortal gods … Earth first of all bore starry Sky, equal to herself, to cover her on every side, so that she would be the ever immovable seat for the blessed gods; and she bore the high mountains, the graceful haunts of the goddesses, Nymphs who dwell on the wooded mountains. And she also bore the barren sea seething with its swells, Pontus, without delightful love; and then, having bedded with Sky, she bore deep-eddying Ocean and Coenus and Crius and Hyperion and Iapetus and Theia and Rhea and Themis and Mnemosyne and golden-crowned Phoebe and lovely Tethys. After these, Chronos was born, the youngest of all, crooked-counseled, the most terrible of her children; and he hated his vigorous father.' Translated by Glenn W. Most (Cambridge, MA: Harvard University Press, 2006).
6. Martin Heidegger, 'The Origin of the Work of Art', in *Poetry, Language, Thought*, trans. Albert Hofstadter (New York: Harper & Row, 1971), 45.
7. Heidegger, 'The Origin of the Work of Art', 45, 59–61.
8. Heidegger, 'The Origin of the Work of Art', 47: 'World and earth are essentially different from one another and yet are never separated. The world grounds itself on the earth, and earth juts through world. But the relation between world and earth does not wither away into the empty unity of opposites unconcerned with one another. The world, in resting upon the earth, strives to surmount it. As self-opening it cannot endure anything closed. The earth, however, as sheltering and concealing, tends always to draws the world into itself and keep it there.'
9. Heidegger, *De l'origine de l'œuvre d'art. Première version (1935)*, ed. and trans. Emmanuel Martineau (Paris: Authentica, 1987), 32. See also Andrew J. Mitchell, *The Fourfold: Reading the Late Heidegger* (Evanston, IL: Northwestern University Press, 2015), 75.
10. See Erich Neumann, *The Origin and History of Consciousness*, trans. R. F. C. Hull (Princeton, NJ: Princeton University Press, 2014), 102–30.
11. Heidegger, 'The Origin of the Work of Art', 45.

12. Heidegger, 'Building Dwelling Thinking', in *Poetry, Language, Thought*, trans. Albert Hofstadter (New York: Harper & Row, 1971), 152.
13. Heidegger, 'The Origin of the Work of Art', 45.
14. Heidegger, 'The Thing', in *Poetry, Language, Thought*, trans. Albert Hofstadter (New York: Harper & Row, 1971), 170.
15. Heidegger, 'The Thing', 170.
16. Heidegger, 'Building Dwelling Thinking', 152.
17. On this point see the first chapter, 'Phenomenology to its Limit', of Emmanuel Falque's *The Wedding Feast of the Lamb: Eros, the Body, and the Eucharist* (New York: Fordham University Press, 2016), 11–30.
18. 'The Thing', 177.
19. For an overview of this theme, see especially Richard Capobianco, *Heidegger's Being: The Shimmering Unfolding* (Toronto: University of Toronto Press, 2022), 9–22 and 71–7.
20. See Capobianco, *Heidegger's Being*, 61–70.
21. M. L. West, *The Orphic Poems* (Oxford: Clarendon Press, 1983), 119–20; Jean Rudhardt. *Le thème de l'eau primordiale dans la mythologie grecque* (Berne: Éditions Franke, 1971).
22. Emmanuel Levinas, *De l'existence à l'existant* (Paris: Vrin, 2013), 83/73. Pagination for this edition followed by original pagination.
23. Levinas, *De l'existence à l'existant*, 73/84.
24. Levinas, *De l'existence à l'existant*, 79/91.
25. Levinas, *De l'existence à l'existant*, 79–80/91–2.
26. Emmanuel Levinas, *Totality and Infinity: An Essay on Exteriority*, trans. Alphonso Lingis (Pittsburgh: Duquesne University Press, 1996), 130–42.
27. See Guthrie, *Orpheus and Greek Religion*, 79, 94, 102. And Luc Brisson, 'Les théogonies Orphiques et le papyrus de Derveni: notes critiques'.
28. '… the fathomless depth of the element, coming from an opaque density without origin, the bad infinite or the indefinite, the *apeiron*' (158–9); '… possession, accomplished by the quasi-miraculous grasp of a thing in the night, in the *apeiron* of prime matter, discovers a world. The grasp of a thing illuminates the very night of the *apeiron*: it is not the world that makes things possible' (163).
29. Levinas, *Totality and Infinity*, 142: 'The nocturnal prolongation of the element is the reign of mythical gods.'
30. Levinas, *De l'existence à l'existant*, 65/74.
31. Levinas, *De l'existence à l'existant*, 66/75.
32. Levinas, *De l'existence à l'existant*, 66/75.
33. Dante Alighieri. *Inferno*, trans. Mark Musa (New York: Penguin, 2003), I. 1–3, p. 67.
34. Levinas, *De l'existence à l'existant*, 83/95.
35. Levinas, *De l'existence à l'existant*, 83/96.
36. Levinas, *De l'existence à l'existant*, 83/95–6.
37. Levinas, *Totality and Infinity*, 158.
38. Quotation from Paul Valéry's 'La Cimetière marin', *Œuvres de Paul Valéry* (Paris: Éditions du Sagittaire, 1933).
39. For an English translation, see N. K Sandars, trans., *Poems of Heaven and Hell from Ancient Mesopotamia* (Baltimore: Penguin, 1970), 73.
40. Rudhardt, *Le thème de l'eau primordiale dans la mythologie grecque*, 32.
41. Homer, *The Iliad*, trans. Peter Green (Oakland: University of California Press, 2015), 14, 244–7 (trans. mod.).
42. 'I am going to visit the ends of the bounteous earth, Ocean, the father of the gods, and Tethys, their mother.' *Iliad*, trans. Peter Green, 14, 200–1 (trans. mod.).
43. Plato, *Thaetetus*, 180c–d; cf. 152e.
44. N, 194.
45. Heraclitus, Fragment B76. Translation from Patricia Curd, ed., *A Presocratic Reader*, (Indianapolis: Hackett Publishing, 2011).

46. Bachelard, *L'eau et les rêves*, 130.
47. Bachelard, *L'eau et les rêves*, 142.
48. For a more sustained version of this argument, see Gilbert Simondon, *L'Individuation à la lumière des notions de forme et d'information* (Grenoble: Millon, 2013), 39–60.
49. N, 190.
50. Heidegger, 'Building Dwelling Thinking', 152.
51. VI, 315/267.
52. VI, 159/121.
53. OE, 65.
54. OE, 31.
55. SN, 30.
56. SN, 30.
57. SN, 23.
58. On this point see Alfred North Whitehead, *The Concept of Nature* (Cambridge: Cambridge University Press, 1920), 16–21.
59. *Poimandres*, 4–5a. Quoted at OE, 70.
60. For more on this, including Merleau-Ponty's source for this quotation, see Mauro Carbone, *La chair des images* (Paris: Vrin, 2011), 141–6.
61. OE, 70.
62. OE, 70–1.
63. *Poimandres*, 4–5a. Translation from *Hermetica 1*, trans. Walter Scott (Oxford: Clarendon Press, 1924).
64. OE, 77.
65. Quoted at OE, 72.
66. OE, 77.
67. OE, 85.
68. OE, 70–1.

Chapter 5

The Savagery of the Symbol: The Barbarian Principle and Elemental Negation

In the final pages of the 1815 draft of *The Ages of the World*, descending into a rhapsodic meditation on the primordial ground, Schelling alludes to 'a barbaric principle ... that could be stifled, but never suppressed'.[1] This principle, this wild essence at the heart of all existence, became a cornerstone idea of Merleau-Ponty's later writings. The 'principe barbare', 'être sauvage', or 'esprit sauvage', all are of Schellingian provenance. Many articles have been written on Merleau-Ponty's appropriation of Schelling's barbarian principle.[2] It should be noted from the outset that, although the exact term *das barbarische Prinzip* appears only in these final pages of the third and final draft of the *Weltalter*, it is an idea that spans the course of Schelling's career, from his early Naturphilosophie to his Freedom essay and into his later works on the philosophy of mythology.[3] In the Freedom essay (1809) he calls it 'erste Natur' (primal Nature) – an 'incomprehensible ground' and an 'irreducible remainder'.[4]

It is unclear exactly how much Schelling Merleau-Ponty read. Many of his references are mediated through Karl Jaspers book on Schelling[5] and Karl Löwith's *Nietzsche's Philosophy of the Eternal Recurrence of the Same*.[6] Both these texts are cited plentifully in the section on Schelling in the *Nature* course. Samuel Jankélévitch's selected translations of Schelling seems to be the most important collection of primary source reading for Merleau-Ponty. This volume includes selections from the Naturphilosophie works (*Ideas for a Philosophy of Nature, First Outline of a Philosophy of Nature* and *On the World Soul*) as well as excerpts from the *Freedom* essay. Additionally, he may have read the same Jankélévitch's translation of *Ages of the World* and consulted a copy of Samuel's eminent son, Vladimir Jankélévitch's early book *L'Odyssée de la conscience dans la dernière Schelling*.[7]

Ever since Hegel dethroned Schelling from the pinnacle of German philosophy in the 1810s, Schelling worked without approbation, relatively unknown and publishing nothing from that time forward.[8] At his death he was dismissed as a minor figure attached to the coat-tails of Fichte and Hegel. This view persisted until mid-twentieth-century scholars began to recognise the significant advance he made in his late courses on the philosophy of revelation and the philosophy of mythology. The 1950s particularly saw a revival of interest in Schelling, after a century and a half of Hegelianism. Yet at this time Schelling was read through an existentialist lens, as, for example, in Jaspers, who (like the Schellingians of the next half-century) was reluctant to consider the Naturphilosophie as 'the core of Schellingianism rather than just a phase'.[9] Because Merleau-Ponty's reading was partly filtered through Jaspers, we ought to take it with a grain of salt. Yet, it remains the case that, in an existentialist decade, few were more 'presciently receptive to the problem of nature in Schelling's thinking' than Merleau-Ponty.[10] It takes only a brief glance at Merleau-Ponty's disputes with Sartre to see that Merleau-Ponty was no proponent of existentialism.

William Hamrick and Jan Van der Veken contend that Merleau-Ponty's narrow reading of Schelling through Samuel Jankélévitch's *Essais* shows that Merleau-Ponty does not recognise that these works, eclectically put together from different periods of Schelling's career, 'cannot be harmonized'.[11] Thus they contend that Merleau-Ponty is not a close reader of Schelling, but only appropriates what he finds useful for his own philosophical project. If we read Schelling in the light of the more recent literature, particularly the work of Iain Hamilton Grant, we might come to a different position on Merleau-Ponty: that Merleau-Ponty's eclectic reading of Schelling was fortuitous. Having no clear regard for the trajectory of Schelling's project and its 'phases' allowed him to continue to read Schelling's later work in light of his early Naturphilosophie, a position that Grant contends is the right way to read Schelling but had not been the prevailing reading in the fifties. Read in light of Grant's continuity thesis – that nature remains the unifying core even in Schelling's later phases – the eclecticism of Janklevitch's *Essais* fortuitously helps Merleau-Ponty avoid an overemphasis on discontinuity between phases, and the idea of an increasing 'existentialism' from the *Freedom* essay onwards. Unburdened by scholarly disputes on this issue, Merleau-Ponty gets straight to the heart of Schelling's project when he identifies him as a thinker of the irreducibility and physicality of form. 'The key to the Naturphilosophie', Merleau-Ponty writes, 'is to consider the existence of God as an empirical fact, or even to understand that it is at the base of all experience. Whoever has understood this has understood the Naturphilosophie, which is in no way a theory, but a life interior to Nature.'[12]

An essential reason Merleau-Ponty resources Schelling is their common aim to overcome the correlationism intrinsic to philosophy after Kant. Schelling's understanding of nature as a weight that 'can never be annihilated, even when it is surpassed' is, according to Merleau-Ponty, 'the only possible form of realism'.[13] This weight of nature, beyond correlation, is central to overcoming a philosophy of subjectivity, like that of Fichte, which is 'curiously incapable of expressing action, exactly because it ensconces itself in subjectivity'.[14] Merleau-Ponty sees that this correlationism includes his own tradition – phenomenology. He realises that phenomenology itself lacked a concept of nature and that this was its essential weakness. Phenomenology needs the barbarian principle, that which is 'non-phenomenology', a weight of things beyond the airy weightlessness of the phenomenological correlation. This non-phenomenological principle is essential for phenomenology to retain its own coherence:

> What resists phenomenology within us – natural being, the 'barbarian' source Schelling spoke of – cannot remain outside phenomenology and should have its place within it. The philosopher must bear his shadow, which is not simply the factual absence of future light.[15]

Schelling's own critique of Hegel and Fichte had contained a similar goal: that of overcoming correlationism. It is the correlation of mind and world that finally converts the concept into the consummation not only of philosophy but of history itself. Contained within Schelling's idea of nature is something that resists this correlationism. It is why he takes nature as the fundamental starting point. It is a term that better comprehends the principle of the All than does the term Esse, which too easily is converted into a concept. Further, being-as-All cannot comprehend non-being and negation as participants in the whole.

The present chapter contains two theses. The first concerns Schelling and it is something that has been hinted at in Schelling scholarship but has never been stated outright: namely his understanding of the barbarian principle cannot be separated from his understanding of symbol. I see this thesis as a working out of recent developments in Schelling studies, which have made this claim defensible through two main arguments. The first is the argument for a continuity that runs through all of Schelling's work: that with the *Essay on Human Freedom*, Schelling does not in fact change gears and move away from his Naturphilosophie principles, becoming a philosopher of freedom *instead of* a philosopher of nature. Above all, the publication of Iain Hamilton Grant's *Philosophies of Nature after Schelling* (2006) marked a watershed moment towards taking Schelling's Naturphilosophical starting point as that which remains constant through the later 'phases' of his thought.[16] For Schelling, nature remains *the* starting point: not freedom, not revelation, but nature. Nature is a principle, not a particular domain of being. Strictly speaking, Schelling's Naturphilosophie is not a philosophy *of* nature. Nature is fundament, the *Grund*. It is the ground of freedom. It is freedom itself in its spontaneous passage into existence. The most basic principle of being, nature is the *arché* of metaphysics as such.

Building off Grant there has been a new emphasis on the concept of symbol as a Naturphilosophie concept. While it may seem that symbol ought to be relegated to philosophy of language or philosophy of religion, symbol has a certain thickness to it that I will argue brings it into intimate relation not just with the understanding of Naturphilosophie as a whole, but with the notion of the barbarian principle in particular. What this certainly does not mean is that what is wild or savage is 'tending towards' meaning, a type of 'pre-sense' that eventually becomes meaningful. In fact, this is precisely what the idea of symbol in contrast to the sign resists. What I would argue instead is that both the barbarian principle and the symbol are essential concepts for Schelling's understanding of powers, but that the duality is insurmountable. It is impossible to think the barbarian principle without at the same time thinking the symbol and vice versa.

This point becomes crucial when thinking about the barbarian principle in relation to Merleau-Ponty. Thus my second thesis: Merleau-Ponty's understanding of the barbarian principle is, like Schelling's, connected to a concept of symbol. This thesis would be obvious if the connection between the barbarian principle and symbol were clear in Schelling and if Merleau-Ponty himself made it clear. While symbolism indeed becomes central in Merleau-Ponty's late thought, the relation between the barbarian principle and the use of symbol in Merleau-Ponty needs to be made explicit. Ultimately what I will suggest is that Merleau-Ponty's notion of the flesh as a 'sensible generality' or 'concrete emblem' ought to be understood to operate according to the logic of the symbol and its powers, but in a way modified from how Schelling formulates it. He isn't a Schellingian of the strict observance. Indeed, the transition from Schelling's notion of symbol as tautegory to Merleau-Ponty's notion of flesh as chiasm offers a critique of Schelling's way of practising metaphysics 'from above' (*une philosophie de survol*) and an attempt to think 'from the middle'. Nevertheless, the flesh as natural milieu maintains a deeply Schellingian and Romantic heritage. For this reason, we need to go into some detail on Schelling.

What is without doubt clear is that, as Emmanuel Falque has emphasised, for Merleau-Ponty, the world is never totally without sense, whereas, as we have seen already, Levinas is able to posit the possibility of a purely meaningless 'night of phenomenology' where no horizon appears at all: the night of trauma, the abyss without horizon (see Chapter 4, section 3).[17]

Though Merleau-Ponty speaks of the barbarian principle and of wild being as what resists the meaningful and ordered, the barbarian in Merleau-Ponty nevertheless does retain a certain status as 'pre-sense'. Though Merleau-Ponty 'remains the phenomenologist that leaves the most space for darkness', it is a darkness that always 'prepares for the light'.[18] Falque's objection to the limits imposed on the barbarian principle as something always 'for' meaning, is part of what I want to respond to in this chapter by developing the dynamics of the barbarian principle with respect to the term proper to what makes meaning in it, namely, the symbol. After all, Merleau-Ponty calls brute being 'the umbilical cord of our knowledge and the source of meaning for us'.[19] If everything is always directed towards sense, this directedness is nevertheless resisted by the origin's duality, the unsurpassability of the barbarian ground.

Already in Schelling the notion of the barbarian principle is connected with that which is coming to light. What I want to show is that the economy of the symbol expresses the way in which wild being is not exclusively 'pre-sense' or coming to light. It is an error to suppose that the principle, any principle, is entirely made manifest, or even could theoretically be made manifest. What allows the barbaric to remain barbaric is precisely a theory of symbol as opposed to sign, a philosophy of form as opposed to content, and a thinking of powers as opposed to correlation.

1. Symbol as Naturphilosophie concept

Symbol features prominently in Schelling's theory of art. He does not, however, relegate it to aesthetics. His manner of deploying it within his aesthetics illustrates precisely in what way symbol, above the other aesthetic categories, expresses the proper way to conceptualise the emergent properties of nature. In Schelling's philosophy of art, there are three species of image that correspond to the three modes of being in his Naturphilosophie: Schematism, Allegory and Symbol.[20] The first, Schematism, or *Einbildung*, is a universal that signifies a particular thing. The second, Allegory, is a particular thing that has universal meaning, which is to say, a particular that points to a schema. Later Schelling will speak of tautegory in contradistinction to the second category, that of allegory.[21] Tautegory is a neologism that he begins to use for what he speaks of here as the third mode of imaging: the Symbol. Allegory literally means 'to say something other than' what is (literally) said. Tautegory means 'to say the same'. While the allegory points to something other than what it says, the tautegory points to the very thing that it says. It does not point elsewhere. It signifies itself.

When Schelling moved to Jena in 1798 as Extraordinary Professor of Philosophy, he and Goethe discussed at some length the nature of symbol and allegory.[22] The consensus between these two great German thinkers was that, as a means of artistic expression, symbol was far superior to allegory:

> There are also works of art that shine by means of understanding, wit and gallantry, in which we also include all allegory. Very little good can be expected from these, because they destroy the interest of the presentation itself and, as it were, repel the spirit into itself and withdraw one's eyes from what is really presented. The allegorical is differentiated from the symbolical by the fact that the former signifies indirectly, the latter directly.[23]

There were no doubt differences between the theories of symbol held by the various thinkers of the age of Romanticism, but the essence of the symbol was always the same: the indifference of meaning and being. The discovery of this notion of symbol so excited Goethe precisely because before he came upon this idea he was 'beset with dualisms between thought and the empirical world: each subsisted in an independent realm and reconciliation seemed impossible'.[24] Schelling calls this indifference of meaning and being 'tautegory'.

Seen anachronistically through the eyes of a Weberian secularisation thesis, twentieth-century scholars often read the Romantic 'symbol' as a reactionary concept deployed to 're-enchant' a world that had been denuded of sense by modern science and Cartesian or idealist philosophies. While the Romantic tradition no doubt rejected the mechanical understanding of nature dominant in the eighteenth century, recent scholarship has challenged the interpretation of the Romantic symbol as mystical reversion to pre-modern ways of thinking. Daniel Whistler, for instance, argues instead that the idea of symbol was deployed precisely as the way of expressing how meaning emerged *naturally* rather than from, say, a spirit-world separated from the physical world. It is his commitment to understanding nature as a comprehensive term from which everything emerges, including sense, that makes Schelling so attached to the symbol, as a physics of emergence. Schelling was as committed to a naturalistic starting point as the scientists of his day. He just contested the mechanical paradigm of nature.

This reading of symbol as Naturphilosophie concept *against* 'Romantic re-enchantment', may present a false dichotomy. After all, what re-enchantment narratives combat is the same mechanical view of nature as that contested by Naturphilosophie. Nevertheless, the Naturephilosophical context is essential. Without it, we cannot understand how the symbol relates to the barbarian principle. What is important is that the symbol expresses a physics more than a metaphysics. It doesn't descend from on high, nor does it indicate a realm of transcendence. The Schellingian symbol always remains fully within nature. The symbol is the finite manifestation of the infinite, but the infinite is not the infinitude of God. It is the indefiniteness of the *apeiron*. The symbol enables nature to manifest its productive power rather than to exhaust it. Schlegel poses the question in indirect dialogue with Schelling, 'How can the infinite be brought to the surface, to appearance? Only symbolically.'[25] Here we are speaking precisely of the infinite power of nature, which comes up to the surface through a negation of its indefiniteness. It is by the symbol that the infinite rises to the surface: the elemental abyss brought to concrete manifestation.

Symbols are often confused with signs or considered a subspecies of signs.[26] For Schelling, the irreducible union of form and content in the symbol shows that the symbol is something entirely unique. Signs point to a signified. The sign is not in itself the signified but indicates it. Like a trail marker pointing the way to the top of a mountain, the sign does not share in the essence of what it signifies. There is nothing 'mountain-like' in the trail marker. For Schelling, a true symbol does not symbolise something other than itself. It does not point to a signified. To know the symbol requires going into the symbol, not beyond it. As Stefano Biancu puts it, 'Unlike the sign, which refers to something else, the symbol invites us to enter into and participate in itself.'[27]

This idea of symbol was developed in the context of German Romanticism. It is no doubt a particular and perhaps polemical conceptualisation of symbol. Schelling himself first toyed with the theory of Georg Friedrich Creuzer, which puts symbol in closer relationship to a semiological account.[28] But the influence of Creuzer, integrated into Schelling's tautegorical account, would be a large part of what gave the symbol the same dynamism of emergence as *physis*. Creuzer considered symbols as codes that needed to be deciphered. He linked symbols to a type of hieroglyphism and hermeneutics. He argued that ancient priests were the first exegetes, able to decipher the religious symbols and thus provide privileged access to an esoteric realm. This hermeneutical approach was also applied to myth, which was said to teach something that could be abstracted from the story. The doctrine to be acquired was cloaked in mythological language. To get at the message, the hermeneut only needed to undress it from its mythological trappings. Like the mythologists of the day, Creuzer's theory suggested that imagery aims to suppress itself. 'The image cedes its autonomy to the profit of sense, of which the image becomes a sign.'[29] While Schelling will reject this semiological understanding of the symbol and the accompanying 'Protestantisation' of ancient cultures, he retained from Creuzer the idea of an exoteric and esoteric world, which is most manifest in the *Bruno*.[30] Appropriated in a new way, this exoteric-esoteric duplicity gives Schelling a means of restoring spiritual thickness to things without a dualism of spirit and nature. Schelling uses the example of prophetic writings. The exoteric meaning of an apocalyptic text is the present event. It is what the text literally says. The esoteric meaning, by contrast, points to the future event insofar as it is contained within the present. The esoteric does not replace and cancel the exoteric as much as the exoteric propels us towards the esoteric.

Symbol is a Naturphilosophie concept because its temporal dynamism expressed in the exoteric-esoteric dynamism of prophecy is more fundamentally the dynamism of *physis* itself. The fact that symbol has no content separable from its form may make it seem similar to an Aristotelian hylomorphism. Schelling, however, means something quite different. Symbolic unity originates from his ontology of powers rather than an Aristotelian or Newtonian ontology in which bodies are ultimate. For Schelling, 'force is the ultimate [...] to which all our physical explanations must return'.[31] The recent return to thinking Schelling's formalism flies in the face of two centuries of Hegelianism and of interpreting Schelling through a dominantly Hegelian lens.[32] If there was a certain formalism in art and art theory at the beginning of the twentieth century, it has nevertheless turned out to be a century of semiotics, hermeneutics and deconstruction of forms. Structuralism was followed by post-structuralism. In the wake of a century of political violence and an accompanying suspicion of institutions perhaps this was inevitable. Paul de Man, a prototypical antagonist to the symbolic theory of language, attacks the symbol as a violent 'suppression' of the difference between meaning and being in language, calling it a 'tenacious self-mystification'.[33] De Man asserts that the fact that 'sign and meaning can never coincide is precisely what should be taken for granted'.[34] As Whistler notes, from a Schellingian point of view, de Man entirely misses the point. Language understood as symbolic does not at all mean to say that it is a representation of nature, nor a correspondence or identity with it. It is instead a repetition of nature.[35] The symbol activates, expands and empowers rather than signifies or represents. Far from saying the symbol is severed from nature, the logic of symbol insists that language, as with other symbolic forms, does not have a representational relationship with nature. The relationship is deeper. Language is, as it were, a second *physis*.

To say that language is symbolic in the Schellingian sense is first of all to say that nature is itself symbolic all the way through. The symbol replicates itself before any split between being and meaning can be postulated. I use the verb *to replicate* though we have also referred to repetition. The meanings of the two terms have significant overlap, but I will privilege the term *replication* because it refers to the organic, but non-sexed, essence of both nature and the symbol: nature as symbol is like a virus, bacteria or fungus that replicates without sexual duality. This claim will soon become clearer both with respect to Schelling's own thinking and how it might be understood through Merleau-Ponty's introduction of the concepts of institution and chiasm (see Chapter 6, section 5).

2. Symbolic replication and the birth of the gods

To understand symbolic replication with respect to Schelling's own work, we first need to delve into his use of tautegory. Replication and augmentation, the symbol's work of activation and expansion in the replicated products, come into focus in his philosophy of mythology. We do not have to go beyond *The Deities of Samothrace* (1815), which was originally written as a companion piece to *Ages of the World*, but which was in the end published separately. The French version to which Merleau-Ponty had access includes both texts.[36] For Schelling, symbol is described as tautegorical because tautegory expresses the internal dynamism of *physis*. It refers to itself and therefore creates from itself. Nature, in other words, operates symbolically. Forms are not put together by a process of synthesis from disparate parts but repeat themselves in creating new forms from their internal dynamism.

I have already suggested that Schelling should be understood as a thinker of form rather than a hermeneut. This is the fundamental feature of his style of thought that distinguishes it from the critical tradition inaugurated with Kant. In order to overcome the Hegelian apotheosis of the concept, Schelling resists deconstructing physical form. The symbol should be understood as what performs this resistance to Hegelianism – the system that has remained dominant to our day. The Schellingian symbol might be conceived as a pre-critical concept – having much in common with Leibniz and Spinoza – perpetuated in a post-critical context (insofar as symbolic theory was developed only in the wake of Kant).

The hermeneutical approach deconstructs form to get at an underlying content. It moves from the text as sign to the signified underneath. The signified is esoteric in the sense that the hermeneut assumes that the true meaning isn't the explicit meaning. The text must be interpreted in order for the true signified to be revealed. The esoteric meaning need not be the meaning intended by the author. It might not be a meaning the author intentionally hides under a text, like a puzzle he asks his readers to solve. A Freudian hermeneutic, for example, suggests that the real meaning of a text is always an *unintended* meaning that reveals the unconscious of the author, something the author reveals in spite of him- or herself. The mythologists of Schelling's day aimed to look behind the various myths of world cultures in order to see one universal meaning behind all mythologies: that all the myths signify the same thing, or that all the divinities of polytheism were really just different manifestations of the same god.[37] Schelling adamantly rejected this approach, for he thought it devalued the mythical form for the sake of some hidden message behind the form. Instead, he considered myths as real events – real physical things that must be taken with the sense proper to themselves, not the sense proper to another (as the allegorical interpretation demanded). For Schelling, there was no ideal essence behind the myth. In other words, they must be taken as tautegories rather than allegories.

By retaining the form rather than looking behind it for a secret content – by retaining the form rather than taking it apart analytically – Schelling was able to see something quite different than what the critical tradition can see. The symbolic progresses forwards with an upwards thrust. Schelling's move to what he calls positive philosophy against the purely negative philosophy of Hegel is grounded in this retention of symbol as a site of power as much as a site of meaning. Indeed, the tautegorical is fundamental to his philosophy of myth in which he argues for a certain literalist reading of *successive* polytheism against an atemporal and spatialised *simultaneous* polytheism. As he outlines it in the *Deities of Samothrace*, the age of Night is followed by the age of Chronos who is in turn castrated by his son Zeus, who then seizes the cosmic throne. Successive polytheism for Schelling is an example of symbolic repetition or replication. Each generation inaugurates a new age which is also an augmentation of the power of the last one. This newness and augmentation is accomplished through a primordial deed that acts against the power that founds it: the castration of the father.

Allegorising interpretations have always seen the plurality of gods to be mere phantasmic emanations of the one God who abides in a permanent stasis. The gods, in such interpretations, are the various powers of a singular god or a singular nature. Schelling's dynamic approach, however, takes the succession of gods literally because it takes the becoming of *physis* seriously. The idea of successive deities rather than simultaneous deities expresses the physics of becoming. Indeed, in direct opposition to an emanationist account from a divine above, the gods do not descend as phantasmic representations of the one God. They ascend from the most primordial and the lowest divinity – 'it is a misrepresentation if one also regards this first being as the highest' – to the last god who is, even then, 'the herald of a coming god'.[38] In the *Ages of the World* (1811) Schelling explains the inadequacy of a system of descent, like certain Neoplatonic systems:

> The systems which want to explain the origin of things by descent from above, necessarily arrive at the thought that the outflowings of the highest original power must finally lose themselves in a certain outermost extremity, where there was only, so to speak, a shadow of essence, the slightest leftover of reality ... This is the meaning of non-being for the Neoplatonists who no longer understood the truth in Plato. We, following the opposite direction, also maintain an outermost, beyond which there is nothing; but for us this is not the ultimate reach of an outward flow, but the first, from which everything begins, not pure lack or a reality almost wholly robbed of existence, but an active negation.[39]

Because Schelling wants to maintain maximum reality at both ends of the spectrum – on the one extreme the highest god and consciousness and at the other extreme the first god and the unconscious – he seeks to establish a shared principle: nature itself, which remains robustly real precisely because only an *active* negation could overcome nature's primordial and unconscious freedom.

The allegorising interpretation of mythology finds its consummation in a concept. First, the meaning is abstracted to arrive at a schema: the unity of the gods in a God. But this one God was not a living God but an idea such that the God himself is finally tossed aside for the concept pure and simple. Schelling's move to 'positive philosophy' is a move towards a philosophy of existence and away from Hegel's philosophy of essence with its allegorising and schematising method. It is a means of thinking the life of God or the ground of freedom – an existence that grounds essence rather than an essence that grounds existence.

While dialectic maintains an essential role in his philosophy, Schelling, like Plato, realised he must turn to myth when dialectic ceases to function. Myth is the language of becoming. Dialectic is the language of unchangeable things.[40] For Schelling, the theogonies are really theogonies. They tell of the actual birth of the gods and are not mere projections of the human mind. What this means is first of all that they are physical, historical realities within a process of becoming, and secondly, that the unity of the whole is not in human consciousness, projecting reality, but in nature from which all emerges.

> The theogonic process, through which mythology emerges, is a *subjective* one insofar as it takes place in *consciousness* and shows itself through the generating of representations: but the causes and thus also the objects of those representations are the *actually* and *in themselves* theogonic powers ... The content of the process are not merely *imagined* potencies, but rather the *potencies themselves* – which create consciousness and which create nature (because consciousness is only the end of nature), and for this reason are also actual powers. The mythological process does not have to do with natural *objects*, but rather with the pure creating potencies whose original product is consciousness itself.[41]

Schelling does not mean to say that the theogonies are not stories. He wants to address a problem that cannot be confronted if the theogonies are understood as *mere* stories. When the narratives are thought to signify something other than what they actually say, then they lose their power to create. They lose their power to express nature and to generate consciousness. Mythology explains itself (is tautegorical) because, as Xavier Tilliette says, 'it is itself an "explication," that is, a development, a history, a process'.[42]

The act of allegorisation can produce two different displacements of meaning from the actual thing at hand. The first displacement is emanationist: thinking the divinities in descending order, or thinking creation as a fragmentation of the divine. As it fragments or refracts, it moves further and further away from the really real, which in this case is God or the One. The second displacement is the theory of projection, where one thinks the mytho-theological as a projection of human consciousness. We look within our concepts and images of the divine for a hidden, merely human, content. While the first displacement considers God as the real and consciousness/world as suffering so much unreality, the second retains all the reality for consciousness and its correlates. The first displacement is characteristic of Neoplatonism, and a large portion of the philosophical tradition more broadly. It is also characteristic of certain strains of Christianity. The second displacement tends to be characteristic of modernity. For Schelling, the problem with both of these dualistic models is not merely that one term of the relation loses all reality to its other – dualisms that in the end turn out to be monisms. The real problem is that there is no place for an authentic active power. To understand the theological and mythological naturalistically (in Schelling's sense) does not equate to an allegorisation à la Feuerbach, who, following Hegel, splits sense and appearance, the real and the perceived, thereby psychologising rather than naturalising the mytho-theological. Schellingian literalism holds the two together – sense/image – by thinking the relation's unity through powers rather than through correlation of mind and world as if mind or world were some sort of 'container' for meaning which settles into conditions of possibility like so many objects settling into object-shaped holes. Thinking meaning-being unity through powers means that there is never a pure coincidence – being/meaning or being/thinking. The relation is always asymmetrical since powers are by nature infinite and the bodies which bear them are finite.

It is in this way that Schelling sidesteps the 'access problem' that has defined philosophy as correlative since Kant inserted the idea of the thing-in-itself as a 'hard core' of reality which mind or language could not reach. In posing the thing as some sort of centre of darkness, Kant presupposed that consciousness, by contrast to the tenebrous thing, is absolutely translucent – that consciousness is all light standing up against the opacity of the thing. Kant transfers the problem of the 'dark' onto the thing, where Schelling saw that consciousness too is grounded in shadow. Its origin and its freedom is in the night. This night is neither of consciousness nor of being and things. The Schellingian night is the indeterminability of originary force: the night of the unconscious and the unthinged. Equally, any attempt to 'go back' (by reduction) from an appearance to an inapparent but fully graspable meaning is misguided. The irreducibility of forms is essential for Schelling's dynamic philosophy of existence. The form is not an end but a medium. It does not exhaust its reserve of darkness. Quite the opposite: in relation to consciousness it amplifies this reserve, which creates an augmentation of consciousness that is not an augmentation of cognitive information, but which stirs up a force slumbering within mind. As Edward Allen Beach describes it, 'the function of myths in religions', according to Schelling, 'was not to impart information or to reach an intellectual understanding of the world, but rather had something to do with stimulating a special kind of psychological response within the listener'.[43] In this way symbols are future-oriented and prophetic – launching us into temporality through the dynamism of exoteric and esoteric disequilibrium – containing both the depth of the past and the inscrutability of the future. As a concrete datum of human culture, myth is a reduplication of nature. It cannot be explained away by advancing towards some static essence behind it. It is an irreducible remainder buried in our past, an active harbinger of the present, which continues to beckon towards the future, heralding the coming god.

3. Nature against correlation

In his reading of Schelling in the *Nature* course, the first thing that Merleau-Ponty emphasises is that Naturphilosophie was a means of overcoming the pure present that correlationism implies. *Erste nature* is the most ancient element, an 'abyss of the past'.[44] To think nature as irrecoverable past sets the thought of nature against reflexive philosophies where being is coterminous with reflection. Nature's temporality is that of a radical past: not a past that was once present but a past that was always past – the very rocks of the earth that preceded every past possibly experienced by anyone. It is as immemorial past that nature is something irreducible to reflexive thought – outside of the control of consciousness, and yet not unrelated to consciousness, for consciousness itself is one of its products and therefore one of the things for which Nature is always experienced as a past. The time of nature is as it were the castrated Chronos. From a living temporality, it becomes an immemorial past, an unlivable past on which our living is grounded.

The turn against correlation and against transcendental idealism, is not, for Merleau-Ponty a turn against relation. Neither is it a turn against relation for Schelling. What I am suggesting is that Schelling formulates symbol as a concept of *physis* that directly opposes the correlationist Kantian theory of knowledge without losing the link of *physis* to consciousness and meaning. If correlation is surpassed by nature, it is also surpassed by the symbol and its irreducible earthiness. For Schelling, however, his notion of symbol as tautegory – entirely undiscussed by Merleau-Ponty – leaves him little room to explore the kind of relation symbolism implies (though we do know what kind of relation he is against – the relation of correlation and representational theories of perception). The relation between consciousness and what is not consciousness is absolutely central, but the turn from the relation of consciousness and (its) world to the relationship between consciousness and nature leads Merleau-Ponty to understand this relation as chiasm. In order to understand the relation implied in the dynamism of symbolic repetition, I will suggest that we need the Merleau-Pontian concept of chiasm.

The kind of relation described is one in which the barbarian principle – what is not correlated – cannot be surpassed or converted into relation. Though we can 'exceed' the barbarian principle, it can never be put aside. Merleau-Ponty understands the barbarian principle to be Schelling's effort to explain this 'pre-being which, as soon as we arrive, it is already there'.[45] It is not however a problem of 'access' to the hard thing itself. It is the 'ground from which' (see Chapter 3, section 3). Merleau-Ponty sees here an ally for his perceptual ontology which starts from the togetherness of being and meaning rather than from their separation. The barbarian principle's unsurpassibility has to do with its nature as primordial power from which all being, even conscious being derives. What is perceived is primordial with respect to the act of perceiving: *Erste Nature* is 'an excess of Being over consciousness of Being'[46] first due to power – the inexhaustibility of what is primordially there – and second due to pastness – its irrecoverability as principle of life. Every time I extend my perceptive faculties out into the world, I perceive something pulsing with antiquity, something that seems to have already been there, the perception of which therefore plunges me back into the depths of time. This already-having-been is not merely the past of a discrete object perceived. It is the pastness of the whole field in which it arises, its being 'caught up in a logic', caught in a system of visibility which does not appear quite eternal, but immemorially ancient. The visible surpasses the vision by means of its antiquity not its 'reality'.

It is encircled with the invisibility of the immemorial past that shines forth nevertheless in its visibility. This is not an argument for a realism of the object, but a means of integrating temporality into perception. Because the perceiver is temporally late, always after what he or she perceives, correlation no longer makes sense as the means of constructing the relation between perceived and perceiver, visible and vision.

The question of some a priori power that resists us and which is something we resist is essential to Schelling's prioritisation of existence over essence. The philosophy of existence becomes the foundation of his 'positive philosophy', which he posits against Hegelian essentialism. For Schelling, the philosophy of existence represents the prioritisation of nature over the idea. In the Freedom essay, freedom only takes its place as ground insofar as it surges up from the unruly abyss:

> The world as we now behold it is all rule, order and form; but the unruly lies ever in the depths as though it might break through, and order and form nowhere appear to have been original, but it seems as though what had been initially unruly had been brought to order. This is the incomprehensible basis of reality in things, the irreducible remainder which cannot be resolved into reason by the greatest exertion but always remains in the depths. Out of this which is unreasonable, reason in the true sense is born. Without this preceding gloom, creation would have no reality; darkness is its necessary heritage.[47]

The transcendental philosophy of Kant, Fichte and Hegel tended to split the world between the subject who predicates and the objects it is able to predicate, i.e. the transcendental subject and the world it knows. The copula is what binds them together. Schelling, for his part, rejected this binary which put consciousness on the subjective side and all knowable things on the side of the predicate. Instead he posed nature itself as subject. This should not be understood as a strict reversal, but as a wholly different structure.

The doctrine of nature as subject is not a 'senseless ... Romantic anthropomorphism' as many have argued.[48] In thinking nature as subject Schelling indicates the autonomy of nature: nature 'not as it appears to Mind, but *nature itself*'.[49] Nature as subject is not a personal subject. It should be remembered that Aristotle thought matter as subject, that is, as something indefinite, 'that of which things are predicated', able to take on a variety of forms.[50] While Schelling's nature is by contrast an active principle of emergence like the Ionian idea of nature, its subjectivity should be understood as something more similar to Aristotle's understanding of the subjectivity of matter than to the subjectivity of post-Kantian transcendentalism. In thinking nature as subject, Schelling's primary aim is to uncondition nature, to overcome the limits imposed on nature by Kant – the limits of a priori conditions of the possibility of experience. Grant suggests that it is this struggle to delimit nature that makes Schellingianism 'resurgent every time philosophy reaches beyond the Kant-inspired critique of metaphysics, its subjectivist-epistemological transcendentalism, and its isolation of metaphysics from physics'.[51] This is certainly the case with Merleau-Ponty, who, by the time of *The Visible and the Invisible*, was radically questioning the very foundational presuppositions of his earlier work precisely to the degree that it relied on Husserl's philosophy of consciousness which thought the being of things primarily as a 'presence to': things as present to consciousness and consciousness as present to things. If much of the rest of the French philosophical tradition struggled against Kant through an attempt to uncondition the phenomenon,[52] Merleau-Ponty follows Schelling's goal of unconditioning nature, which is to say, of un-phenomenalising it without severing it from a logic of appearing – neither simply the things that exist nor the hard core known as essence.

This context is essential to understanding what Merleau-Ponty intends with the 'pre-' in pre-sence, pre-subjective, pre-objective – no longer as 'presence to' or conditioning towards a correlation – where 'world' correlates to sense. Pre-sense plays with the word presence – a pure unconditioned 'now' which is not a 'presence to'. It designates nature as an 'absolute of presence'.[53] In that it is both pre-subjective and pre-objective, the ground of both subject and object, it is unconditioned – not produced by a relation (of predication). But it is equally not the 'thing in itself' of Kant, for it doesn't have the limits of a thing. It is subject as indefinite and predicable. As Merleau-Ponty describes the question of his late philosophy:

> For us the essential is to know precisely what the being of the world means. Here we presuppose nothing – neither the naïve idea of being in itself, therefore, nor the correlative idea of a being of representation, of a being for the consciousness, of a being for man: these along with the being of the world are all notions we have to rethink with regard to our experience of the world.[54]

Understanding correlation less as a completion (an act) and more as an activation of certain powers leads to the necessity of thinking a ground that precedes any correlation – a ground of freedom, a ground that is utterly unconscious. In short, a barbarian ground that would not enclose all existence in a concept but would retain what is in Plato's *Timaeus* a 'physics of the Idea'.[55] Indeed, the very return of a way of thinking nature as the guiding thread throughout Schelling's career demands conceiving force as something before correlation. It would not make sense to say that the barbarian is 'for' sense as perhaps the existentialist readings of the fifties might. If there is a 'tending towards' and a 'not yet' in the pre-sense of wild being, it is nevertheless a 'not yet' and 'never' at once. The barbarian principle will never become sense although it always foretells it.

Grant sees that Platonic physics of the Idea is essential to Schelling's theory. He contrasts an Aristotelian 'physics of all things' (*ta physika panta pragmatica*)[56] to Plato's 'physics of the All' (*tou panto physeos*).[57] Aristotelianism divides physics from metaphysics because 'what underlies' (*hypokeimenon, subjectum*) is 'what is common to all the things of Nature'.[58] Aristotelian nature has no dynamic principle to create things precisely because 'all things' are presupposed as already existing. Plato's khora by contrast is an all beyond 'all things' because it is their principle of emergence and so is excluded from being among the things that exist. For Grant, Aristotle's interpretation of Plato stripped the forms of their materiality by reducing physics to a science of bodies. Because Aristotle thinks the correlation of sensation as the accomplishment of an act (see Chapter 2, section 1), powers are exhausted in their completion there. They find their *telos* in this act. Likewise, if all that really exists are bodies, then there is at the most fundamental level no movement and no powers. In this model, powers only operate within a regulated domain and are fulfilled in bodies. Beyond this regulated domain of bodies (Aristotelian physics) is the realm of Aristotelian metaphysics – being as such – for which the becoming of physics does not apply. Schelling is inspired by Plato because for Plato forces are as real as bodies. And further, there must be originally a multitude of powers since a power without something to resist it is no longer a power (*Sophist* 247d–e), for it would do absolutely nothing.[59] In this case, it would no longer be a power. If a force is coincident with its product, no force has taken place. Consequently, in order for there to be finite products, forces must be infinite – not coinciding with their finite product. If they can exhaust themselves in their products, bringing the product to completion, then it would coincide with the product it generates, and would no longer be a force but a body. Not only do forces precede bodies, they proceed bodies as radically unconditioned. This Platonic insistence on primordial, unconditioned force underlies Schelling's primary thesis: that the world first comes to be through an act of negation, a resistance to the unconditioned power of the Ground. It is thus the force of the element, not the pure possibility of prime matter that is Subject.

4. Unmotivated upsurge: The freedom of nature and the primordial negation

Schelling's most fundamental contribution to philosophy was the disassociation of freedom and consciousness. In the modern tradition, exemplified by Fichte and Kant, freedom and consciousness were fused such that freedom was understood as a becoming-conscious.[60] Sean McGrath summarises, 'The transcendental identification of freedom and consciousness, initiated by Descartes and reaching its apogee in Fichte, split nature and subjectivity into irreconcilable opposites. Nature became the exterior order of causality, the order of things that are bound by their essences; subjectivity was the interior order of spontaneity.'[61] For Schelling, at the ground of personhood is an act of freedom, which, 'in its origin, is entirely unconscious'.[62] Schelling's early understanding of the unconscious aims to overcome Descartes in thinking the 'primordial oneness of subject and object, consciousness and matter'.[63] It is in light of this primordial unity that we can define the unconscious as materiality – a realm of indefinite power that becomes conscious through an act of decision. There will be more on Schelling's notion of the unconscious in the last chapter (section 1), but it is necessary to bring this up here in order to be able to talk about why Schelling links freedom with unconscious nature rather than with consciousness.

For Schelling, freedom is not achieved by surpassing or contradicting necessity. Freedom is fundamental and absolute. The contradiction arises with the assertion of necessity upon a ground of freedom. In Schelling, there is an inversion of the usual order. Nature is typically the realm of necessity and human subjectivity the realm of spontaneity and freedom. Instead, in Schelling everything depends upon a ground of freedom such that freedom is no longer ontologically after necessity. The surprising thing, Schelling remarks, is that, in spite of their initial freedom, everything is caught in the 'web' of reason.[64] How then, we must ask, did everything get into this web? Nature is this ground of freedom – that which has no sufficient reason. Nature is like the rose – without why. Human freedom then is not consciousness, but self-appropriation, the primordial act of decision upon a ground of freedom. It realises its freedom through determining it – converting the infinite unruly forces into a definite form, thereby turning initial freedom into ancillary necessity. It is in this way that Schelling secures nature's status as an absolute. He renders it something that arises before reason. As a 'web', reason is relational, while Nature, being free and absolute, must decide for reason. Nature is free of any correlation to consciousness and its reasons, and yet after the fact always caught in a web of reasons. The ground of freedom is hidden under the emergence of necessity.

Freedom is thus not linked with personal subjectivity, but it postulates a new subjectivity. Nature as *subjectum*, that is to say, as unconscious ground, is utterly free. While the ground is a ground of freedom, the ground is freedom not because it is conscious but because it is the churning of indeterminate, infinite powers – a certain rotary motion. The infinitude of these powers are not exhausted in the act of self-appropriation. Consequently, they yield an 'irreducible remainder' which is an earlier expression of what Schelling will later term the barbaric principle.[65] The severing of freedom from consciousness is what returns Schelling to the old idea of nature as subject. While Aristotle did not associate it with freedom, the subjectivity of matter in Aristotle already implies a kind of negation in many ways analogous to Schelling's formulation of the primordial negating deed, an analogy which enables us to show a radical difference. Aristotle links matter's potential to become with the logical notion of contrariety. Aristotle tells us that contrariety is a different form of negation than that of contradiction, and that contradiction only obtains for statements (it is only logical or noetic) while contrariety can obtain for things (it can be logical and ontological).[66] A contradiction obtains if the truth of one statement implies that the other statement is false and if the falsity of the first statement implies that the second is true: 'Socrates is a man' and 'Socrates is not a man' are contradictory statements (if it is the case that Socrates must be either a man or not a man). The contrariety, by contrast, refers to two statements that cannot both be true, but can both be false. If the delimitation of a subject of a predicate is a genus that contains more than the two predicates of two positive statements, they are contrarieties. 'This animal is a bear' implies that 'This animal is a lion' is necessarily false. The animal cannot be both a lion and a bear. But the animal still could be neither a bear nor a lion. The animal could be a walrus.

Even though Schelling, like Merleau-Ponty, is 'not a great Aristotelian', contrariety is an essential part of the logic of the Schellingian original act of negation. The negation, which is the passage from a primordial chaos of forces (elemental non-being), does not abolish the infinite power of nature that it negates when it asserts itself as something definite and finite. The negation obtained through the assertion of a contrary term retains what is negated. It does not retain it as actual, but in its virtue or potency. It still *could* be something else. The assertion of one possible predicate ('This animal is a bear') does not exhaust the possibilities of the subject 'animal', but it does negate their actual existence for the duration that it is a bear. The non-exhaustion of *logical* possibilities in the act of predication is analogously related to the non-exhaustion of *ontological* potencies in the original act of negation. In both cases, the assertion of a negation retains what is negated in virtuality. The subject 'animal' still has the virtue of naming bears, lions and walruses, even though it is predicated of a bear in this particular sentence. Likewise, when a certain bit of matter becomes a bear, it cannot at the same time actually *be* a lion. But that very same matter could be a lion if it ceases to be a bear. Logical, predicative contrariety retains the *possibility* of what is not, ontological contrariety retains the *potency* of what is not.

Aristotle recognises the relation between logical predication and ontological structures.[67] He understood there to be an intrinsic relation between matter and contrariety. Particularly, he understood privation, matter's lack of form, to be the primary contrariety. For Aristotle, matter was infinite (*apeiron*) because it lacked form. Matter is infinite by privation of form. This means that Aristotelian prime matter could take on an infinite number of different forms. It was infinitely malleable. Yet while matter could potentially take on an infinite variety of forms, the activation of any single form would exclude the activation of all the others. While this particular bit of matter does not have to be either a lion or a bear, if it does have the form of a lion at this time, it cannot have the form of a bear at the same time. Nor can it have any other form at the same time. In actuality, it can only be one form, but in possibility, it retains the power to be infinite other forms. The negation of contrariety thus negates the actualisation of all other possibilities while retaining those possibilities in potentiality.

Schelling's original act of negation should be understood first of all as contrariety rather than a contradiction, though contradiction is the term he uses. By negating the indefiniteness of nature, it becomes one thing to the detriment of all other possible things. But it does not eliminate the ground of possibility from which it arises. It does not eliminate the infinite power of that ground. Although they share a common understanding of the material ground as contrariety, Schelling's physics of the ground is fundamentally opposed to Aristotle's division of physics from metaphysics because he understands the elemental ground as infinite power to be. What is unconditioned about nature is its force underlying all bodies – a sort of form of forms. There is a certain torsion within the physical object in Schelling that is not there in Aristotle, a continual upward thrust insofar as it is from the base that forms arise and not from above. And it is clear that he uses the term contradiction thus in a Heraclitean dynamic logic (see Chapter 1, section 5) that neither adheres to Aristotelian noncontradiction, nor breaks its rules. But the contrariety better explains the continued existence in power of what is negated. In power, the ground endures within the very thing that negates it. Because the ground is power, a principle of becoming, rather than a ground like Aristotelian matter, which is a principle of sameness across change,[68] the ground continues to (non)exist in everything it grounds. But it persists in this way as absolutely separated. Nature, by becoming one thing, still contains the other things, not only privatively (in the sense that, if it ceases to be one thing, it can then become another). It contains those possibilities in power. The thing that emerges from the negation is never an absolutely accomplished thing. It remains in transition. It retains nature's power vibrating within it. In Schelling's physics, the thing does not need to lose its form in order to become something else. The form itself becomes a site of power. It replicates *physis* as a second *physis*.

This point is essential for understanding how, for Schelling, symbols are able to activate unrealised possibilities. The Ground is a germ rather than a cause. It produces by being negated. The seed dies and recedes so that the product might be. While Merleau-Ponty, echoing Schelling's own language, calls it a 'fecund contradiction',[69] the negation enacted upon the ground is that of a contrariety – a positive, fecund contrariety. Perhaps even better: fecund contradiction is the definition of contrariety as such. In any case, the fecund contradiction expresses the latency from which the product emerges but which the product does not exhaust. Understood as subject, the Ground is the *apeiron* – unconscious rather than conscious, indifferent to the forms it will bear. As seminal principle of existence, the Ground 'is ambiguous like the possible itself, of which it is the generating and, so to speak, maternal form'.[70] Insofar as the symbol is the finite manifestation of an infinite ground, primordial negation is the act of the symbolic. The symbol thus operates like a logical contrariety. In coming to the surface, it does not abolish the material power by converting it into form. It manifests that power by holding the indefinite base together with the finite form.

Merleau-Ponty takes up Schelling's notion of freedom to show that nature can be thought neither through mechanism nor finality since neither mode of causality can go back to a beginning a 'surgissement immotivé'[71] and an understanding of God not as *causa sui* (Spinoza) but as Abyss – from the *ens necessarium* to 'what exists without reason'.[72] Schelling's move from a philosophy of essence (and its *ens necessarium*) to a philosophy of existence (and its unmotivated upsurge) is not only a means of thinking God as a living God who surges up from a ground of freedom. It is already for Schelling a way to escape the God of the philosophers 'before whom we can neither dance nor pray', as is manifested in the theological theme of the 'barbarian principle' paragraph (which we will get to in section 6 below).

The succession of monarchical divinities, one succeeding to the throne by castration of the previous is a way of describing becoming, for 'becoming needs victims', as V. Jankélévitch puts it.[73] Becoming rests upon the negating act. The symbolic interpretation of successive polytheism against the allegorical interpretation of simultaneous polytheism shows that the operation of symbolic replication is for Schelling identical to the operation of *physis*. It also demonstrates the central place of negation. Emergence requires a primordial negation of the unruly abyss. But the emergence of successive symbolic forms through the act of negation nevertheless does not annihilate the barbarian ground that it negates. It continues to resource this barbarian ground as a site of power. From his earliest philosophy, the symbol had been the self-same revelation of the infinite in the finite. In the later works, *Ages of the World* and *The Deities of Samothrace*, the primordial negation stands in this same place. Simply put, symbolic emergence is characterised by negation.

Schelling's philosophy of life takes the symbolic realm of myth as the realm of the primordial, a realm which is at once wild and symbolic through and through, activating and augmenting the powers of becoming which the concept dissolves and exhausts. The temporality of becoming does not erase the past but builds upon it in a constructive antagonism. The past becomes the Ground. Ejected into the past, the ground is the irreducible remainder, a heap of divine carcasses from which the world was made. The Ground cannot be understood as the cause of its products. In a certain way it is produced by them. The Ground is not Ground until the product emerges, just as a walnut is a nut and not a seed until it dies in the ground and the tree emerges: 'It is from the inside that the shadowy principle transforms itself into light, that the germ breaks forth within the obscurity of the soil.'[74] The Ground has a double aspect. The organism is pre-formed tacitly in the Ground as germ. All its possibilities are contained virtually in the germ. But the ground is also contrary to the development it engenders since 'development needs resistance'.[75] Organic development requires darkness. The Ground is both the intrinsic power of the grounded and the paternal essence that must be killed off. The paternal deity must be castrated to be dethroned. The Ground is replicated in every becoming. It is the virtual principle in every form. Jankélévitch sees that the seminal principle unleashes 'a contrary force that will suppress it'.[76] Schelling overcame correlation through the idea of the primordial negation – at once the emergence of consciousness and the guarantee that something (the negated) remains beyond the scope of the (personal/ even transcendental) subject's intentions. Merleau-Ponty saw how this negation was the only escape from the solipsism of correlationism and its exhaustion of force. The subject imagines itself in a world but because the powers of nature do not precede it as irreducible weight, the world that it believes it is 'in' is merely epiphenomenal, a product of mind, at best a correlate of consciousness. The folly of subjectivity – and this applies to a certain extent to precedent phenomenologies – is 'to think it is in the midst of a world when it is really only in itself'.[77]

One important step Merleau-Ponty makes towards a philosophy from the middle involves the way he understands how the relation of the infinite and finite is not hierarchical in Schelling. We cannot say which comes first, for they are not held together by a causal relation. The finite is produced by an 'internal scission' of the infinite, 'the result of a fecund contradiction'.[78] Since there is no linear order or causality, we cannot say that the finite is *only* negation since it cannot be 'analytically pulled out of the infinite'.[79] In other words, thinking the being-meaning coincidence from power leads back to an originary fusion of the finite with the infinite, and never to an analytic concept. The very commitment to originary force (rather than a world of bodies) leads back to the originary productive union. This union is the symbol. Symbol does not so much oppose concept but precedes it at every step.

5. The interiority of nature: From representation to repetition

With regard to his understanding of nature as subject, Merleau-Ponty sees that Schelling is in the lineage of theosophy more than Aristotelianism. Subjectivity is not only the retention of possible predicates. It is the structure of the relation between the macrocosmic – nature – and the microcosmic – the human being. In other words, what is 'common' between nature and humanity is not matter – the pure exterior – but a certain interiority that is amplified in nature's creations. This interiority is also linked to Merleau-Ponty's reading of Whitehead's critique of unique emplacement: 'What I perceive is both for me and in the things. Perception is made starting from the interior of Nature.'[80] In other words, to view a point on a coordinate grid of space as the concrete reality underlying the sensible thing is the wrong way to look at reality. The coordinate system of exteriority views each point as absolutely separated from every other point. This view makes exteriority the real, but once we overcome the fallacy of misplaced concreteness, we can no longer view exteriority as original. We arrive at an interiority of nature that coincides with its sensibility rather than its measurability. Perception starting from nature means that the thing perceived is in multiple places at once. It is for me and in the things.

The relation of nature to consciousness is neither one of exteriority nor an exteriorising of a not-me projected outside of me. The relation is a shared interiority that emerges in both microcosm and macrocosm. Both nature and the human being have the same capacity to take on and produce being: 'what we call the me and what we call the living being have a common root in pre-objective Being'.[81] For Schelling, contrary to Fichte, there is an interiority not only in the human subject but in nature itself.

The interiority of nature is the origin of human interiority. This shows that human subjectivity itself – its capacity to reflect the universe – is not a personal subjectivity opposite to Nature's objectivity. Human subjectivity is itself linked to nature's impersonal capacity to take on an infinite variety of forms through 'fecund contradiction'.[82]

Despite his critique of final causality, Merleau-Ponty sees a place for it here. The finality that he sees in Schelling at this point still would not be a finality that attains an end absolutely. It is always blended with a wildness that cannot be overcome. Nature's seeming 'blind mechanism' is never surpassed but it is also constitutive of its internal drive. 'Nature, in its blind and mechanical finality', Schelling writes, 'represents for me a primal unity of consciousness activity and of the unconscious, but it does not represent it in a way that I could say that its last reason resides in me.'[83] This unconscious is the shared interiority of nature and man alike, where participation of the me with the not-me is possible as a primordial 'milieu of experience' in which 'my life participates in each thing and reciprocally' [each thing participates in my life].[84] There is already in Schelling the primordial togetherness of mind and matter. This is formulated elsewhere in Schelling as the unity of symbol. The irreducibly material, unruly ground is primordially together with sense.

Transcendental subjectivity – subjectivity from on high – is replaced with a subjectivity of the below, the primordial interior capacity not only to take on predication, but to negate the primordial unconscious in order to create being and consciousness. It is in this precise case that the distinction organic-inorganic is invalid for Schelling. At least since *On the World Soul* (1798), he understood 'that the perimeter dividing organic from "anorganic" Nature' was 'naturalistically untenable and philosophically vicious'.[85] This is to say that he contests the opposition between mechanically operating physics and the self-organisation characteristic of biological life. By understanding the universe as self-organising, and thus organic in the widest sense, Schelling overcomes in advance the dichotomies maintained in later philosophies of life (Schopenhauer, Nietzsche, among others) which take for granted mechanical causality within physics and chemistry, but claim biology as a philosophical discipline.[86] Schelling rejects such a 'biocentrism' precisely by thinking symbol as a Naturphilosophie concept: self-organisation is not the remit of *bios*, but of *physis*. These later philosophies still assume that physics operates mechanically and save freedom for the biological. Schelling wants to show that not even physics should be understood mechanically. In this way he was far ahead of his time, showing that self-organisation (organism) was not 'an exception to a mechanistic natural order, but rather the *principle* of nature itself'.[87] That forces exceed mind and bodies enables *physis* to be a principle of self-organisation where this self-organising would always depend upon something unable to be integrated into the organised whole, namely the forces themselves – the most interior principle.

The passage from the non-biological realm into biological life is not made through a transition from mechanical, blind causality that rules over physical things to an internal finality that motivates biological organisms. 'It is by an internal development and not by a rupture that we pass from the physical being to the living being', as Merleau-Ponty states.[88] It is precisely because Schelling refuses to make a distinction along the lines of organic-inorganic that he cannot be either finalist or vitalist. Biological life and sensible qualities are 'two different "powers" of the same Nature'.[89] What Merleau-Ponty means here is that things, even when they are not perceived, have the power of sensibility. Life in its development from non-life takes to a second degree this power of sensible things: sensibility is turned back on itself to be sensed in its becoming a sensitive life. But this is not to turn nature into the *élan vital* of Bergsonian vitalism, a life force that runs in one direction and for which forms are only so many obstacles to its continuous flow.

> We are the parents of a Nature of which we are the children. It is in man that the things become conscious in themselves, but the relation is reciprocal: Man is the becoming conscious of the things. Nature travels by a series of disequilibriums, toward the realisation of man who becomes the dialectical term for it. It is only in man that the opening of the process is determined. But we can say that man is the *Mitwissenschaft* (knowing with) of the Creation. He bears the traces of all that Nature has been. He is the recapitulation and the contemporary of Creation. Schelling follows here the thinkers of the Renaissance, like Bruno, for whom man is a microcosm, and not, as in Kant, an empty freedom, an *antiphysis*.[90]

This emphasis on *physis* as what holds all things together despite their differentiated powers makes Merleau-Ponty's reading of Schelling similar in a significant way to Grant's 'continuity thesis' – showing that nature, not freedom, remains the unifying concept even into Schelling's middle and late periods. The world cannot be divided into what is natural and mechanical on the one hand and what is biological and free on the other. Freedom is in *physis* itself. It is not the exclusive domain of biological life.

6. Symbol and barbarian principle

It is not by accident that the paragraph in which Schelling invokes the *Barbarische Prinzip* includes a critique of modern theology's tendency to strip God of power and force. Moreover, this stripping of force is tied to allegory and 'empty schematizing', the eternal foe of symbol in Schelling's system:

> However, this idealism that has appeared among us is just the expressed mystery of the entire direction that has been for a long time more and more prevailing in other sciences, in the arts, and in public life. What was the endeavor of all modern theology other than a gradual idealization and emptying of Christianity? Character, competence, and force are getting less and less in both life and public opinion, but so-called 'humanity,' for which the above qualities would have to serve as ground, counted for everything. Likewise, this age could only avail itself of a God from whose concept all power and force had been removed. This is a God whose highest force or expression of life consists in thinking or knowing and which, besides this, is nothing but an empty schematizing of itself. This is a world that is still just an image, nay, an image of an image, a nothing of nothing, a shadow of a shadow. These are people who are nothing but images, just dreams of shadows. This is a people that, in the good-natured endeavor toward so-called Enlightenment, really arrived at the dissolution of everything in itself into thoughts. But, along with the darkness, they lost all might and that (let the right word stand here) barbaric principle that, when overcome but not annihilated, is the foundation of all greatness and beauty.[91]

Schelling is particularly critiquing the allegorisation of the Christian story in the theology of his day, a theology already moving towards nineteenth-century liberal theology. Allegory and its philosophical form, idealism, converts Christianity into an empty construct without real content. The barbarian principle is invoked to oppose this allegorising habit of idealist theology: 'Without this principle which resists thinking', Schelling continues, 'the world would actually already be dissolved into nothing.'[92] Given that the insertion of the barbarian principle provides an alternative to the allegorising or 'empty schematizing' of the idealist theological trends that strip God of power, it is evident that the recovery of 'wild being' cannot be separated from symbol. If the barbarian principle's enemy is theological allegorising, its primary ally is symbol.

Without an essentially symbolic understanding of nature, the barbarian principle, its resistance to 'empty schematizing',[93] does not hold together. Reciprocally, the symbol, even as self-referential 'tautegory', could not make sense without the barbarian principle: its irreducible concreteness, its productive power, and its power of resistance. In this paragraph, Schelling implies that the barbarian principle is not a pure chaos or meaningless force. It has a primordial qualitative dimension: the barbarian principle is the 'wrath of God'. This wrathful dimension, the 'irascibility' of nature, is not accidental, but characterises the essence in its infinitude:

> Hence, immediately with the relationship of external Being to the Godhead, without change or alteration in the Godhead itself, the Godhead in this relationship is a consuming No, an eternally wrathful force that tolerates no Being outside of itself. This consequently also admits of an inverse formulation. This wrathful force is not merely a quality, principle, or part of the Godhead. It is, rather, the entire Godhead, insofar as it consists of itself and is the most essential Being. For it is self-evident that this essential Being is something inaccessible to everything else, an irresistible ferocity, a fire in which nothing can live.[94]

Further on he says:

> There must be Might before there is Leniency and Stringency before Gentleness. There is first Wrath, then Love. Only with Love does the wrathful actually become God.[95]

Merleau-Ponty comments on the importance of the idea of the wrath of God for properly thinking *erste Nature*: 'There is nothing solid in the history of Nature, where this no doubt destructive and wild, but necessary, force is ignored.'[96] Here Merleau-Ponty draws attention to, and imitates in the structure of his sentence, Schelling's critique of his own century for having lost sight of nature's or God's essential irascibility.

Without doubt, this idea of the wrath of God as ground of nature stems from Böhme, who writes:

> The wrath (the fire) is the root of all things and the origin of all life; in it is the cause of all strength and power, and from it are issuing all the wonders (manifestations of power). Without that fire there would be no consciousness, but everywhere a mere nothing.[97]

Schelling's formulation of the barbaric principle directly echoes Böhme's description of the divine wrath. Just as the barbaric principle is 'the foundation of all greatness and beauty', so the divine wrath is 'the cause of all strength and power, and from it are issuing all the wonders'. It is unclear whether Merleau-Ponty's reference to Böhme stems from his reading of these other passages in *Ages of the World* which are no doubt inspired by Böhme's concept of God as fire-ground, or whether Merleau-Ponty refers to it simply because he knows of Böhme's broader influence on Schelling. In the latter case, his own reference to the wrath of God could have been supplemented by his reading of Alexander Koryé's book on Böhme.[98]

It should also be noted at this point that for Merleau-Ponty the idea of wrath would have also been mediated through Bachelard, for whom the irascible nature of the elements was a major theme. In a chapter on 'violent waters', Bachelard suggests that 'as a source of energy, being is an a priori anger'.[99] It is perhaps because Bachelard had already argued for a non-anthropomorphic view of material irascibility that the theme of the wrath of God in Schelling and Böhme would have particularly stood out for Merleau-Ponty. While Merleau-Ponty himself does not allude to symbol in his reference to the wrath of God, it is clear that in Böhme, Schelling and Bachelard, it is a symbology that is operative from the deepest levels of elemental powers – that the emotive is just as real as any other quality of the material, for the emotive lies neither in things nor in subjects. Elemental power is fundamentally symbolic because it is irascible to its core: what the element means to us – its overwhelming irascible nature – coincides with what it actually is. Only the irreducibility of its wrathful essence prevents the kinds of idealisations that empty out material existence. We might then make a stronger claim than we have thus far made: *wild being is not only intrinsically related to the symbolic, it is the symbolic through and through.*

The inversion brought about by the primordial negation makes the symbol emphatically originary. It is not something that consciousness tacks on to materiality afterwards. The symbolic is an irrecoverable beginning which rises up primordially and then sinks back into the obscurity of an irrecoverable past. Where the Hegelian concept is an end towards which all things tend and in which all things find their fulfilment, the symbol is a beginning, a site of power and generation. But the symbol must be *accomplished* as a beginning. It is ground only as repetition. The eternal rotary motion of drives and forces is negated by the primordial deed which marks the commencement of the world as such. Although this deed is truly beginning, before which nothing was, it cannot be understood as beginning except insofar as it is *passage to the beginning*. If the symbolic is from the beginning, if nature is symbolic all the way down, the question must arise at some point: *where is the real, that eternal opponent of the symbolic?* We will only be able to give a thorough answer to such a question towards the end of the next chapter.

Notes

1. F. W. J. Schelling, *Les Ages du monde* suivis de *Les Divinités de Samothrace*, trans. Samuel Jankélévitch (Paris: Aubier, 1949), 187. English translation: *The Ages of the World*, trans. Jason Wirth (Albany: SUNY Press, 2000), 106.
2. See, for example, the edited collection: *The Barbarian Principle: Merleau-Ponty, Schelling and the Question of Nature*, ed. Jason Wirth (Albany: SUNY, 2013).
3. Jason Wirth, 'The Reawakening of the Barbarian Principle', in *The Barbarian Principle: Merleau-Ponty, Schelling and the Question of Nature*, ed. Jason Wirth (Albany: SUNY, 2013), 4.
4. *Schellings Werke: Nach der Originalausgabe in neuer Anordnung*, ed. Manfred Schröter (Munich: C. H. Beck, 1927), 360.

5. Karl Jaspers, *Schelling: Grosse und Verhängnis* (München, Piper Verlag, 1955).
6. English translation by J. Harvey Lomax (Berkeley: California University Press, 1997).
7. See Robert Vallier, 'Être sauvage and the Barbarian Principle', in *The Barbarian Principle: Merleau-Ponty, Schelling and the Question of Nature*, ed. Jason Wirth (Albany: SUNY, 2013).
8. See Grant, *Philosophies of Nature after Schelling*, 1–25.
9. Grant, *Philosophies of Nature after Schelling*, 3. See also Daniel Whistler's recent article on precisely this subject: 'The Schelling of religious existentialism', *International Journal of Philosophy and Theology* 80.1–2 (2019): 178–95.
10. Wirth, 'The Reawakening of the Barbarian Principle', 5.
11. William S. Hamrick and Jan Van der Veken, *Nature and Logos: A Whiteheadian Key to Merleau-Ponty's Fundamental Thought* (Albany: SUNY Press, 2011), 124.
12. N, 73.
13. N, 77.
14. *La Nature ou le monde du silence*, ed. Emmanuel de Saint Aubert (Paris: Hermann, 2008), 49.
15. From 'La philosophe et son ombre' (S, 290).
16. See especially, Grant, *Philosophies of Nature after Schelling*, 14–21.
17. See Emmanuel Falque, 'Principe barbare et il y a', *Revista Portuguesa de Filosofia* 78.3 (2022): 673–96.
18. Falque, 'Principe barbare et il y a'.
19. VI, 207/157.
20. Schelling, *Philosophy of Art*, trans. D. W. Stott (Minneapolis: Minnesota University Press, 1989), 46 (§39).
21. Schelling takes this term from Coleridge, who first coins the word as a concept articulating some of Schelling's own earlier philosophical principles. See Coleridge's 'On the Prometheus of Aeschylus', in *Literary Remains*, vol. 2, ed. H. N. Coleridge (London: Pickering, 1839), 296. Schelling acknowledges the borrowing of the term 'tautegory' from Coleridge in a footnote to the Lectures on the Philosophy of Mythology, *Historical-critical Introduction to the Philosophy of Mythology* (Albany: SUNY Press, 2007), 187.
22. See Daniel Whistler, *Schelling's Theory of Symbolic Language: Forming the System of Identity* (Oxford: Oxford University Press, 2013), 8–9.
23. Goethe, 'Über die Gegenstände der bildenden Kunst', in B. A. Sørensen, ed., *Allegorie und Symbol: Texte zur Theorie des dichterischen Bildes im 18. Und frühen 19. Jahrhundert* (Frankfurt am Main: Athenum, 1972), 130. This text was written in 1797. I have borrowed Whistler's translation from 'Naturalism and Symbolism', *Angelaki* 21.4 (2016): 91–109.
24. Whistler, *Schelling's Theory of Symbolic Language*, 8.
25. A. W. Schlegel, 'Theory of Art (Selections from 1798–1803)', in Jochen Schulte-Sasse et al, eds, *Theory as Practice: A Critical Anthology of Early German Romantic Writings* (Minneapolis: University of Minnesota Press, 1997), 207.
26. See Dan Sperber, *Le symbolisme en général* (Hermann : Paris, 1974), 29–62.
27. Stefano Biancu, 'Competing Paradigms: A Century of Humanism and *homo symbolicus*', *Munera* (2019): 125.
28. Georg Friedrich Creuzer, *Symbolik und Mythologie der alten Völker, besonders der Griechen: in Vorträgen und Entwürfen* (Leipzig and Darmstadt: Leske, 1810).
29. Vladamir Jankélévitch, *L'odyssée de la conscience dans la dernière philosophie de Schelling* (Paris: F. Alquin, 1933), 254–5, in which Creuzer and Schelling are discussed.
30. V. Jankélévitch, *L'odyssée de la conscience*, 254.
31. Schelling, *Ideas for a Philosophy of Nature*, trans. Errol E. Harris and Peter Heath (Cambridge: Cambridge University Press, 1988), 37.
32. On Schelling as a thinker of form, see Bruce Matthews, *Schelling's Organic Form of Philosophy* (Albany: SUNY, 2011) and Whistler, *Schelling's Theory of Symbolic Language*, 226–8.

33. Paul de Man, *Blindness and Insight: Essays in the Rhetoric of Contemporary Criticism*, 2nd edition (London: Methuen, 1983), 208.
34. De Man, *Blindness and Insight*, 17.
35. See Whistler, 'Symbolism and Naturalism', *Angelaki* 21.4 (2016): 91–109.
36. Schelling, *Les Ages du monde* suivis de *Les Divinités de Samothrace*.
37. 'The Deities of Samothrace' is an accessible and brief example of his approach to mythology and his critique of his contemporaries. The English translation I use is: Robert F. Brown, *Schelling's Treatise on 'The Deities of Samothrace': A Translation and an Interpretation* (Missoula, MO: Scholars Press, 1977).
38. 'The Deities of Samothrace', 22.
39. There is no published English translation of the 1811 draft, so I am borrowing Matt Ffytche's translation of this passages provided at p. 110 of his excellent study, *The Foundation of the Unconscious: Schelling, Freud, and the Birth of the Modern Psyche* (Cambridge: Cambridge University Press, 2012). The original can be found here: *Die Weltalter, Urfassungen*, ed. Manfred Schröter (Munich: Biederstein/Leibniz, 1946), 230.
40. V. Jankelevitch, *L'odyssée de la conscience*, 6.
41. Schelling, *Philosophy of Mythology*, 144 [XI 207].
42. Xavier Tilliette, *Schelling: une philosophie en devenir*, vol. 2 (Paris: Vrin, 1992), 414.
43. Edward Allen Beach, *The Potencies of God(s): Schelling's Philosophy of Mythology* (New York: SUNY, 1994), 34.
44. N, 61.
45. N, 62.
46. N, 62.
47. Schelling, *Philosophical Inquiries into the Nature of Human Freedom*, trans. James Gutmann (La Salle, IL: Open Court, 2003), 34.
48. Hermann Krings, in Reinhard Heckmann, Hermann Krings, Rudolf W. Meyer, eds, *Natur und Subjektivität: zur Auseinandersetzung mit der Naturphilosophie des jungen Schelling* (Stuttgart-Bad Cannstatt: Fromann-Holzboog, 1985), 111–12. Reference taken from Grant, *Philosophies of Nature after Schelling*, 2.
49. Grant, *Philosophies of Nature after Schelling*, 2.
50. Aristotle, *Metaphysics*, 1037b3–1038b12.
51. Grant, *Philosophies of Nature after Schelling*, 5.
52. In the theological turn, especially, Jean-Luc Marion's saturated phenomenon, but even Levinas from *Totality and Infinity* onwards.
53. S, 278.
54. VI, 21/6.
55. *Timaeus*, 49a4–7. See Grant, *Philosophies of Nature after Schelling*, 34–5.
56. Formula of the Aristotelian Simplicius, *In physicam*, 198.28.
57. *Timaeus*, 47a9, 27a5.
58. *Physics*, 192a.
59. See Iain Hamilton Grant, 'The Remains of the World: Grounds and Powers in Schelling's Later *Naturphilosophie*', in *Schelling Studien* 1 (2014): 3–24.
60. S. J. McGrath, 'Schelling on the Unconscious', *Research in Phenomenology* 40 (2010): 72.
61. McGrath, 'Schelling on the Unconscious', 73–4.
62. Schelling, *Philosophical Inquiries into the Nature of Human Freedom*, trans. Gutmann, 65.
63. McGrath, 'Schelling on the Unconscious', 74.
64. Schelling, *Grundelegung der Positiven Philosophie* (Torino: Bottega d'Erasmo, 1972), 222. 'Web' seems to be the best translation here for 'Netz', to grasp the double meaning of being 'caught' [gefangen] in reason as in a spider's web, but, once caught, participating in a web of relations, i.e. a network. Translating it with the English word 'net' doesn't capture the second meaning and the word 'network' doesn't capture the

first. Schelling's exact phraseology is: 'Die ganze Welt liegt gleichsam in der Vernunft gefangen, aber die Frage ist: wie ist sie in dieses Netz gekommen ...'
65. Schelling, *Philosophical Inquiries into the Nature of Human Freedom*, trans. Gutmann, 34.
66. *Metaphysics* X, 4, 1055a34
67. *Metaphysics* X, 4, 1055a34.
68. *Physics* I, 7, 190a13–191a22.
69. N, 61.
70. V. Jankélévitch, *L'odyssée de la conscience*, 38.
71. VI, 261/211.
72. N, 60.
73. V. Jankélévitch, *L'odyssée de la conscience*, 41.
74. V. Jankélévitch, *L'odyssée de la conscience*, 40.
75. V. Jankélévitch, *L'odyssée de la conscience*, 40.
76. V. Jankélévitch, *L'odyssée de la conscience*, 41. Despite a clear understanding of the grounding of the ground by the grounded, Jankélévitch still seems to have a confused understanding of the barbarian principle when he writes of it as a 'marvelous mischievousness': 'The spirit, as reasonable as it is, is not immaculate. In it stirs a wild and very ancient principle, a witness to the origin of time which perpetually threatens our interior civilization. There is in the most regulated mind (*esprit*) the marvelous mischievousness that declares itself sometimes in making the peace-keeping forces keep silent. *Necessity subsists thus in freedom, Nature in the spirit and the non-me in the me*; the barbary of the irrational principle resists the appeals of the spirit' (44, my emphasis). While necessity subsisting in liberty is undoubtably a Schellingian thesis, the parallelisms '*Nature subsists in the spirit and the non-me in the me*', do not seem to coincide with Schelling at all, but rather with a mid-twentieth-century existentialist reading that puts him much too close to Fichte. There is in Schelling a theosophic man-as-microcosm containing the whole universe within himself. But to put 'Nature subsisting in spirit' as parallel to 'necessity subsists in freedom' seems to be a clear misreading of Schelling through a too transcendentalist lens. After all, are not Nature and freedom (not Nature and necessity) the corresponding terms in Schelling, the first philosopher who does not relegate freedom to spirit and consciousness, but identifies it with unconscious Nature?
77. *La Nature ou le monde du silence*, 49.
78. N, 61.
79. N, 61.
80. N, 159/117.
81. N, 64.
82. N, 61.
83. From Schelling's *System of Transcendental Idealism (1800)*. Translated by Peter Heath. Charlottesville: University of Virginia Press, 1978. S. Jankélévitch's French translation (*Essais*, 161), is cited by the editor of *La Nature* at p. 67.
84. N, 64.
85. Grant, *Philosophies of Nature after Schelling*, 10.
86. Grant, *Philosophies of Nature after Schelling*, 10.
87. Grant, *Philosophies of Nature after Schelling*, 10.
88. N, 65.
89. N, 65.
90. N, 68–9.
91. *Ages of the World* (1815), 106.
92. *Ages of the World* (1815), 107.
93. *Ages of the World* (1815), 106.
94. *Ages of the World* (1815), 73.
95. *Ages of the World* (1815), 83.

96. N, 62.
97. Jacob Böhme, Concerning the *Three Principles of Divine Essence*, trans. John Sparrow (London: John M. Watkins, 1910), xxi, 14. For Böhme, even God's Love, which is his very essence, is dependent upon this fire-ground, which is Nature: 'No created spirit can exist without the fire-world. Even the love of God could not exist, if not the wrath of God, or the world of fire, were existing in Him; for the wrath or the fire of God is a cause of light, strength, power, and omnipotence' (ii, 4).
98. Koyré analyses Böhme's understanding of God's nature as fire ground at p. 360 of *La Philosophie de Jacob Böhme* (Paris: Vrin, 1929).
99. Bachelard, *L'eau et les rêves*, 214.

Chapter 6

Symbolics of the Flesh: From Tautegory to Chiasm

Merleau-Ponty finds in Schelling a forerunner of his own understanding of flesh as an 'adhesion to Being'. As Jankélévitch describes of Schelling: 'there is first of all Being, and then consciousness – better still: thinking is nothing but a particular case of Being'.[1] For Schelling this adhesion to being is at once upheld on the barbarian ground and expressed through dynamic symbology. Does Merleau-Ponty merely copy Schelling to this extent? If we interrogate his concept of flesh in light of Schelling's understanding of symbol, we see both similarity and difference. The difference might even be interpreted as a development. In its pre-individual 'adhesion to Being', flesh functions in the place of a Schellingian symbol but radicalises it. The radicalisation has to do precisely with the move from *khora* (and Schelling's dependence on the physics of the Idea in Plato's *Timaeus*) to the chiastic structures of the flesh as a 'middle' and a web of relations, as a milieu and a copula.

If there is a critique of the German philosopher in Merleau-Ponty, it is that Schelling theorises nature 'from on high' (a 'high altitude thinking'). These concepts, chiasm, flesh, institution, should be seen as an attempt to reconfigure what Schelling means by symbol within a phenomenology that aims to think from being's centre. In other words, if 'institution is nearly the opposite of constitution' and 'chiasm is nearly the opposite of correlation',[2] these terms are deployed to grasp the emergence of meaning and of structure from a purely natural starting point, a starting point that is natural in Schelling's sense: not the mechanical nature of naturalism, but the singular principle from which both mind and matter emerge, in other words, from the unity in duality of the symbolic which thinks meaning and structure's generation together with a barbarous source.

The goal of the previous chapter was to delineate the nature of the symbolic in order to finally show that Merleau-Ponty's ontology, particularly the notion of pre-sense, pre-objective being, and the like – the way in which everything is 'moving towards sense' – can only be understood if the notion of sense is understood through the symbol rather than through the sign. Symbolics enables an understanding of pre-sense within a 'not-yet/never' dialectic: the symbol at once creates meaning by propelling us towards a future state and retains a barbarian core that will never be reduced to meaning but which is the naturalistic site of the production of meaning. To understand the flesh as 'element of being' is to understand the flesh as symbol. What we have expounded thus far shows just what the flesh of the world has in common with the flesh of the body. The elemental 'flesh of the world' shares interiority with personal subjectivity in the same way as Schelling's nature has interiority and subjectivity. This is why it can be called a flesh. This interiority is replicated or doubled in the production of consciousness. The liquid elemental copula, the mirror phenomenon, is repeated in the microcosmic copula – the human being. The flesh of the world is thus fundamentally symbolic insofar as 'repetition' is the operation that the symbol performs. Merleau-Ponty does not call it a symbol but 'a concrete emblem', although this is just another name for a symbol. That the flesh of the world doubles itself in the flesh of the body is a fundamental symbolic operation:

> What we are calling flesh, this interiorly worked-over mass, has no name in any philosophy. As the formative medium of the object and the subject, it is not the atom of being, the hard in itself that resides in a unique place and moment: one can indeed say of my body that it is not elsewhere, but one cannot say that it is here or now in the sense that objects are; and yet my vision does not soar over them, it is not the being that is wholly knowing, for it has its own inertia, its ties. We must not think the flesh starting from substances, from body and spirit – for then it would be the union of contradictories – but we must think it, as we said, as an element, as the concrete emblem of a general manner of being.[3]

The flesh as element is understood as 'concrete emblem' rather than as materiality pure and simple. Materiality is not a sufficient description of the element because it strips the physical of its essential power, which is symbolic. Symbol is the Naturphilosophical concept which thinks nature's generative power as prior to the passive formability of matter. It is the means by which nature's interiority expresses itself in the exterior world.

When Merleau-Ponty defines the flesh as a 'sensible generality' or 'concrete emblem', it corresponds precisely to Schelling's definition of a symbol: sensible and therefore particular in some way, but not a particular thing. It is an encompassing atmospheric texture. The flesh is neither particularity nor generality, but both before they can separate. It is a physical idea that does not point beyond itself towards a form of which the particular is but an instance. Nor is it a schema in which particulars fit. The flesh institutes itself. It does not receive its form from elsewhere. It is not passive matter combined with active form. The passivity that the flesh possesses does not point to an active principle somewhere else. It precedes the active-passive distinction. Unlike Aristotelian hylomorphism, the flesh remains in the field of becoming and not in the field of pure presence because its elemental power is never exhausted in the form. The Merleau-Pontian flesh is most marked by chiastic structures – its opening out onto another. Does this therefore contradict Schelling's definition of the tautegorical symbol? To the contrary, I would contend that we must understand chiasm precisely as a development of tautegory and not what opposes it, a development that is essentially already present to the degree that Schellingian symbolic dynamism is linked to primordial negation. Above all, the commonality of the two concepts can be seen in their common goal. Both chiasm and symbol aim to overcome the idealist understanding of world as correlate of mind. At the same time, both chiasm and symbol resist the so-called realist rejection of correlationism.

Merleau-Ponty considered chiasm to be his contribution to the problem of the same and the other: 'that the same be the other than the other, and identity difference of difference'.[4] This definition discloses at once its relation to the Schellingian symbol and its subtle but significant difference from it. Like the Schellingian symbol which repeats itself in the mind rather than makes a mental representation of the world, so the chiasm is primordial and 'does not realize a surpassing, a dialectic in the Hegelian sense'. Instead, Merleau-Ponty says that it is 'realized on the spot, by encroachment, thickness, *spatiality* –'.[5] To fully understand the world neither as the hard in itself (realism) nor as correlate of consciousness (idealism), we have to examine the way chiasm is linked to both vision and time – vision as the core of his ontology of perceptual exchange; time in his notion of a past that was never present, an immemorial time that was before any human consciousness could constitute the visible. It is here that the notion of chiasm becomes central and that we can grasp its continuity and difference with the Schellingian conception of symbol.

1. Sharing the visible world: Vision as paradigm of chiasm

Merleau-Ponty rejected an idea of a nature radically separated from our consciousness of it: 'It is quite clear that Nature in itself is not given to us', he writes. 'There is only the human experience of Nature of which nearly all the elements are symbols that it would be absurd to transcribe into "natural" realities and which, as one says, don't have physical signification.'[6] The intrinsically symbolic reception of what we call nature shows that the very concept of nature is 'not only an artifact of a disinterested scientific consciousness, but is a myth where historical subjectivities project and hide their conflicts at each moment'.[7] This proposition does not seek to uphold a Kantian 'thing in itself' view of the inaccessibility of nature. The hard core does not sit behind a priori knowledge. Its non-correlative aspect is instead expressed through nature's temporality and its visibility. These aspects remain deeply tied to its symbolic expression and thus to culture. Nature as symbol links it to history and sensible emergence, tearing it away from the idea of nature as pure presence. It therefore reconfigures what is non-correlative in nature.

The concept of chiasm in Merleau-Ponty has both rhetorical and anatomical inspiration.[8] His first use of the term chiasm is inspired by Paul Valéry, whom he quotes in 'Man and Adversity' (1951). Valéry's deployment of the term is also ambiguous, seeming to be inspired by both the terms chiasmus and chiasma. The chiasmus is an X-shaped rhetorical structure where the first phrase mirrors the last and the middle two are parallel, i.e. a CDDC structure. Rodolphe Gasché suggests that the chiasm was so important not only to ancient poetry (the Hebrew psalms use it regularly), but also to ancient philosophy because it is not *only rhetorical* but

> reveals itself as an original form of thought, of *dianoia*. As a form of thought, as *the* form of thought, chiasm is what allows oppositions to be bound into a unity in the first place. It is a form that makes it possible to determine differences with respect to an underlying unity.[9]

Chiasm is what enables Heraclitus to think the primordial unity of opposites. It is what makes analogy primary in Aristotle and Plato.[10]

Vision is particularly exemplary of the way the anatomical *chiasma* works. The chiasma of the optical nerves is their point of crossing from the left eye to the right brain and the right eye to the left brain. While one normally tends to think of the world we see as a synthesis of two monocular visions, Merleau-Ponty suggests this is the wrong way to look at it. 'The binocular perception is not made up of two monocular visions surmounted; it is of another order. The monocular images are not in the same sense that the thing perceived with both eyes *is*. They are phantoms and it is the real.'[11] Merleau-Ponty argues that monocular visions cannot be understood to be synthesised in the singular vision precisely because they remain distinct. They 'encroach' upon one another but do not fully unite. The crossed gaze, where the boundary between the one and the other is blurred without losing their distinction, is the 'real' perception.

Merleau-Ponty alludes to this chiasm in one of his working notes on the relation of my view of the world to the view of another: '[L]ike the chiasm of the eyes, this one is also what makes us belong to the same world – a world which is not projective but forms its unity across incompossibilities such as that of *my* world and the world of the other.'[12] Just as each eye functions to see the one world, so my vision and the vision of another are joined in the vision of the single world such that the real world is neither my perspective nor the others perspective on her own, nor the synthesis of our two gazes, but the single world from which both our visions emerge and separate. For Merleau-Ponty this helps to overcome a 'me-other rivalry' since it is founded on a co-functioning where 'we function as one unique body'.[13] The sole perceived world is not synthesised after the fact into a common world. The singular world that I share with the other comes before our division into separated entities.

2. Plunging perception into the elemental past: Time as paradigm of chiasm

For Merleau-Ponty, all the difference between constitution and institution, between correlation and chiasm, lies in the shift from a phenomenological world which is understood to be a world constituted by knowledge (such that the world of knowledge is *the* world *tout court*) to a phenomenological world understood as perceptual exchange, 'exchange between a world ready to be perceived and a perception that relies upon it'.[14] Thus Merleau-Ponty says that 'Constitution is nearly the opposite of institution: the instituted makes sense without me, the constituted makes sense only for me and for the me of this instant.'[15] And Ted Toadvine adds, 'correlation is nearly the opposite of chiasm'.[16] Perceiving crosses with the world that precedes it so that the demarcation of the two becomes vague. Merleau-Ponty links the ideas of institution and chiasm closely with his concept of time. In his lecture course *La Passivité* he writes that 'time is the very model of institution'.[17] And in his working notes to *The Visible and the Invisible*: 'time is not an absolute series of events, a tempo – not even the tempo of consciousness – it is an institution, a system of equivalences'.[18] In another note entitled 'Time and Chiasm' (November 1960), he writes:

> The *Stiftung* of a point of time can be transmitted to the others without 'continuity' without 'conservation,' without fictitious 'support' in the psyche the moment that one understands time as chiasm
>
> Then past and present are *Ineinander*, each enveloping-enveloped – and that itself is the flesh[19]

The paradigm of time as institution and chiasm helps us to understand Merleau-Ponty's fundamental question regarding the past as something really present to perception.

In the 'Temporality' chapter of *Phenomenology of Perception*, Merleau-Ponty had argued against the idea of a world 'prior to man'.[20] There his argument takes a fairly traditional phenomenological form, arguing that it makes no sense to speak of a 'world without an Existence that bears its structure'.[21] While he modifies his position as he begins to think from a naturalistic starting point (rather than from the phenomenological concept of 'world'), he never gives up the phenomenological position, maintaining again in 1951 that it would be absurd to think that the sun existed before men existed.[22] And yet also in the *Phenomenology* he already speaks of an 'absolute past of Nature', a past which was never present. Ted Toadvine describes it as 'an asubjective time, a time without a world, at the heart of lived time'.[23] The 'memory of the world' is the memory of 'an impossible past' that 'anticipates an impossible future'.[24] Merleau-Ponty remains committed to perception as a starting point. It is impossible to imagine a sun that were not, at least, in theory, visible. His late turn to nature and the barbarian principle is not a turn away from this commitment to perception as origin of the world. Rather what changes is the way in which the relation of nature and perception is constructed. In short, he moves away from the traditional phenomenological and idealist relations of correlation and constitution to *empiètement*, chiasm and institution. Surpassing the thought of nature as a correlate of consciousness, this new way of understanding the relation to perception enables Merleau-Ponty to reintroduce a concept of nature that precedes the concept of world. This concept will bring nature into the very heart of phenomenology. It is precisely the historical aspect – that the symbols through which nature is given to us are 'not without relations to those that make the fabric of our history'[25] – that demonstrates that the symbolic as such (and thus nature as such) exceeds a correlationist view without abolishing the intrinsically sensible interior dimension of nature.

We have suggested that his reading of nature as the abyss of the past critiques a correlationism which finds natural objects to be mere correlates of mind. And yet because their non-correlative property is exemplified by *pastness*, in the two senses of passivity and of antiquity, natural objects do not escape the logic of sensibility altogether. Ted Toadvine, following Merleau-Ponty, notes a serious problem with a purely scientific analysis of geological time (the deep past of the earth before humans even existed): science simply cannot think this time as past. Science can only propose a perpetual present and the past as an extension of the present extended along a coordinate system that spatialises time in both directions.

The immemorial pastness of the earth is related to the visible because its pastness can only be grasped in perceptual terms. It is a visibility from which we see but which we do not constitute or even experience. The chiasm of time cannot be separated from the chiasm of the visible. 'If there is emergence', Merleau-Ponty writes in his 1954–5 course, *La passivité*, 'this means that man will never be able to think a Nature without man, and ultimately that the pure in-itself is a myth. Every cosmogony is thought in perceptual terms.'[26] We know from the touching-touched analysis that the sentient must be of the sensible, but it is also more than that. The repetition of the sensible intrinsic to the sentient includes the emergence of an irreducible surplus that is not even 'caused' by the sensible, that is not 'like' the sensible but is radically cut off from it, that is torn from it and is 'of another order'.[27] Since all touching must be touchable, there is a kinship between the touching and the touched. Yet it is a kinship that produces a certain alienation, an at-homeness that leads to the feeling of not-being-at-home: the uncanniness of the immemorial past.

It is thus that Toadvine poses Merleau-Ponty's notions of chiasm and institution as the best means of comprehending the past of nature. It is the concept most adequate to surpassing the understanding of nature as a perpetual present, the singular now. Institution and chiasm, Toadvine contends, are the only means of thinking the deep, geological past as really past – neither correlate of mind nor mere scientific objective data point.[28] If correlation risks turning all temporality into a perpetual present, it is chiasm that allows us to think the pastness of the past, something a naïve realism could never do. To understand the chiastic structure of time we might refer to the example of a fossil or a stone arrowhead found in a creek bed.[29] These symbols of a past that was never present to us send our minds reeling, creating a vertiginous experience of the past that quivers with intimations of our pre-history – a pre-history which is 'ours' only so far as we derive from it. Our bodies go back further than these artefacts even into the past of no one. We carry this anonymous past, an elemental past, in the materiality of our bodies – bodies that are constituted out of mineral and water. Just as we do not and cannot experience the deep past, we do not even experience the minerals that constitute our flesh and bones, or the thickened waters that course through our veins and saturate our cells. Most basic to our life, they are nevertheless not present to experience. In this way, they are only vaguely present as a presence, the opaque presence of a past which we do not and cannot experience. Even if, in a certain sense, there is a sun before humans walked the earth under it, Merleau-Ponty argues that we cannot imagine a sun that is not visible just as we cannot imagine an earth that isn't tangible. Our imaginations stretch towards interstellar silences, but we cannot imagine a world that is entirely inarticulable and soundless, a world in which no voice carries, no wind whistles through a narrow canyon or roars over bare peaks. Even the word of our own mouth sometimes seems to bring to the surface something ancient, the voice of the waves, and of the forest. Institution as opposed to constitution is precisely this asymmetrical overlapping into the past with a trajectory towards the future. What makes the idea of a sun before humans 'mentally disturbing, unbalancing' (Bataille) is 'not the violation of logic' but 'the dissolution of subjectivity into the worldlessness of the elemental'.[30]

Ultimately Merleau-Ponty challenges any realism based on scientific objectivity because even the objectivity of science is grounded in our life on the transcendental earth and under the transcendental sun.[31] As Toadvine describes this experience of a past that is the past of no one:

> [W]hat characterizes the experience of the deep past is precisely its unsettling, vertiginous character, the loss of all common markers and measures. It is our ability to open onto a past that was never our own possibility, never our own memory – an impossible and immemorial past – that makes any scientific investigation or mathematical representation of such a past possible.[32]

The deep past is a perceptual past, not an objective past. The depth of the past places us in an uneasy relationship to nature – neither belonging to it, nor separate from it. We look into a past that does not belong to us. Yet in its fluidity, minerality, and even its sensibility, our bodies bear traces of this elemental past that is not ours. For Toadvine, it is this 'transcendental contradiction'[33] – a past that only gains its true sense in relation to experience and yet is not an experienced past – that makes phenomenology, especially a Merleau-Pontian phenomenology, the only way to truly understand the past of nature. Only the chiasm can comprehend materiality as 'our liability to the forgotten past of the elements themselves'.[34] Only the structures of institution and chiasm can make sense of geology as past, as *our* past, as the past of life that was never present for any living being, the deep past of the earth itself. If the earth existed before humans in a certain sense, it existed as something tangible, visible, sensible. Even an absolute past, a past that has never been present for anyone, still exists in relation to our senses for it is from the sensible earth that our sensation arises. Our life stretches back into a past that has never been present because sensibility stretches all the way to the very beginning. What we mark as the beginning is nothing at all if it is not something sensible. It is nothing at all if it is not the primordial explosion of being into visibility.

Time is not something that merely passes, but which gathers and generates the depth of space that we call place, but place also precedes time in order that time might gather there: 'there is from me to the past a thickness that isn't made from a series of perspectives nor of the consciousness of their relation, which is obstacle and liaison'.[35] The thickness of time is only guaranteed if time is not the product of a consciousness which feels time passing (time according to the principle of immanence (see Chapter 3, section 2), which disregards this thickness).[36] Time passes on its own and therefore is felt not only by us but also by the world of nature. We are one of the products of time feeling itself passing – a product of this friction like an eddy on a river's edge. Time is the very thickness of nature. But this thickness then is instituted. In place of the alternation between subject and object, institution allows us to share an 'intersubjective or symbolic field, [that of] cultural objects, which is our milieu, our hinge, our joint' in which we relate to one another and share the same world.[37] What chiasm helps preserve is the thickness of time and the 'generative difference of the past'[38] expressed in the 'ever newness' of 'the first day'.

3. From collision to sensation: Symbol as chiastic relation

In his reading of Schelling in the *Nature* course, Merleau-Ponty leaves some hints that suggest he would connect the notion of chiasm to a Schellingian understanding of symbol. This reading is speculative insofar as Merleau-Ponty never actually addresses Schelling's understanding of symbol, nor does he use the term chiasm here. But the reasons I think this reading is still legitimate will become clear as the argument develops. Certainly there are other passages, as I have begun to demonstrate, that ground this connection in more than speculation. We examine this particular passage, however, because it helps justify my thesis that symbol is not merely a linguistic category but is something that designates how reality functions: it designates a cosmogonic operation. As another word for *physis*, it is ontologically basic.

In the passages on Schelling, Merleau-Ponty deploys the term symbol three times, though of these three times, not one is in direct reference to Schelling.[39] The only time we get anything positive and useful out of the term is in reference to Leibniz. Leibniz describes how, in every movement, there is a desire of the moving for what it moves towards. What moves is as much drawn into the empty space before it (pulled towards futurity) as it is propelled or pushed by its past. A circular trajectory, for Leibniz, expresses a kind of memory. What the thing desires – its future – it returns to again and again. Merleau-Ponty remarks that Leibniz's definition of matter as *mens momentanea*, 'fleeting' or 'momentary' mind, could be easily dismissed as 'a contradiction in terms'.[40] Mind is not momentary but is precisely what remembers, what holds in memory, and therefore what endures. That 'momentary mind' is a contradictory definition of matter means, however, that Leibniz 'sees symbols there' [in matter], that is, Merleau-Ponty clarifies, 'a sense that adheres to the thing itself, something that makes sense [*renvoie à son sens*]'. Now this definition of symbol – 'a sense that adheres to the thing itself' resonates with Schelling's understanding.

The English idiom of 'making sense' should be taken in its non-idiomatic literal meaning to translate the play of this French idiom. 'Making sense' is 'having a sense' but literally in this case sense is 'made' in the very act of movement. For Leibniz, what we think of as the most purely physical and without sense – a body careening through space – is the site where sense is in the process of being created. This is precisely because movement becomes memory, if only for a moment. Merleau-Ponty is playing with the literal meaning of the French: *renvoie à son sens* – that is: being sent back to its sense. While the singular movement may not be meaningful in itself, it becomes meaningful as soon as it repeats itself, for it then expresses an order and a making of order. The first time it is 'sent back' produces a paradox, for it is only in the repetition and not in the first time, that there is a sense. To be sent 'back' to its sense is the first formation of sense. The first sense is also then a 'return' to sense. Repetition is the beginning of sense formation:

> What indwells Nature is not spirit but this beginning of sense starting to arrange itself but not separated yet from the matter. It is for the monad that matter is *mens*. The subject must intervene to pull out the sense, but this drawing out of sense is not constituting.[41]

So while the meaning is formed within the physical movement itself, the ego makes a meaning explicit by 'liberating' the meaning that is 'captive in the natural thing'.[42] We must emphasise again that the ego here is not all consciousness and light, heroically confronting the darkness of matter. The ego is instead an *I* that is 'primordial and unconscious'.[43] Matter as *mens momentanea* is symbol not only because the sense adheres to the thing, but also because it is emergent. Matter understood as momentary mind is a symbol insofar as it continuously and actually produces mind. Only the symbolic is productive in this way, albeit here the production is instantaneous and instantaneously vanishes. But how exactly does this work for Leibniz? To see this, we need to go beyond Merleau-Ponty's text and look at Leibniz for himself.

The text to which Merleau-Ponty refers is a brief work, the 'Theory of Abstract Motion'.[44] Leibniz views motion as a certain impulsion forward that he calls conatus (after Spinoza). The motion or conatus of any single body is produced neither on its own, nor entirely from outside, but in relation to the movement of other bodies. A body at rest must come into contact with a conatus in motion in order to begin to move. The relation of one conatus to the other is *mens momentanea*. Action and reaction are always included in a pair and constitute all physical motion. But action and reaction also constitute sensation. The feeling of pain, Leibniz tells us, is directly related to some physical entity striking or piercing the flesh. The difference between sensation and the relation of two physical bodies striking each other is that the physical bodies do not retain the relation after impact.[45] At the point of impact, however, the correlation of sensation and physical collision are identical. In physical collision, the two conatuses are joined only for an instant, but for that instant the physical is identical to what constitutes 'mind', i.e. sensation. Movement is that in which the physical is identical to the sensitive, hence Leibniz's definition of the physical as momentary mind.

The difference between sentient and non-sentient being then is this: in sentience the momentary union of two conatuses is retained through memory. Only memory is able to retain the coincidence of two conatuses over time. In this account, sensation is attributable to matter itself because sensation is the union of two conatuses, even if sensation is always immediately lost. We might see that the immediate loss of sensation, in Leibniz's understanding of physical action and reaction is necessarily contested in Merleau-Ponty's late conception of the 'memory of the world'.[46] Yet Merleau-Ponty can still deploy Leibniz's insight: that the continuity between mind and physics is a continuity of sensation. In Leibniz's account, sensation is retained over time only in sentient beings. Perception is the retention of sensation over time, manifested in the hesitation intrinsic to thinking itself. The perceiver's retention of sensation *over time* in turn allows the perceiver to perceive *time itself* in the thing perceived. This perception of time is the perception of the depth of things: that things are deep with antiquity and portentous with futurity. In other words, the perception of time spatialises time as depth rather than spatialising it as a line of succession. For Leibniz, every body with force is minimal sensation since conatus is the beginning of motion. While the beginning is not extended, it is also not zero. It is instead a minimum. This minimum is the edge between every pair of entities, where two conatuses are in momentary union. But the edge becomes a depth when the spatial union is continued over time. Time reconfigures space, such that an edge becomes a deep edge, an intensive milieu. The beginning is contained in every limit. It is the contact between any two conatuses. Temporality makes the beginning coincident with the unlimited abyss: the deep edge.

There are three aspects by which we could say that momentary mind exemplifies the symbol. First, it is a productive union of two concrete entities. The clash of two conatuses creates mind, if only fleetingly. Second, it is at once at the limit and infinitely beyond the limit. It is an instance of the infinite in the finite. Leibniz speaks of the relation of the conatus as beginning of motion to motion itself as a ratio: its ratio is one to infinity like the ratio of a point to space. In contrast the ratio of rest to motion is 0 to 1. In other words, conatus is intrinsically a manifestation of the coincidence of the infinite and the finite. This ratio is manifest at the point of impact of two conatuses. This 'beginning of sense', Merleau-Ponty says, is what indwells nature. All is not mind as such, and yet the physical is already related to mind as a premonition of mind – momentary mind. It becomes the work of mind to 'draw out' sense. Yet the mind that draws out sense is not somewhere other than the physical world. It repeats the primordial link which was first of all in the physics of collision. Mind is implicated in this beginning, the fleeting mind, bringing a finitude to the infinity of motion. 'Drawing out' is, to begin with, nothing more than to retain the instantaneous, to remember it, to return to it. It is to retain finitude over time. The instantaneous is grounded in the abyssal depth of place. To retain the instantaneous is not to extend it in space. Mind has no spatial extension, for it arises at the site of a minimum, thereby exceeding all quantity. Even the circular motion that remembers by repeating does not do so in space but in time: the return to the same place at a different time. Mind is an extension of the instantaneous in time. It does not extend space. It makes space deep with temporality. The beginning is never overcome but remains as an intensive milieu from which we draw out meanings. This then is the third aspect of symbol in the *mens momentanea*: the sense adherent to the thing itself is drawn out so that a second union of concrete entities can emerge through mind's return to its origin where it feeds on the symbolism intrinsic to matter. First the physical creates mind through a symbolic operation and then mind creates further symbols through the latency that remains in matter. As repetition of the primordial link, mind is no longer the union of sensation, but the union of the sense drawn out with the one who draws it, in short, mind takes on an active rather than passive role. This union is the edge between two laterally related entities that gives an upward thrust both for nature and mind because it is the site where the physical becomes the psychic.

While Schelling does refer to Leibniz several times in *The Ages of the World*, a more likely source of Merleau-Ponty's Leibnizian interjection is the passage in Schelling's *On the World Soul* to which Merleau-Ponty alludes two paragraphs earlier, where he refers to Schelling's use of the image of light and air as 'images of God'.[47] If we refer back to the passage in *On the World Soul*, we see that it too speaks of movement. Schelling tells us that the movement of a thing is 'nothing other than the expression of the link that attaches it to other things'.⁴⁸ Although Merleau-Ponty does not mention this, we can see how Schelling's account of movement would have invoked Leibniz's account of movement. While Fichte and Kant use light as an image to speak of consciousness (its access to eternal truth, and its freedom from matter), for Schelling the light expresses itself as image of eternity only in its link to the gravity (heaviness) of the material. Gravity is the representation of time, change and movement. It is the bond between airy luminosity and the heaviness of the solid that 'results in the beautiful appearance of life, it is because of their union that the thing becomes real in the true sense of the word'.⁴⁹ While (1) the darkness of the earth springs towards the light like a plant emerging from earth, and (2) the light reveals the whole in every particular because of its eternal essence which universally penetrates all things, it is (3) water, Schelling tells us, that represents the link between the eternal light (universality) and the perpetual movement of the earth (particular things). In its divisibility into droplets, water mirrors the heavy finitude of the earth, its capacities of fragmentation and movement. In the fact that each of its parts is equivalent to the whole, it retains the eternal luminosity of the air. Water is the copula in its purity 'that from which all productivity departs and to which it returns'.⁵⁰

In describing their mutual relations, Schelling associates light, earth and water each with a different form of life. He connects the heaviness of the earth with the branchings of vegetation stretching towards the light. He links animal mobility with the light turning towards earth. But the absolute copula of the two, elementally represented in water, is now the domain of the human being because 'the bond bears completely on what is bonded and returns to its eternal liberty'.⁵¹ As in Leibniz, the union that binds movement with eternal duration is expressed in memory. The mind is what unites movement and eternity, but it does so through a certain physics deeply tied to the power of the symbolic, just as water unites the principle of earth (movement and individuation) with the principle of air (eternity and universality).

The *mens momentanea* is chiasmic because (1) the two conatuses never coincide but retain a minimum difference and (2) the collision itself is primary, where the separation is secondary. Finally, (3) it generates another order – the passage from physical bodies to mind. The gap or divergence (*écart*) of chiasm is not merely non-coincidence as in the example of the touching-touched. Non-coincidence is derived from the fact that there is always a space of transition between the hand as touching and the hand as touched. Beyond non-coincidence and the equality of reciprocal exchange, the *écart* is a rising up into 'another order' of being – from sensible being, to sensing being, from colliding particles to memory. It is of utmost importance to notice that in the very reciprocity of chiasmic exchange, a hierarchy emerges. It is not a hierarchy that descends from above, but one that emerges from the primordial ground. This primordial emergence is analogous to Schelling's tautegorical interpretation of mythology: the emerging primordial divinities. Similarly, the *écart* creates a cut in being so that what emerges from below does not causally depend on the below. Even though visibility, tangibility or sensibility comes first, touching is not caused by the body. It is 'as if [the body] were built around the perception that dawns through it'.[52] Suddenly, the below (the body) depends upon the above (perception) which it created. The sensible rises up into sensitivity, and sensitivity circles back to pull the sensible up to it. While sentience must be *of* the sensible, it is also more. Its repetition of the sensible includes the emergence of an irreducible surplus that is not *like* the visible world but is absolutely cut off from it. It is a kinship that produces a certain alienation, an at-home-ness that produces the feeling of not being at home. This generation of another order expresses both the intrinsic potency of chiasm and that of the symbol. But the chiasm in this way challenges the Schellingian definition of symbol as tautegory, not because the symbol functions like a sign, pointing to another but because the symbol is itself the relationship. It is the overlapping, ambiguous domain that precedes any separation: the binocular that is not a synthesis of the monocular.

4. The radically incomplete: Symbol and relationship

Schelling's polemical opposition between the symbol and the sign might be considered a rhetorical exaggeration. The sign is no doubt *primarily* transparent and deflective, self-effacing and pointing towards another. The symbol is *primarily* opaque and concrete. One must first go into the symbol in order to go beyond it. Nevertheless, the symbol is not totally alone in its self-reference. It has certain characteristics of a sign. Eugene Fink recognised that although the symbol cannot have the same 'abstract function of the sign' (which signifies without partaking in the signified), the symbol nevertheless 'was initially precisely a sign'. Fink uses the example of a coin broken in two, each piece carried by two friends who are separated by a great distance, as an example of what a 'symbolon' originally was to the Greeks:

> If one sent a visitor to his friend, he gave him the one half to take along as infallible proof: the places where the coin had been split into two had to be matched to each other, the one half had to be completed by the other. Now, both features were significant for the symbol: the 'fragmentation' and the 'completion.' *Symbolon* comes from *symballein*, 'coinciding,' and signifies a coinciding of the fragment with what completes it.[53]

What Fink is describing is more or less the original meaning of *symbolon* in Greek: a sign that guaranteed the veracity of a contract between two parties.[54] The meaning had no doubt changed considerably by the time the Romantics began using it to champion ambiguous and plural meanings in opposition to allegorical determinative clarity. The original symbol, after all, was meant to eliminate all ambiguity through the matching of the two fragments.

Fink himself seems to try to reconcile the original relational meaning of the symbol with Romantic productive indeterminacy guaranteed through tautegory. Following Plato's deployment of the relational aspect of symbol to denote the incompletion of the sexual being (through the voice of Aristophanes in the *Symposium*), Fink reads the fragmentary nature of the symbol as latent with erotic yearning. The man and the woman, sundered into two by the gods, are '*symbola*', precisely insofar as they are 'halves of life arranged for completion, which first constitute the whole human being only when they fit together properly'.[55] On the one hand, these fragments fit together, forming a whole. On the other hand, even the whole remains a fragment. 'In a deeper sense, all finite things in general are fragments – whether they are determined to be maimed or intact, whole or in privation … Being, to the extent that it belongs to finite things, is a variously fractured and restricted Being; it is fragmentary, splintered, rent apart and cleaved asunder.'[56] The fragmentary nature of the sexes repeats the fragmentary nature of finitude as such. As fragment, finitude should not be understood as a mere sign (the incomplete pointing to the complete). The completion 'does not add something that until now had been missing', nor does it abolish the fragmentary nature of the finite.

> Here it is not a matter of making some rubble whole again in the sense of the wholeness of inner-worldly things, but rather precisely of conceiving inner-worldly wholeness as such as a fragment. Things then become *symbola* – not as signs for something different; they are *symbola* as themselves, inasmuch as they exhibit their finitude as intraworldliness.[57]

In this way, what Fink outlines as the symbol's fragmentary 'significative' nature circles back to the self-reference of Schellingian tautegory. The symbol in its signification marks a relationship not a representation of something other. Even as it marks a relationship, it continues to refer to itself. Its other does not determine it externally, artificially, mechanically. The fragmentary nature of the symbol implies that, in its very being, it is propelled towards its other. We will see momentarily that Schelling's view is more 'tortured'. There is an intrinsically *diseased* relation between nature and life that makes the symbolic itself a sickness and produces sickness.

The things that a symbol puts into relation are irreducibly concrete. It is the relation of these two entities that generates meaning. The concrete quality of each cannot be dissolved without dissolving the relationship and thus the symbolic's capacity to produce meaning. In creating a pact or alliance, the symbol 'ruptures a semantic field to the point of installing a new grammar and syntax'.[58] We could take the discovery of gold in the American West as an example of the instituting function of the symbol. Gold bears within itself a symbolic resonance, the shining forth of being itself. It symbolises the possibility of wealth. In its original, non-technical meaning, the Greek word for being, *ousia*, was a word that meant property. *Ousia* was a substance that could be owned, especially metallic and other fire-resistant substances. In alchemy, *ousia* referred to 'a material thing by which a connection is established between the person to be acted upon and the supernatural agent'.[59] *Ousia* was the symbol par excellence. While gold has never stood in for being as such, it nevertheless carries with it most of these original meanings of *ousia*. Gold not only symbolises the possibility of wealth. It *is* wealth. Its glimmer is the radiation of prosperity. To find gold is to become wealthy. But the symbolism is not in the gold by itself. There must be both the gold and people who want gold for gold to function as a symbol. Only then does gold mediate the blessings of the gods.

For centuries a certain calm reigned over the sleepy riverbeds in the backwoods of the American wilderness. A family of deer would come to the river every morning to drink. Perhaps a Sioux Indian, having learned about the habits of this cervine family unit, lurks nearby. The whizz of his arrow, the cry of the unfortunate buck, the crackle of branches as the other deer scatter into the woods. Then the return of calm. This idyllic scene vanished forever when gold was discovered scattered through the silt of these winding rivers. Something new began. Tens of thousands of fortune-seekers rushed to buy land and to sift the river. A new community formed. Laws were founded, even as justice was carried out by whoever had the quickest draw. Doctors, prostitutes, businessmen and all the unruly crowd that we call society came to what was just moments ago a quiet backwater. The community of the Sioux was entirely disrupted though not abolished: it persisted in a new relation to the gold-seeking community.

We might call this change from one situation to another an 'event'. Yet because it happened from the ground up, that is, from the river bottoms to the trees (which soon became a hastily constructed wood-planked town), the event must be understood as inaugurating something new by means of the power of the symbolic and not by the top-down reception of the unforeseen. It therefore does not fit the definition of an event set out by Romano and Marion.[60] Sense, community, language form precisely around the non-sense of the gold. And we might call gold both non-sense and nonsense. It is just a shiny rock after all. But to say it is *just* a rock entirely misses the point, for why is it that the non-sense of gold can institute sense? It is indeed precisely its barbarian nature, its concreteness and its meaningless shimmer, that makes it operative as a producer of meaning. Unlike a sign whose aim is complete transparency, complete self-effacement before the signified, the symbol's opacity is what ruptures the semantic field and enraptures us with its shine, its mesmerising effect going so far as to give us a new semantic field altogether, so that a world without shine seems bereft of life.

This example demonstrates that the barbarian principle cannot be understood as a pre-sense that becomes sense. It is a hard core around which sense is instituted and which itself never becomes intelligible. Why do men kill each other for gold? This is an unanswerable question. From one angle, gold will always be just a shiny rock. The opaque meaninglessness of the symbolic material produces as much murderous nonsense as sense, but the symbol itself is never converted into the nonsense that it produces. The symbol is inexhaustible not because it points to a spiritual mystery, something incorporeal and insensible that is always beyond what we can grasp intellectually. It is inexhaustible because of its materiality, which is at once an object of desire and evades assimilation into the one that desires it.[61] If the symbol can maintain the ambiguity of Romantic tautegory and the relational aspect of the original concept of *symbolon*, would not chiasm, the notion of an ambiguous original togetherness, not have something to say about the nature of the symbol? Would not chiasm be the symbolic par excellence? What leads us towards symbol as chiasm is the combination of the fragment with productive negation, for it is only this conjunction that makes the symbol radically productive. If the sign can be indeterminate insofar as it does not adequate to its object, the productive indeterminacy of the tautegorical is produced from a chiasmic togetherness of two concrete realities. It is the indeterminacy of that which is 'cleaved asunder' rather than that which begins as separate and seeks a union. It is thus at once the pure self-reference (tautegory) of what is originally together and a violent drive towards its other.

5. Contaminated by nature: Symbolic repetition and viral replication[62]

From Schelling's earliest Naturphilosophie writings, symbol is connected to organism and self-organisation:

> If the human spirit is of an *organic* nature, nothing will enter into it *mechanically from the outside*; whatever is in it, [the spirit] has configured to itself *from the inside out* in accordance with an inner principle ... Whatever is absolutely purposive *is in itself complete and perfected*. It contains within itself the origin and the final purpose of its existence ... In purposiveness, form and matter, concept and intuition interpenetrate. Precisely this is the character of the spirit wherein the Ideal and the Real are absolutely united. Hence there is something *symbolic* in every organism, and every plant is, so to speak, *an arabesque delineation of the soul*.[63]

Every organism is a symbol, having its development from within itself. Jankélévitch writes that for Schelling 'the world grows old like an organism' which itself implies 'an irrational element that is never entirely surpassed'.[64] Growing old is one aspect by which the irrationality intrinsic to the organism is expressed. While Schelling championed a philosophy of becoming, it is the belief in the world as something inherently organic that leads Schelling to argue against a constructivist account of evolution. He argued against Rousseau's belief that the earliest humans were 'savages' – that there was a type of *tabula rasa* from which civilisation emerged by collecting pieces at random. Instead, he argued that the interior principle of evolution (what we would now call endogenesis) evolves 'from the gigantic to the integrated'.[65]

If the symbol institutes 'a new grammar and a new syntax', it does so by 'rupturing' a preceding semantic field. This is the primordial negation, the castration of the father, on which the becoming of *physis* is founded. Up to this point we have little explored the negative side of this negation: what remains behind. What is it that is ejected into the past? I will make a brief foray into Slavoj Žižek and Jacques Lacan because of certain thematic resonances with Merleau-Ponty. This is justified, on the one hand, by the mutual influence between Merleau-Ponty and Lacan,[66] and, on the other, by certain resonances between Lacan and Schelling that Žižek draws out. The reason Žižek can so often draw simultaneously on both Schelling and Lacan is that what is true of the Lacanian Real can, at least to a certain extent, be said of Schelling's barbarian principle.[67] The Real, as Žižek puts it, 'is a much more complex category than the idea of a fixed trans-historical "hard core" that forever eludes symbolization; it has nothing to do with what Immanuel Kant called the "Thing-in-itself," reality the way it is out there, independently of us, prior to being distorted by our perceptions'.[68] For Lacan the Real is not prior to symbolisation, but after it. It is parasitic on the symbolic. 'What all this amounts to', Žižek writes, 'is that, for Lacan, the Real, at its most radical, has to be totally de-substantialized. It is not an external thing that resists being caught in the symbolic network, but the crack within the symbolic network itself.'[69]

This sense of the Real – that it is not a resistance to conceptualisation but the incapacity of any system to close in upon itself – draws attention, in my eyes, to a potential problem with Schellingian organicism. To draw this problem out, a brief synopsis of Žižek's use of Ridley Scott's *Alien* will be immensely helpful inasmuch as he uses this film to explain the Lacanian *objet petit a*. This analysis is not merely tangential. Lacan's concept of *objet petit a* was influenced by Merleau-Ponty's concept of chiasm.[70] While it certainly isn't correct to read Schelling's barbarian principle as Lacan's *objet petit a*, the comparison nevertheless helps to bring out certain aspects that would otherwise remain hidden concerning its relation to the symbol. Further, it isn't unreasonable to assume that one of the metaphysical sources for the *objet petit a*, as for the barbarian principle, was Böhme's understanding of the fire-ground.[71]

Žižek draws on a quotation from Lacan concerning the lamella and compares Lacan's lamella to the alien which in Ridley Scott's original 1978 film mutates into various forms as the film progresses. The story takes place around the crew of a cargo spaceship who are awoken from their deep-slumber pods because the ship's system has picked up an unknown signal from a passing planet. Descending to the planet to investigate, one of the crew members, acting as lead reconnaissance, climbs down into a warm, womb-like cavern, filled with slime and reptilian eggs. As he reaches out to touch some pulsing organic tissue, something leaps out at him, and the screen goes black. In the next scene, he is lying on a medical examination table back on the ship, his face enveloped by a multi-legged, faceless creature, which has also slid some sort of tentacle down his throat. Later the alien will mutate into a ten-foot-tall monster with a huge phallic head. But it is the 'face-hugger' form that is strikingly resonant with Lacan's text, written ten years before the film was released:

> Whenever the membranes of the egg in which the foetus emerges on its way to becoming a new-born are broken, imagine for a moment that something flies off, and that one can do it with an egg as easily as with a man, namely the hommelette, or the lamella. The lamella is something extra-flat, which moves like the amoeba. It is just a little more complicated. But it goes everywhere. And as it is something – I will tell you shortly why – that is related to what the sexed being loses in sexuality, it is, like the amoeba in relation to sexed beings, immortal – because it survives any division, and scissiparous intervention. And it can turn around.
>
> Well! This is not very reassuring. But suppose it comes and envelopes your face while you are quietly asleep ... I can't see how we would not join battle with a being capable of these properties. But it would not be a very convenient battle. This lamella, this organ, whose characteristic is not to exist, but

> which is nevertheless an organ – I can give you more details as to its zoological place – is the libido.
>
> It is the libido, qua pure life instinct, that is to say, immortal life, irrepressible life, life that has need of no organ, simplified, indestructible life. It is precisely what is subtracted from the living being by virtue of the fact that it is subject to the cycle of sexed reproduction. And it is of this that all the forms of the *objet a* that can be enumerated are the representatives, the equivalents.[72]

As Žižek writes, lamella 'stands for the Real in its most terrifying imaginary dimension, as the primordial abyss which swallows everything, dissolves all identities'.[73]

The relation between the egg image and the unsexed, amoebic replication, is what I want to focus on, particularly in its relation to mythological ideas of the world egg. The world egg is an important image for every philosophical organicism. With any metaphysics in which seminality and self-organisation is intrinsic and original to nature as such, a notion of world egg must be, implicitly or explicitly, attached. It exists in Schelling as in Plato and most Neoplatonic systems and world mythologies. In the *Ages of the World*, Schelling refers to it as 'the primordial seed of visible nature'.[74] But the lamella points to something problematic with the world egg concept. More precisely, it points to the way seminality produces its own problem from within. With the hatching, 'something flies off', as Lacan puts it – a part of the shell or membrane that takes no part in what is born, and which remains alien to that birthed thing, that is to say, it remains alien to the 'world' as such. If nature as organism tends towards death, if the world 'grows old', this is not because it is living, and all living things die. It is because the world-organism is a sexed life. This does not mean that the world is necessarily male or female, but simply that it contains the duality of sex within it. The amoeba is living but does not tend towards death. It is a life without duality. It therefore creates a disturbance in every world organicism. Monistic life, such as an amoeba or a virus, is a nature against nature – a non-differentiating nature. Rather than reflective non-being, it is for sexed life an invasive non-being, a foreign body that disturbs organic emergence.

Both Lacan and Schelling interrogate the relation by which mortality is bound up with sexuality. In the sublime horror of the confrontation with pure life detached from sexual duplicity, Lacan sees a manifestation of vital life flow: the libido. In this regard, he compares the libido to an amoeba. Because the amoeba replicates itself rather than producing a new individual through sexual unification, the amoeba has a kind of immortality. The libido is immortal in the way that an amoeba is immortal. Indifferent to the emergence of forms, it is always the same. In the case of sexual being, the libido preserves itself through a pair of individuals (male-female). It ultimately renews itself in the offspring and discards the individuals for the sake of the perpetuation of the species. Žižek summarises:

> Human sexuality is marked by an irreducible failure, sexual difference is the antagonism of the two sexual positions between which there is no common denominator, enjoyment can be gained only against the background of a fundamental loss. … [T]he myth of lamella presents the fantasmatic entity that gives body to what a living being loses when it enters the (symbolically regulated) regime of sexual difference.[75]

Mortality is built into the very structure of sexed existence because the unsexed essence – monistic nature or vital flow – feasts on the duality for the sake of its own monistic immortality. Unsexed but living beings do not have this same inclination towards death because they do not have the same individuality. As Lacan notes, it is the unsexed being's immortality that evokes the sense of dread in their presence. It is not death that is feared here, but the disruption of the category of life-death. Self-replicating life disturbs the categories that we live by. The self-replicating is the undead. In this respect, self-replicating nature is more like a virus than like a sexed being. The world may grow old, but nature will remain. What this demands first of all, then, is a distinction between what we call world and what we call nature. One universe may split itself off from this one as a reduplication. But what will remain common between the two worlds is nature. The barbaric principle as 'something horrible', may thus be understood as this unsexed life of nature, viral or even fungoid, parasitic on symbolic productivity. In this guise barbarian nature is a sort of contagion that no longer bears the feminine qualities of *khora*. It is neuter, immortal and invasive.

Schelling himself did not precisely have a concept of unsexed, immortal life. He understood this principle in an indirect way when he speaks in his early Naturphilosophie about the monism of nature as a disease in relation to sexual duplicity. For Schelling, sexual maturity is the pinnacle of organic life precisely because nature, at that moment, achieves the unity it was seeking out of the duplicity it had created. 'Nature constantly strives to cancel out [*aufzuheben*] duality and to return into its original identity.'[76] Once the sexes, developing to maturity separately, are joined in sexual union, nature has no more need for the duplicitous. At this point, the individual, the sexed being, begins to die:

> Nature did not intend the separation [of the sexes]. – Nature leads the product in both directions only for the sake of letting it sink back into indifference as soon as it reaches the apex of development.[77]

It is indeed an anomaly rather than the norm, Schelling notes, if the individuals of a species live much beyond the attainment of sexual maturity. Most insects for instance have a long gestation as larvae (sometimes years), but have a very brief mature life (sometimes less than a day) only to mate and die. It is for this reason that, as David Farrell Krell puts it, Schelling sees nature as 'careless of the individual, insofar as the individual is but one half of a sexual pair'.[78] The monism of nature is a contagion that 'consigns the individual, *monos*, to death'.[79] The singular, the *monos*, therefore has something moribund about it. It is intrinsically diseased. Krell describes this as a 'moribund monism'[80] Schelling's notion of life as something that struggles towards individuation against nature's monism makes life itself a kind of disease to nature, and nature a disease to life:

> It is thus totally nonsensical to call disease an unnatural state, for it is precisely just as natural as life. If disease is an unnatural state, then so is life – and admittedly it is unnatural to the extent that life is really a state extorted from Nature, not favored by Nature, but a state enduring against Nature's will, for it is preserved only by means of struggling against Nature. In this sense one can say that life is a perduring sickness, and death only the recuperation from life.[81]

The illness of life is the illness of sensation. To have sensibility is to be alive. But too much sensation is the cause of death. Illness is thus an excess of sensation, but who is to say where life begins to be an excess and thus an illness? Is not sensation itself excessive? Is not life itself a disease? The illness of sensation begins as soon as one is sentient. Krell proposes that in Schelling life itself is a contagion. Nature is contaminated with the contagion of life-death: 'to produce heterogeneity is to allow duplicity to insinuate itself into all avowed identity as an unstoppable contagion'.[82] But might we not pose the reverse: namely, that life is contaminated with nature? Indeed there is a mutual contagion of one by the other: unsexed nature, in its seeking after monistic identity, sees sexuality as a disease it must eradicate, the illness of duplicity and the inverse. For the sexed individual, unsexed nature will always remain a virus seeking to destroy its individuated identity and return it to the origin's monism. But is it articulated here as a virus? Certainly, Schelling did not have a concept of virus. The virus had not been discovered. More importantly, the relation of nature as disease of life and life as a disease of nature seems to be too neatly reflexive. Can we more adequately think of this contagion of nature in a chiastic rather than reflexive way?

In the introduction of a new concept of immortality, we are dealing with a reconceptualisation of *natura naturata* – enduring and unchanging nature – beyond the dynamism of *natura naturans*. This *natura naturata* is not the ordered whole, but something that persists outside of the whole. Lacan's is a concept of immortality based on vital force indifferent to individuated forms. It is the sublime par excellence. Lacan reads amoeba-like immortality as libido and speaks of it as something the sexed being 'loses in sexuality',[83] a driving principle that, while it transcends sexual difference and seeks to dissolve it, is ultimately the guiding principle of sexuality itself. Schelling's is a concept of disease that at once interrupts life and constitutes its possibility. Like Lacan, he speaks of nature's drive towards the obliteration of difference, but he understands this drive as an *infection* within life.[84] The infection, however, does not have supreme rule in the way the libido lords over sexual entities as a pure flow. As contagion, nature is locked in a deadly struggle with the differentiating principle of life. In Schelling, there is a stronger, if implicit, chiasm between the immortal principle of monistic nature and individuating, sexed life. In Lacan, the understanding of the antagonism as that between life flow and individuated forms leaves little room for a possible victory of individuated being against the monstrous libido. While Schelling does not have a notion of nature as virus, a concept of nature as disease provides a way to get beyond the sublime obliteration of the individual in Lacan. If in Schelling life is contaminated with nature, nature is also contaminated with life. The way to overcome the problems with a pure reciprocity is to introduce a contaminant, which would lead towards chiasmic impingement of the one on the other as a certain diseased productivity (or disease at the heart of production) rather than an obliteration of the product into the pure life force.

It is difficult to get beyond the pure sublime destruction of the individual so long as we think this antagonism of nature and life only through the drive towards monism implicit in sexual duplicity. The concept of a virus gives us an understanding of an immortal principle that is radically opposed to sexual differentiation and to individuation more broadly, but which is not merely libido. Viral immortality cannot be understood as an immortality that has been lost (in a fall from amoeba-like, androgynous unity). It is something outside sexuality altogether, something properly foreign and invasive. Consequently, mortal life (sexed, individuated existence) is rethought with respect to a contaminating immortality rather than in reflective opposition to an eternal and inert order. It is a mortality that is opposed to another vitality, a vitality that is radically foreign to it. But isn't this a better description of the image that Lacan already gave us? The immortal principle of nature, if time and the stability of forms is not to be utterly obliterated, must itself be understood as outside the horizon of what we call the world: that which is produced in the hatching of the world egg and that which remains in a continual state of productivity.

In other words, the element – if it is continuous production as 'primal seed of the visible' – also produces a by-product, the foreign body, the thorn in the side of the world.

How then do we understand the relation of the symbol particularly to this disease of life contaminated with nature and nature contaminated with life? If nature is the Real, the barbarian principle that 'flies off', the passage to sexuality is the opening to the symbolic as an originary passage: the hatching of the world egg which leaves behind an irreducible remainder. The perpetual strife between nature's viral replication and sexual difference requires an understanding of the world as symbol and an understanding of disease as the crack in the symbolic order. Viral replication is the condition of the possibility of the symbol's tautegorical status. That the symbol repeats itself tautegorically in each new individual and does not refer elsewhere means that it retains the irreducible contagion of nature – the monistic principle that resists individuation. Being individuates in a primordial antagonism with a nature that drives towards a 'moribund monism'. That it retains the contagion of nature then means that every passage into being is symbolic and tautegorical. The secret to nature's productive power is this very antagonism:

> It indeed sounds paradoxical, but it is no less true, that through the influences which are contrary to life, life is sustained. – Life is nothing other than a productivity held back from the absolute transition into its product. The absolute transition into its product is death. That which interrupts productivity, therefore, sustains life.[85]

Can we integrate the contaminate back into Schelling's concept here in order to avoid a pure reciprocity between sexual individuated life and its sublime obliteration in the 'moribund monism'? For Schelling, that which interrupts nature's productivity is sexual duplicity. But only in sexual duplicity does nature achieve the monism it seeks to produce – the unity of the sexes which destroys their duality in the offspring. Reciprocally, the individuation that sexed being seeks is interrupted by nature's drive to monism, a drive expressed within sexed being's seeking of sexual union. But it is only in this interruption that the individual becomes utterly other than its product, that its product itself is another individuated being. It is through this resistance that self-reference others itself, i.e. that tautegory spawns viral replication. If it can be understood as precisely that – as a resistance and something we resist – then we can at once exceed the tendency towards self-obliteration that is the logical outcome of philosophies of reflection. Because the contagion persists at the innermost heart of the contaminated, the contagion is the originary chiasm: life impinging on nature and nature encroaching on life. Such an encroachment no longer obliterates the product precisely because, as foreign body, it resists it. Symbolic repetition reproduces this resistance, which the pure transparency of the sign cannot reproduce. In other words, symbolic repetition is a form of viral replication.

We might take this analysis one step further if we look at connection between the unsexed life of the lamella and Emmanuel Falque's concept of the spread body (*corps épandu*). Falque develops the spread body as a third term of thinking about the body between the extended, objective body (*corps étendu*) and the flesh or lived body (*la chair, corps vécu*), noting that 'phenomenology does not know how the body is material unless it is made objective'.[86] As exemplar of the spread body, Falque speaks of the medicalised body, the body stretched upon the examination table. For our purposes, I want to note that the medicalised body is a body that is no longer sexed but is not a dead body. Even if medical practice often understands the body as an 'anticipatory corpse',[87] its corpse-likeness partially lies in the fact that it is no longer eroticised. It is in an in-between zone. Like the virus that it fights against, the medicalised body is undead. In *Alien*, the character with the lamella hugging his face is also on an examination table, hospitalised, anonymised and neutered – the alien penetrates his mouth, emasculating him, and planting the seed that will later erupt out of his stomach. The alien itself moves back and forth between feminine, womblike manifestations, and masculine phallic sublime horror. Life's amoeba-like aspects, usually abjected into the past of our experience, burst into the present. This irruption is not the body itself, but a certain clinging to the body that becomes all too present. It is indeed *more present* than the body, for the lived body, as we will see in Chapter 7, section 3, can only be lived as a past.

For Lacan it is the immortal libido for which the sexed being is only the servant. The sexed being is what the libido feeds upon and discards for the sake of its own perpetual replication. Falque writes of the aspect of *having* a body, rather than *being* a body – that the body imposes itself upon us, and that 'my own body penetrates me, even annihilates me, as the fingernail becomes ingrown (*s'incarne*) in my flesh'.[88] This imposition of the spread body is much more of a presence than the lived body, which is immemorially past – that from which we live. Falque's understanding of the body as something invading me is reminiscent of Schelling. The very possession of sensation is to have a disease invading our very life. Intrinsic to the body is not only self-constitution but self-destruction.[89] Aristotle and Schelling both note this paradox, that the very means by which we have contact with and can manipulate the world is the means of our destruction. If we are touched with too much force, we die.[90] It is the very crossing, the disease, the chiasm, that is the most present to us. It is a 'fecund contradiction',⁹¹ a negation that is more present than the positive body. This interruption is in fact sustained by nature's monistic tendency against sexed life. It is thus disease that makes possible life's productive capacity. Life depends upon what destroys it.

The individuation intrinsic to sexed existence needs this resistance to sexuality in order for sexuality to act as force, that is, in order for sexed beings to individuate without being absorbed back into the immortal libido. In the primordial negation, the barbarous is split into originary force, on the one hand, which is creative, and, on the other hand, something that reduplicates itself or mutates and remains a foreign body at the heart of life. These two dimensions at once resist and make possible the very creation of being. The repetition of the symbolic produces individuation, but in each repetition, 'something flies off'. Each individuation also replicates the resistance of the real. In this way, *natura naturata* remains an active force rather than a stable regulating order, even as it struggles against the creative, individuating impulse of *natura naturans*. The tautegorical nature of dynamic symbolism must hold onto these two opposing dimensions. The symbol repeats or replicates rather than assembles or represents. Symbolic repetition understood as viral replication however thus reveals the moribund aspect of the dynamism of *physis* as an originary chiasm which individuates life and ejects immortal nature. The virus lives in this fissure. The very sameness of being, the originary chiasm before difference, the quality that is passed on through change, is a disease within the individuated being, but a disease that cannot but be perpetuated, a parasitic non-being that clings to a being parasitic on it.

With respect to the symbol, the barbarian is both principle and product. It is both pre-objective and meta-objective – resistance and remainder. Schelling's understanding of nature refuses the possibility of the concept as consummation. The very scission of existence – the passage of the beginning – produces an irreducible remainder that cannot be incorporated. Literally: that cannot become the body that I am, nor even the body that I have. It is a body that has me, a radically foreign body that is nevertheless the principle from which and against which I live my life.

Notes

1. V. Jankélévitch, *L'odyssée de la conscience*, 328.
2. Toadvine, 'The Elemental Past', 271.
3. VI, 191/147.
4. VI, 312/264.
5. VI, 312/264.
6. Merleau-Ponty, *La Nature ou le monde du silence*, 44–5.

7. Merleau-Ponty, *La Nature ou le monde du silence*, 45.
8. Saint Aubert, *Le Scénario cartésien. Recherches sur la formation et la cohérence de l'intention philosophique de Merleau-Ponty* (Paris: Vrin, 2005), 165–6.
9. Rodolphe Gasché, 'Reading Chiasms', in *Of Minimal Things: Studies on the Notion of Relation* (Stanford, CA: Stanford University Press, 1999), 273.
10. Ted Toadvine, 'The Chiasm', in *The Routledge Companion to Phenomenology*, ed. Sebastian Luft and Søren Overgaard (London: Routledge, 2012), 337.
11. VI, 22/7.
12. VI, 264/215.
13. VI, 264/215.
14. IP, 172/128.
15. IP, 37/8.
16. Toadvine, 'The Elemental Past', 271.
17. IP, 36/7.
18. VI, 235/184.
19. VI, 315/267–8.
20. PP, 494/502.
21. PP, 494/502.
22. In an anecdote that begins his lecture, 'Les consequences du non-savoir', Georges Bataille recounts a barroom debate in which he, Merleau-Ponty, the British philosopher, A. J. Ayer, and the atomic physicist Georges Ambrosino participated. While Ayer held that 'there was a sun before men existed', the three Frenchmen rejected this claim. Bataille argues that Ayer's seemingly common-sense statement, though 'logically unassailable', is nevertheless an instance of 'non-knowledge' because it is 'an object independent of any subject' and therefore 'perfect non-sense' (in *Oeuvres complètes*, vol. 8 (Paris: Gallimard, 1976)). Translated by Michelle Kendell and Stuart Kendall as 'The Consequence of Nonknowledge', in Georges Bataille, *The Unfinished System of Nonknowledge*, ed. Stuart Kendell (Minneapolis: University of Minnesota Press, 2001), 111. See Toadvine, 'The Elemental Past', 262–4.
23. Toadvine, 'The Elemental Past', 266.
24. VI, 296/243; 163/123.
25. Merleau-Ponty, *La Nature ou le monde du silence*, 45.
26. IP, 172/128.
27. IP, 172/128.
28. Toadvine, 'The Elemental Past', 273ff.
29. Toadvine, 'The Elemental Past', 274–9.
30. Toadvine, 'The Elemental Past', 276.
31. IP, 171–2/128.
32. Toadvine, 'The Elemental Past', 271.
33. On the distinction between the 'sterile non-contradiction of formal logic' and 'the justified contradictions of transcendental logic', see Merleau-Ponty, 'Le primat de la perception et ses conséquences philosophique', *Bullétin de la société française de philosophie* 49 (1947): 126.
34. Toadvine, 'The Elemental Past', 274.
35. IP, 36/7.
36. The lack of temporal thickness is another point on which Merleau-Ponty critiques Husserl's conception of the immanence of phenomenality (in addition to the development of the 'in betweenness' of the originary bond (see Chapter 3, section 3)): 'Husserl's error is to have described the interlocking starting points from a *Präsensfeld* considered as without thickness, as immanent consciousness ... [T]ime ... is the model of these symbolic matrices, which are openness upon being' (VI, 224–5/173).
37. IP, 35/6.
38. Phraseology of Ted Toadvine, 'Natural Time and Immemorial Nature', *Philosophy Today* 53 (2009): 219, but he is alluding to a passage of Claudel: 'The past is an

incantation of things to come, the generating difference they need, the forever growing sum of future conditions. It determines the *sense*, and, in this light, it does not cease existing anymore than the first words of a sentence when the eye reaches the last ones. Better still, it does not stop developing, organizing within itself, like a building, whose role and aspect is changed by new constructions, or like a sentence made clearer by another sentence. In a word, what has been once, never loses its operating virtue; it increases with each moment's contribution. The present minute is different from all other minutes, in that it does not border on the same quantity of past. ... At every breath, the world remains as new as it was at the first gulp of air out of which the first man made his first expiration', Paul Claudel, *Art Poétique* (Paris: Mercure de France, 1929); translated by Renée Spodheim as *Poetic Art* (New York: Philosophical Library, 1948), 44–5/27.

39. Once in reference to Kant (N, 60); once in reference to Fichte (N, 66); and once in reference to Leibniz (N, 68).
40. N, 68.
41. N, 68.
42. N, 67.
43. N, 67.
44. Gottfried Wilhelm Leibniz, 'Theory of Abstract Motion', in *Philosophical Papers and Letters*, ed. and trans. Leroy E. Loemker (Dordrecht: Kluwer Academic Publishers, 1989), 139–42.
45. 'Theory of Abstract Motion', 141 (§17).
46. VI, 247/194; N, 163/120.
47. N, 67.
48. Schelling, *Essais*, trans. S. Jankélévitch, 113.
49. Schelling, *Essais*, 113.
50. Schelling, *Essais*, 116.
51. Schelling, *Essais*, 119.
52. VI, 24/9.
53. Eugene Fink, *Play as Symbol of the World*, trans. Ian Alexander Moore and Christopher Turner (Bloomington: Indiana University Press, 2010), 120.
54. For an account of how the term *symbolon* began to take on quite a different (and in certain ways opposite) meaning from post-classical Greece onwards, see Peter T. Struck, *Birth of the Symbol: Ancient Readers at the Limits of their Texts* (Princeton, NJ: Princeton University Press, 2004), 72–99.
55. Fink, *Play as Symbol of the World*, 120.
56. Fink, *Play as Symbol of the World*, 120.
57. Fink, *Play as Symbol of the World*, 121.
58. Biancu, 'Competing Paradigms', 126. See also Biancu's more recent article 'Le symbole donne (encore) à penser', *Revue de théologie et de philosophie* 148 (2016): 755–67.
59. Dictionary entry in Liddell and Scott: 'ousia'. Robert Scott and Henry G. Liddell, *A Lexicon Abridged from Liddell and Scott's Greek-English Lexicon* (Oxford: The Clarendon Press, 1944).
60. Claude Romano, *Event and World*, trans. Shane MacKinley (New York: Fordham University Press, 2009); Jean-Luc Marion, *In Excess: Studies of Saturated Phenomena*, trans. Robyn Horner and Vincent Berraud (New York: Fordham University Press, 2002).
61. See Biancu, 'Le symbole donne (encore) à penser', 763.
62. A version of this section has been published as "Contaminated by Nature: Rethinking Mortal Life and Immortal Nature with Schelling, Lacan and Merleau-Ponty". Crossing: The INPR Journal (2023): 83-94.
63. 'Treatise Explicatory of the Idealism in the Science of Knowledge', in Thomas Pfau, *Idealism and the Endgame of Theory* (Albany: SUNY Press, 1994), 92.
64. V. Jankélévitch, *L'odyssée de la conscience*, 6.

65. V. Jankélévitch, *L'odyssée de la conscience*, 270.
66. See Emmanuel de Saint Aubert, *Être et Chair*, 165–200 (among many other passages). Also, Alexandra Renault, 'Merleau-Ponty et Lacan: un dialogue possible?', in *Merleau-Ponty aux frontières de l'invisible*, ed. Marie Cariou et al. (Milan: Associazione Culturale Mimesis, 2003); Guy Félix Duportail, 'Le Chiasme d'une amitie: Lacan et Merleau-Ponty', *Chiasmi international 6: Entre Esthétique et psychanalyse* (2005): 345–67.
67. See especially the first chapter of Slavoj Žižek, *The Indivisible Remainder: On Schelling and Related Matters* (London: Verson, 1996), 11–91.
68. Slavoj Žižek, 'Troubles with the Real: Lacan as a Viewer of Alien', in *How to Read Lacan* (London: Granta Publishing, 2006), 65.
69. Žižek, 'Troubles with the Real', 72.
70. Bernard Baas, 'L'Élaboration phénoménologique de "l'objet a": Lacan avec Kant et Merleau-Ponty', in Baas, ed., *De la chose a' l'objet: Jacques Lacan et la traversée de la phénoménologie* (Leuven, Peeters, 1998), 41–87.
71. Dany-Robert Dufour argues that Böhme (through Koyré) is a potential source for Lacan's mirror stage: 'Lacan et le miroir sophianique du Boehme' (Paris: Éditions et publications de l'École lacanienne, 1998). Given the influence of Koyré on Lacan, Dufour's argument can be extended to the *objet petit a*.
72. Jacques Lacan, 'From Love to the Libido', in *The Seminar of Jacques Lacan: Book XI: The Four Fundamental Concepts of Psychoanalysis, 1964* (New York: W. W. Norton and Company, 1977), 197–8. See also, 'Position of the Unconscious', in *Écrits: The First Complete Edition in English* (New York: W. W. Norton and Company, 2006), 703–21.
73. Žižek, 'Troubles with the Real', 64.
74. Schelling, *Ages of the World* (1815), 30.
75. Žižek, 'Troubles with the Real', 65.
76. Schelling, *First Outline of a System of the Philosophy of Nature*, trans. Keith R. Peterson (Albany: SUNY Press, 2004), 40n.
77. Schelling, *First Outline*, 40n.
78. David Farrell Krell, *Contagion: Sexuality, Disease, and Death in German Idealism and Romanticism* (Bloomington: Indiana University Press, 1998), 95.
79. Krell, *Contagion*, 95.
80. Krell, *Contagion*, 95.
81. Schelling, *First Outline*, 160n.
82. Krell, *Contagion*, 112.
83. Lacan, *The Four Fundamental Concepts of Psychoanalysis*, 197.
84. Schelling, *First Outline*, 41n.
85. Schelling, *First Outline*, 62n.
86. Falque, *The Wedding Feast of the Lamb*, 14.
87. See Jeffrey P. Bishop, *The Anticipatory Corpse: Medicine, Power, and the Care of the Dying* (Notre Dame, IN: Notre Dame University Press, 2011).
88. Falque, 'Éthique du corps épandu', *Revue d'éthique et de théologie morale* 288 (2016): 60.
89. Falque, 'Éthique du corps épandu', 60–1.
90. Aristotle, *De anima*, 413–14, 421–3 and 435.
91. N, 61.

Chapter 7

What the Sea Left Behind: The Element as the Unconscious

> Since our philosophy has given us no better way to express that intemporal, that indestructible element in us which, says Freud, is the unconscious itself, perhaps we should continue calling it the unconscious – so long as we do not forget that the word is the index of an enigma – because the term retains, like the algae or the stone that one drags up, something of the sea from which it was taken.[1]

This chapter begins with an explication of two relationships: (1) the relationship between two competing traditions of the unconscious, one that begins with Schelling and the other with Freud; (2) the relationship between two philosophies of consciousness, one that begins with Freud (psychoanalysis) and the other with Husserl (phenomenology). It is the intersection of the relationships between these competing theories that, I will argue, is central to understanding and developing Merleau-Ponty's own articulation of the unconscious and his understanding of symbolism within it. Through understanding these relationships, we will contest and enlarge upon previous interpretations of Merleau-Ponty's unconscious and begin to analyse certain deficiencies within his late thought, particularly a certain inconsistency between Merleau-Ponty's thinking of the body and of elemental power. In sum: to the degree that Merleau-Ponty is a thinker of the elemental, he is able to retain the insights of the Freudian drive, but at the same time his phenomenology of the body risks flattening out the unconscious by reducing it to the unconscious of the phenomenal field.

1. A divergence and a meeting point: Freud and Schelling on the unconscious

It is common to group theories of the unconscious into two primary categories: the productive unconscious and the repressive or reactive unconscious.[2] The former has a genealogy that has its origin in Schelling and passes to Jung and Deleuze. The latter is developed by Freud. Freud seems to have taken nothing from Schelling despite some references to Schelling's corpus in other regards.[3] The primary influence on Freud's theory was Schopenhauer.[4] For Freud, the unconscious was understood to be those past events that could not come to the surface. They could not be made conscious because the mind actively kept them from rising up into the clear light of day. The unconscious thus inhibits free conscious action and only reveals itself in behaviour latent with the (energetic) *structures* but not the *content* of past events, especially traumatic ones. The unconscious is of course also latent with wishes and desires which society's prohibitions and taboos push down into darkness.

For Schelling, by contrast, as we have already seen, restriction has a positive meaning. The unconscious is not a site where consciousness gets buried. It is a site of unrestricted force. Restriction is the coming into consciousness of this force. It is a taking on of form by negating the primordial formlessness of the unconscious. For him, the unconscious is identified with nature:

> The intrinsic notion of everything merely *objective* in our knowledge, we may speak of as *nature*. The notion of everything *subjective* is called, on the contrary, the *self* [Ich], or the *intelligence*. The two concepts are mutually opposed. The intelligence is initially conceived of as the purely presentative [Vorstellende], nature purely as what can be presented [Vorstellbare]; the one as the conscious [Bewuste], the other as the unconscious [Bewustlose]. But now in every *knowing* a reciprocal concurrence of the two (the conscious and the intrinsically unconscious) is necessary; the problem is to explain this concurrence.[5]

Negation's fundamentally positive role is the self-assertion of spirit that depends on nature for its fecundity, but which is truly productive only by negating nature to the point of an absolute scission. This negating therefore is not repressive but creative. Unconscious nature must be restricted for being to emerge.

Both Freud and Schelling hold that there is a reality to forces, not just to bodies. Platonists that they are, forces in a certain way exceed bodies. This position is exceptional rather than the norm within modern philosophy and science and so the commonality should not be taken lightly.

Psychoanalysis and Schellingianism both speak of the unconscious because they are both philosophies of force. For Schelling, this force is nature itself. For Freud, it is the drive. This forceful dynamism is connected to another point: the unconscious in both cases is intrinsically linked to temporality. For Freud, it is connected to the temporality of the past—how things get buried but somehow remain present. The Schellingian unconscious is bound to the temporality of the future. It is the fertile ground in which any future production has its source.

Despite opposed understandings of the unconscious, both Freud and Schelling understand the unconscious to be somehow related to the symbolic. For Freud, symbolic dream content reveals the structures of the unconscious. Freud's use of the term symbol, however, has been controversial from the beginning.[6] Jung criticised Freud's practice of reducing all dream symbols to the expression of a wish. His objection was not that dreams were not symbolic. Rather, Jung believed that Freud got the definition of symbol wrong, and so Freudian interpretation of dream symbols resulted in a reductive interpretation:

> The essential thing in Freud's reductive method is to collect all the clues pointing to the unconscious background, and then, through the analysis and interpretation of this material, to reconstruct the elementary and instinctual processes. Those conscious contents which give us a clue to the unconscious background are incorrectly called *symbols* by Freud. They are not true symbols, however, since according to his theory they have merely the role of *signs* and *symptoms* of the subliminal processes. The true symbol differs essentially from this and should be understood as an expression of an intuitive idea that cannot yet be formulated in any other or better way.[7]

Roland Dalbiez, in 1936, remarked that the psychoanalytic meaning of symbol 'constitutes the exact antithesis' of the ordinary meaning of symbol: 'whereas the ordinary symbol implies no direct causal relation with what it symbolizes, the Freudian symbol is essentially and by definition an effect of what it symbolizes'.[8] For Dalbiez, what Freud calls a symbol is actually an 'effect-sign'. It is directly caused by the unconscious which expresses its wish-fantasy in dream content while the ego's guard is down during sleep. By contrast, we use white as a symbol for moral innocence even though there is no direct causal relation between the symbol (whiteness) and the symbolised (purity).[9]

Jung objects to the Freudian interpretation of dreams as a semiotic rather than symbolic interpretation. Freud misapplies the term symbol for what is really a sign: 'Every view which interprets the symbolic expression as an analogue or an abbreviated designation of a *known* thing is semiotic.'[10] Jung argues that semiotic interpretations of dreams 'reduce' the symbol to a mere signifier of either a repressed (sexual) event or of an infantile fantasy. There is a distinct privilege in Freud of what Merleau-Ponty calls the 'accomplished rationality' of modern man. This rationality uses the symbol to surmount the symbolic and thereby arrive at the objective – to overcome 'infantile' logic, which is symbolic, for the adult logic of scientific objectivity.[11] Schelling's approach to myth insisted that we cannot deconstruct the form to get at a hidden content. Psychoanalysis operates in the demythologising tradition that Schelling resists – the dream symbol is understood as an effect rather than a cause. From a Schellingian perspective, Freudian psychoanalysis allegorises the symbol in order to get at a content that is elsewhere. But we must suspend this critique for a moment to look at another similarity between Freud and Schelling. For while they use symbol differently, what is remarkable is that symbol is in both cases linked to the unconscious and thus to a certain barbaric principle. Freud's version of the barbaric principle is the id. For Freud, the symbol is the eruption of the unconscious into conscious psychic life. It is the way the unconscious is composed in conscious form. For Jung, following Schelling, the symbol cannot be composed. It is not a product of unconscious desire but itself composes desire. Symbolic images are themselves primordial, irreducible and transpersonal. As Deleuze puts it, 'The irreducible datum of the unconscious is the symbol itself, and not an ultimate symbolized. *In truth, all is symbol in the unconscious*, sexuality and death no less than anything else.'[12] Dream symbolism simply repeats the symbolism that already structures unconscious desire.

Freud and Schelling have radically opposed views of the unconscious – at least on the surface. Freud's is repressive and Schelling's is productive. While both connect unconscious to symbol, the symbol in Schelling is irreducible while for Freud it is constructed. From a Schellingian point of view the problem with analysis (*psycho*analysis in this case) is that it always allegorises. It sees dreaming as an effect rather than a cause. It is only the positing of being as intrinsically oneiric that frees dreaming from its reduction to a symptom and instead turns it into a starting point, something productive and generative. It is this *essentially* symbolic and therefore oneiric aspect of being that Merleau-Ponty seeks to draw out of the work of Freud despite Freud's tendency towards allegorisation. When the world is no longer seen as a positive phenomenon – i.e. the object that phenomenological intentionality is directed at (consciousness *of* something) – but is instead a mixture of conscious and unconscious together, Freud's insight leads beyond such allegorising to a 'primordial symbolism' and to a consciousness that must be conceived like the Heraclitean soul, a soul with an inexhaustible depth: 'One would never discover the limits of soul, should one traverse every road – so deep a measure does it possess.'[13] Merleau-Ponty writes in his Preface to Hesnard's 'L'Oeuvre et l'esprit de Freud':

'Consciousness is now "the soul of Heraclitus," and Being which is around it rather than in front of it is an oneiric Being, hidden by definition.'[14]

2. Year zero: Two new philosophies of consciousness

If Freud is bound together with Schelling as founding fathers of alternative traditions of the unconscious, Freud is linked with Husserl as founding fathers of new philosophies of consciousness. The year 1900 marks the publication both of Freud's *Interpretation of Dreams* and Husserl's *Logical Investigations*. The common link between these two philosophies of consciousness which nevertheless 'have remained foreign to one another'[15] is the teaching of Franz Brentano, whose lecture both the young Freud and the young Husserl attended. Brentano's reintroduction of Aristotelian intentionality enabled these two pioneers exploring the frontiers of consciousness to bring an idea of the directedness of action back to philosophy: Husserl with a reconfiguration of the concept of intentionality and Freud with the concept of the drive.

While these two philosophies of consciousness have a common progenitor, the discourse between phenomenology and psychoanalysis has remained at best stilted if not entirely absent. This has been noted recently by Thomas Fuchs on the side of clinical psychology and by Emmanuel Falque on the side of phenomenology.[16] Fuchs argues for a phenomenological correction of Freud's psychology, particularly via Merleau-Ponty, while Falque argues for a psychoanalytic swerve in phenomenology, noting Merleau-Ponty's lifelong interest in Freud, but deploying Freud's idea of the id to contest Merleau-Ponty's commitment to sense and sense-making. Falque argues that Merleau-Ponty, like phenomenology as a whole, does not go far enough into the 'non-sense' and 'non-phenomenology' that psychoanalysis is so apt at interrogating.

Fuchs argues that the main reason there has not been more of a rapprochement between these two philosophies of consciousness is that they have fundamentally conflicting views of the role that consciousness plays. While for psychoanalysis, 'consciousness appeared only as a shimmering varnish concealing psychological forces and processes in unfathomable depths which are what is actually effective', for phenomenology 'consciousness was the medium or the light through which all phenomena come to be seen in the first place and appear as such'.[17] For phenomenology, appearance is manifestation (*Eischeinung*) while for psychoanalysis it is mere semblance (*Schein*) behind which is the really real. I have been arguing that the connection of appearance and manifestation remains the essential insight of phenomenology, but that it is only in interpreting manifestation as originally symbolic manifestation in a Schellingian sense can we overcome the tendency in philosophy (as well as in psychoanalysis), to split semblance and reality. At the same time, the Schellingian interpretation of symbol needs to be radicalised through the Merleau-Ponty notion of chiasm.

Freud's strategy for interpreting dreams was to show that the symbolic content really pointed to mechanisms that functioned in a purely material way but which could only express themselves to us in symbolic form. These mechanisms were outside of our conscious control or even conscious perception. So while the unconscious was the source of psychic life, it was hidden and often in opposition to conscious intention. Husserl, for his part, aimed to overcome any such split between consciousness and a realm outside of consciousness. Yet he strove to exceed the Kantian limits imposed on phenomenality, using the doctrine of intentionality to go 'back to the things themselves' without a reversion to naïve realism. Since *what* we see is still determined by *how* we see, the unconscious could not be some realm inaccessible to consciousness, as it is in Freud. Instead, Husserl described an unconscious which was, in the words of Fuchs, an 'implicit awareness that remained potentially accessible to consciousness or reflection and, in any case, could not be foreign to the subject'.[18] Fuchs thus draws out a third understanding of the unconscious that is neither the 'productive' unconscious nor the 'repressive' unconscious (see section 1 above). This third understanding can be termed the phenomenological unconscious. He opposes the phenomenological unconscious to the psychoanalytic unconscious, but in our account, it would be a third unconscious, next to both Freud's psychoanalytic unconscious and Schelling's understanding of nature as the unconscious ground of all productivity.

Already in Husserl phenomenology has a new account of the unconscious than that of Freud. If Freud and Husserl (and for that matter Schelling) have different accounts of the *un*conscious, what they share is a common account of consciousness: 'the Cartesian view of consciousness as "clear and distinct perception," the assumption that consciousness is transparent to itself insofar as its own contents are concerned'.[19] While consciousness is the space for all the ideas that are present in some form or other, the unconscious is the space that contains all ideas that are not currently before consciousness, but could become present. If Husserl thought it absurd to think of an unconscious as some space apart from consciousness, Freud, for his part, rejected any ambiguity between knowing and not knowing: 'a consciousness of which one knows nothing seems to me many times more absurd than a psychic unconscious'.[20] So while Freud rebels against classical understandings of consciousness, especially against the premise that everything psychic must be conscious,[21] he 'not only failed to overcome it but, without being aware of it, even adopted its premises',[22] thereby turning the body into the site of the meanings projected by the underlying operations of the psyche. Freud thus solves the problem of latency by reinforcing the dualistic paradigm that splits the subject who knows consciously from the objective psychological apparatus which is an 'internal foreign country',[23] that is to say, 'something external within oneself, whose meaning and effect are alien to the subject'.[24]

As any pious academic invested in career advancement, Merleau-Ponty stayed clear of writing anything about Jung. Yet in clear contradistinction to Freud and, for that matter, the mainstream philosophical tradition since Descartes, Merleau-Ponty suggests that the 'accomplished logic' that 'overcomes' the symbol deploying tendency of mythical and infantile thinking also opposes the very logic of perception, for the logic of perception is a logic of symbol. We perceive in symbols. At the same time, Merleau-Ponty recognised the importance of Freud and understood that there was a vital connection between the unconscious and the symbolic. It is precisely within this relation of the unconscious and the symbolic, I would argue, that Merleau-Ponty continues to insist upon *être sauvage*, indeed insists more and more, while at the same time arguing that everything human is cultural, instituted and symbolic. In this light we can begin to understand the relation of Merleau-Ponty to these opposing traditions – that of Schelling and that of Freud – traditions opposed but sharing an understanding of the unconscious as at once wild and connected to symbolism.

Three statements made by Merleau-Ponty from 1948 onwards serve to clarify the way in which he integrates the productive unconscious of Schelling, the reactive unconscious of Freud and the phenomenological unconscious of Husserl.

1. Perception is the true unconscious.
2. Symbol is the most true to perception.
3. Symbol is the true unconscious.

It is from these statements, which essentially form a syllogism, that we can make sense of Merleau-Ponty's own understanding of an unconscious that is elemental and the way in which he integrates these three theories to overcome the Cartesian theory of consciousness that undergirded the philosophies of their originators: Schelling, Husserl and Freud.

3. 'Perception is the true unconscious' (1): Unconscious as body memory

Fuchs sees Merleau-Ponty's understanding of the body schema as a way to overcome the dualism inherent in Freud's doctrine, his dependence on the modern understanding of consciousness as transparent to itself and the consequent *abjection* of the drives into a mechanically operating 'foreign country'. While Merleau-Ponty will use the suggestions of Husserl to develop a phenomenological unconscious, he does so always in light of and in response to Freud, who remains for him a decisive thinker. Merleau-Ponty's engagement with Freud stands in stark contrast to Husserl, who did not significantly engage his psychoanalytic contemporary. Fuchs seems to suggest that body schema in its relation to the world provides a sufficient way of overcoming Freud's dualism, but I would argue that, while it does have strong explanatory power, interpreting the psychoanalytic unconscious phenomenologically comes with a price. Indeed, it tends to obliterate Freud's most significant insight, for this insight emerges from his hybrid method which linked a humanistic philosophy of consciousness with a positivistic theory of force (the mechanistically operating drives).

The phenomenological unconscious remains the weakest sense of the unconscious precisely for the reason that Fuchs values it. It gets rid of dualism and thereby loses the antagonistic power of a force *against* consciousness. By calling it the 'weakest' sense, I do not intend to imply a truth value or even to say that the stronger accounts are better. All I mean at this point is that there is a real opposition at play in both Schelling and Freud, a fecund opposition, because the unconscious and the conscious are incompatible in a certain sense, and therefore locked in antagonistic struggle. Freud's unconscious is a strong sense of unconscious in a second way: it is a substantive – *the* Unconscious, some special mysterious place inaccessible to conscious mind and with a capital U. In phenomenology by contrast, the unconscious is the flip side of consciousness or a kind of ambiguity that perpetually shadows it or keeps it in the shadows. The great strength of the phenomenological unconscious is that it begins to slip away from the modern binary consciousness-unconsciousness towards the ambiguity of 'awareness'. The category of awareness is something between consciousness as clear and distinct and something radically unconscious. While implicit awareness is one aspect of the phenomenological unconscious that must be retained, Merleau-Ponty does not entirely succumb to the pitfalls of de-antagonising consciousness and unconsciousness. His insistence on the barbarian principle is key to retaining this agonistic torsion. To understand Merleau-Ponty's position between Schelling, Husserl and Freud, we first need to explain how Merleau-Ponty revises Freud with the notion of body schema and body memory.

Merleau-Ponty's understanding of the body schema is a way of overcoming the dualism inherent in Freud's dependence on the theory of the subject as 'clear and distinct'. Fuchs deploys Merleau-Ponty on this point by thinking about the relation of the lived body to two types of memory: autobiographical memory and body memory.[25] The lived body is not what is first of all visible, touchable, sentient, as opposed to the incorporeal psyche that lies behind it.[26] The lived body is our capacity to see, touch and feel. The lived body takes on historical dimensions insofar as body memory incorporates our experiences into our capacities. It converts experience into lived body such that what is learned is no longer experienced at all, but becomes a behaviour that expresses the body schema of which it has become an aspect. These two forms of memory turn out to be radically different. While autobiographical memory 'shows a linear form of time, that is to say, the experiences line up in an arrow of time directed into the past and so are remembered, body memory by contrast consists in repetition, the "re-enactment" of the experienced, the learned or habitualized, without the past being still remembered as such'.[27]

Merleau-Ponty sources this distinction from Maine de Biron and Bergson.[28] Bergson makes this distinction between the *souvenir-image* and *mémoire habitude*. In the process of learning, for example, the goal is to move from conscious to unconscious memory of some past event or piece of information. Unconscious memory is achieved by means of repetition whereby we achieve a learning so deep we no longer remember (autobiographically) the process of learning. To have the full capacity to, say, ride a bike, we have to forget the very process of learning. When we ride the bike well, we no longer have to think about information given by an instructor. We no longer think of past experiences of attempting to ride the bike. Remembering how to ride the bike entails forgetting the past events that led up to knowing how to ride. When the body itself knows how to do some learned activity in such a way that we call it instinctive (like the 'instinctive' reactions of an athlete which are the result of much training), there is no longer a remembered image (*souvenir-image*) of the past time in which we learned. It is a habit or a way of conducting oneself that is essentially unconscious. As Fuchs describes it: 'Body memory does not take one back to the past but conveys an implicit effectiveness of the past in the present.'[29] It does not direct us back to the past but 'contains the past latently as a presently effective experience in itself'.[30]

Body memory as habitualised action does not in itself provide a sufficient explanation of what Freud meant by the unconscious. The Freudian unconscious concerns repressed or avoided events rather than learned capacities. Merleau-Ponty contrasts the depth dimension of the psychoanalytic unconscious with the horizontal nature of the phenomenological unconscious:

> the latency of psychoanalysis is an unconscious that is beneath conscious life and within the individual, an intrapsychic reality that leads to a psychology of depth in the vertical dimension. ... [T]he latency of phenomenology is an unconscious which surrounds conscious life, an unconsciousness in the world, between us, an ontological theme that leads to a psychology of depth in the lateral dimension.[31]

There is however a side of implicit bodily memory that concerns no unconscious capacities like riding a bike but instead unconscious avoidance. This would be directly relatable to the Freudian unconscious. One pertinent example of an unconscious avoidance that can be explained better through a Merleau-Pontian paradigm is that of a cultural taboo. A taboo is stronger than a prohibition because we don't even know we are avoiding it. Our avoidance behaviour is structured by the avoidance behaviour of the culture that surrounds us. Because it is socially constructed in such a way that we do not even know we are avoiding the taboo object, the avoidance behaviour is best described as a result of forces operative *in* the perceptive field rather than by means of a psychic mechanism *beyond* consciousness. That the taboo is socially constructed is to say that it is an operation in the perceptive field, but because we do not even know we are avoiding the behaviour, it is unconscious and invisible. The resistance to the taboo is neither conscious nor pre-conscious. Nor is it altogether outside of consciousness. It operates as the negative of consciousness. Consciousness in this account always has a double – those things which are not known and which we do not want to know. The taboo curves our perceptive field around itself so that we not only avoid taboo behaviours but do not even see them as possible behaviours. In another case, that of a Freudian slip, for example, a certain chiastic structure emerges at the site of some ambiguous perception. The ambiguity of the perception allows us to interpret the perception how we want to interpret it and thus a repressed desire might suddenly break through.[32] The Freudian slip is considered a *mis*interpretation or mis-speaking precisely because the negatively perceived (repressed desire) is allowed to break through as a positive phenomenon by attaching itself to something positively perceived which has ambiguous meaning. Thus, Merleau-Ponty explains,

> the unconscious cannot be a process 'in the third person,' since it is the one who decides what will be admitted to official existence, insofar as it detours around thoughts and situations that we resist, and is thus not a *non-knowing* but rather an unacknowledged, unformulated knowledge that we

do not wish to tolerate. In an approximative language, Freud is here in the process of discovering what others more correctly have called an *ambiguous perception*.³³

Freud examines various defence mechanisms in which some sort of experience, memory or emotion has been retained in the structure of the body. When a perceived phenomenon has enough ambiguity to allow us to attach a repressed meaning to it, this meaning bursts out, for repressed wishes contain such a surplus of psychic energy that they will come out in any way possible, despite our best intentions to keep them hidden. A traumatic event can be understood as body memory of this variety. No longer present as a content, it is only present as an energetic structure. In *Phenomenology of Perception*, Merleau-Ponty describes the way in which unconscious fixation is retained as a structure rather than a memory content:

> [T]his fixation is not to be confused with memory; it even excludes memory in so far as the latter spreads out in front of us, like a picture, a former experience, whereas this past which remains our true present does not leave us but remains constantly hidden behind our gaze instead of being displayed before it. The traumatic experience does not survive as a representation in the mode of objective consciousness and as a 'dated' moment; it is of its essence to survive only as a style of being and with a certain degree of generality.³⁴

Traumatic events are translated into body memory – into the corporal schema. The body's general comportment and its ability to translate sensation from one schema to another is what then allows the repressed to emerge in dreams and through the various defence mechanisms like transference and projection. These transferences are analogous to synesthetic translations from one sense to another since 'my body is a system of equivalences and of intersensorial transpositions'.³⁵ There is an essential similarity between learned capacities and repressed memories – both are removed from the realm of explicit memory into body memory, becoming the base from which we see the world. They become the perceptual ground. This ground, however, is revealed in the possibility of transpositions from explicit body structure to various forms of 'acting out'. It is in these transitions and transpositions that the unconscious must be located.

4. 'Perception is the true unconscious' (2): Unconscious as perceptual link

It is the ambiguity of perception that leads Merleau-Ponty to the formulation 'perception is the true unconscious'.³⁶ Because the perceptual unconscious describes how our perception curves around what we do not want to know or experience, unconscious fixations can be understood phenomenologically as 'certain restrictions in a person's space of potentialities produced by an implicit but ever-present past which declines to take part in the continuing progress of life'.[37] These curvatures and restrictions are aspects of the perceptual field rather than something 'behind' consciousness in the way Freud formulates unconscious mechanisms. We see already how Merleau-Ponty's rejection of the Cartesian premise that consciousness must be transparent to itself has enabled him to think consciousness and unconsciousness together, as two sides of the same phenomenon, as positive and negative aspects contained within every perceptual field. The unconsciously perceived envelops every conscious perception precisely because every perception is perception from a body. Perception as such has form – is restricted and limited – only because it is haloed by the unconsciously perceived which restricts and limits it. Consciousness needs body in order to be consciousness of something. It needs resistance. But this implies a certain inversion between consciousness and the unconscious – no longer unconscious of something that ought to become conscious, but consciousness as dependent on a milieu of the unconscious, which is its proper limit and lining. The unconscious is the sensible body itself – its immemorial history, its habits and material antiquity. There are of course certain aspects of what is unconscious which *ought* to become conscious. Making this type of unconscious phenomena conscious remains the therapeutic goal of psychoanalysis. But therapy never results in an absolute abolition of the unconscious, for the unconscious is nothing if it is not the very limits of the body – the site of its transitions.

This broader understanding of the unconscious as limit of the body provides the fullest means of understanding Merleau-Ponty's fundamental thesis: that perception itself is the ground and origin of being. Perception here is not consciousness as it is in classical idealism or in the twentieth century's preoccupation with the disintegration of the distinction between conceiving and perceiving (see Chapter 3, section 2). Perception is fundamentally *unconscious*. 'The unconscious is not a proliferation of thoughts, hidden mechanisms, but the functioning of perceptual links [*des liens perceptifs*] which are always equivocal links offering a univocal spectacle.'[38] By thinking the unconscious link as the borderland between chiasmically related fields, Merleau-Ponty begins to develop the link itself as the fundamental ontological characteristic. It is not an epistemological link – a link between consciousness and thing – but an ontological, originary link. Indeed, his disassociation of perception from consciousness and thus from the (merely) epistemological allows him to talk about the unconscious as 'the excess of the perceptual over the notional'.[39]

5. Symbol as 'most true to perception'

Merleau-Ponty's last lecture course on nature was entitled 'Nature and Logos: The Human Body'. Here Merleau-Ponty's reading of Freud leads him to speak of the body itself as a 'natural symbolism'. The 'natural' symbolism of the body contrasts to the conventional or artificial symbolism of language. Unlike the first two courses, we do not have thorough notes from an auditor of the course. We do have Merleau-Ponty's own notes, but they are merely sketches of what he planned to say. There are eight separate sketches, many of which go over much of the same material. Despite many differences, in each of the first three sketches there is a section entitled 'Body as symbolism', the material of which is partially repeated in each draft, partially revised, and sometimes simply different. Taken in isolation it may seem that Merleau-Ponty wants to say that what distinguishes the human being from the animal is the capacity for symbol. This is indeed the thesis of Ernst Cassirer's three-volume work *The Philosophy of Symbolic Form* that Merleau-Ponty already engages in the *Phenomenology of Perception*. Cassirer, like Merleau-Ponty, sees the importance of the biologist Johannes von Uexküll's notion of *Umwelt*, the lifeworld. Both human and animal see the world in a way fitting to their nature. In the world of a fly there are only 'fly things' in the world of a sea urchin, only 'sea urchin things'.[40] Cassirer sees von Uexküll's understanding of animal worlds as a way of overcoming paradigms that anthropomorphise animal life. Von Uexküll suggests that the relation of animal life to its *Umwelt* is composed of two systems of relation – receptor systems and effector systems, ways of receiving information from the world and ways of effecting change in the world and taking charge of the information one receives. These two systems operate for every animal including the human. For the human being, however, there must be added a third system – the symbolic system.[41]

After certain engagements with von Uexküll in the second lecture course, Merleau-Ponty, for his part, deploys at the very end of the course the work of Konrad Lorenz, a biologist and student of von Uexküll, who uses von Uexküll's notion of *Umwelt*. I would argue that the work of Lorenz, and especially Merleau-Ponty's reading of it, would challenge Cassirer's thesis that symbol is what distinguishes man from animal. Lorenz argues that even animal instinct operates by means of symbolic systems. It is these connections to body schema, including the schema of animal bodies, that makes symbol such a key concept in Merleau-Ponty's late thought, for the body schema enables symbol to escape a merely epistemological determination and to remain a perceptual category, which therefore, following

Merleau-Ponty's perceptual ontology to its end, makes symbol a basic ontological starting point. Thus symbol as 'the most true to perception' tells us not only that we *see* in symbols, but that we *are* in symbols, and that this being is seeing. In the perceptual ontology, symbol is neither on the side of consciousness nor on the side of materiality. It is the link between the two. It is a being that originates from visibility itself. To unpack this claim, we will shortly look at Merleau-Ponty's analysis of Lorenz on animal symbolism and the way animal instinct offers a 'passage' to the symbolism which is the human body.

For now, we return to the third lecture course, where we found the three sketches of the section on the human body as symbolism. In opening this section, Merleau-Ponty speaks of the 'enigma of the body'. The body is at once 'closed and open' – self-organising and reaching out into the world in order to consume it, to know it, to feel it. It is a 'thing and measurer of everything'. To think the body as a symbolism helps clarify this enigma, Merleau-Ponty says, in the same way that we can clarify the meaning of language by calling it a 'second body' or 'open body'.[42] For Merleau-Ponty, language as a second body is also a 'second symbolism', a symbolism that is 'conventional' and artificial in contrast to the body itself.[43] To understand why symbolism helps clarify both the enigma of the body and the enigma of language, we need to look at his use of the term symbolism and how the body-symbol would produce a second 'conventional' body, i.e. language. In the first sketch of the section, 'Human Body as Symbolism', Merleau-Ponty defines symbolism as 'a term taken as representative of another, *Auffssung als* → we refer ourselves to the spirit as bearer of the *als*, to intentionality, to sense'.[44] Without needing a preconception of the signifier or the signified, 'the body passes into the world and the world into the body'.[45] This idea goes back to the *Phenomenology of Perception* and the way one sensory expression can be translated without any representational mediation into another, expressive 'by their insertion into a system of non-conventional equivalences, in the cohesion of the body'.[46] (And it is this passage too in which Merleau-Ponty refers to Cassirer.)

Reintegrating this later analysis of symbol into his earlier analysis of the way one system transfers into another expressive system leads to the most important 'correction' from one sketch of the 'Body as Symbolism' to another. In the second sketch, he will no longer link symbolism to representation. Where in the first sketch he defined it as 'a term representative of another', he retracts this claim, emphasising that it is *not representation*. The human body is a symbolism 'not in the superficial sense = a term representing another, standing in its place, but in the fundamental sense of: expressive of another. Perception and movement symbolise'.[47]

This definition of the symbolic seems to lie somewhere between that of Schelling and that of Freud. In a Schellingian way, he speaks of the symbolism of the body as 'natural' symbolism because it expresses the body's indivision – its sense which is 'latent' and 'blind'. To speak of an expressive 'indivision' is to bring the symbol of the body back to the Greek sense of *physis*. Further, to argue that the 'second symbolism' of language derives from the first symbolism of the body is to make the very Schellingian move by which forms are not aggregated from parts but 'repeat' another symbolic system from which they emerge (see Chapter 5, sections 1 and 2). For Merleau-Ponty here, language has a 'quasi-natural life in the indivision of the signified-signifying. It is like a second nature. It precedes itself. Its origin is mythic.'[48] Freud's influence can be seen in the understanding of symbol through the emphasis on the alterity of the symbolic. That the symbolic 'expresses another' is Freudian in provenance and is contrary to Schelling's notion of the tautegorical. In Freud, dream symbolism is the unconscious trying to get out, expressing the repressed in another medium. For Freud the symbolic is a means of expressing in coded language what cannot get out in the way it wants. We should not however read Freud as asserting the simplistic idea that there is a content hidden under dream symbols. Unconscious wishes are not a content of ideas. It is an energetic structure, such that 'the full meaning of any particular dream is revealed by its place in the whole web of wishes, desires, and other psychic forces'.[49] Nevertheless the symbolic expression is a real energetic discharge of the desire. The desire finds another means of expressing what it wants – it takes recourse in symbol rather than in its 'real' desire. In contrast to Freud, however, Merleau-Ponty does away with the mechanical drive which operates 'underneath' so that every immediate translation from one sensible expression to another lies on the surface of perceptual expression. The secondary symbolism does not lead back to the 'real' working of drives. It leads to the first symbolism – the cohesion of the body itself.

Despite apparently dispensing with the understanding of the drives as a 'foreign country', Merleau-Ponty does not do so in order to eliminate what is wild, brute or unruly. He wants to abolish any merely mechanical production: the idea of the drive as psychic *mechanism* and the unconscious as receptacle for representations. Indeed, at the end of each of the sketches of 'Body as Symbolism' he invokes an *esprit brut et sauvage*.[50] The intertwining of wild being with *logos* is central to the whole project of thinking the symbolism of the body – so much so that when he speaks of nature and *logos* as the theme of his last, incomplete works, we might replace nature with wild being and *logos* with symbolism: 'there is a *logos* of the sensible world and a wild spirit that animates the sensible world'.[51]

And in the first sketch he concludes in remarking that 'we must find this raw and wild spirit under all the cultural material that it displays'.[52] The *logos* of the world is symbol, for the originary cannot point to something beyond itself, something more primordial. It is not a *logos* as signified or signifying, but the irreducible unity of the two: a *logos* that expresses itself.

6. Drive and instinct: Symbolism in the human and the animal

From *The Structure of Behavior* onwards, the Freudian drive was an important concept for Merleau-Ponty. It was particularly fruitful in his work to overcome behaviourism.[53] Further, it provided Merleau-Ponty a means of articulating directed motivation that is non-finalist and which contained a certain element of force that phenomenological intentionality could not. This force was guaranteed by Freud's 'hybrid method', the inherent incompatibility of mechanical drives with a humanistic theory of consciousness. Freud distinguished human behaviour from animal behaviour through the concept of the drive. The drive designates human behaviour whose motivation is fused artificially but forcefully to its object: 'the sexual drive and the sexual object are merely soldered together'.[54] What this means is that, unlike instinct, drive can slip from one object of desire to another. Not naturally attached, it is soldered on after the fact. Animal behaviour by contrast is motivated by instinct, which is natural and therefore lacks the slippery, artificial nature of drive-directed motivation. Freud's assumptions about animal behaviour largely derived from nineteenth-century mechanical views, where the behaviour of an animal was incited automatically from the presence of the object that could fulfil its need. Given the right hormonal conditions, the sexual instinct of the male was activated instantly in the presence of the female. Merleau-Ponty, however, suggests that animal behaviour operates in a way more similar to what Freud describes as drive. This is corroborated by the biological studies that Merleau-Ponty uses, such as Lorenz.

In hindsight, it doesn't matter that Freud got animal instinct wrong. He was able to use it as an effective foil to develop a new understanding of motivated activity that he reserved for humans, but which was later, at least in part, expanded to include animal behaviour. *Trieb* in the German, or drive in English, was used to describe the kind of behaviour that wasn't just a rigid performance of instinctual actions. It helped explain such phenomena as displacement, transference and condensation. The human sex drive, Freud showed, did not have to be enacted in the presence of the opposite sex. It could be sublimated into other activities such as music, poetry or sportive competition. It could show itself in fetishes. According to Freud, the drive was a frontier concept, somewhere 'between the psychic and the physical'.[55]

Instead of the strict dichotomy of instinct and drive, Merleau-Ponty uses the biological studies of Lorenz to show that animal instinct manifests the same fundamental disconnect between desire and its object.[56] Instinct therefore does not operate in a mechanical or finalist way, as Freud thought. 'Instinct is a primordial activity which is objectless', Merleau-Ponty writes.[57] Instinct's objectlessness is exemplified by the fact that in many animals sexual arousal can be activated by the signs of sexuality rather than the actual presence of the other sex. The colour red, for instance, can incite the sexual instinct in certain birds. Homosexuality too can manifest because a female of the species can articulate male behavioural patterns. According to Merleau-Ponty, the instinct should thus be understood as an inner tension that responds to a certain field of textures, manifestations and signs in which this tension can find release. This textural field of signification expresses aspects associated with the opposite sex, which is not an entity or class of entities but a general aspect of being. In the instinctual act, however, Lorenz argues that there are perceptual elements that should not be confused with the instinctual elements.[58] Unlike the instinctual elements, perceptual and motor elements are indeed oriented towards an end. The dive of an eagle towards its prey, Merleau-Ponty explains, is an end-directed action. It aims towards the rabbit in the field. What instigates the dive, however, is not an intrinsic connection to the prey that pulls the eagle towards it. The rabbit is a 'means' of resolving the tension within the eagle 'as if the object intervened as the pivot of a theme which is in the animal as if it brought the animal the fragment of a melody that the animal bore within itself, or suddenly awakened an a priori, provoked a reminiscence'.[59]

To further draw out the endogenous character of instinct, Merleau-Ponty uses the example of an adolescent starling that will pretend to chase and devour a fly when not only has it never seen another starling perform such an action, but there is no fly around to provoke said action. It is an instinct that is not performed with an end in mind, but is 'an activity for pleasure'.[60] Instinct thus has a reference to the inactual, to 'oneiric life'.[61] Even if 'these acts are usually performed with reference to an object, they are something else entirely than the reference to an object, they are a manifestation of a certain style'.[62] Even though instincts usually operate in response to an object, the object should not be understood as a cause but as something that awakens an innate complex. Following Lorenz, Merleau-Ponty thus assigns to instinct many of the characteristics that Freud reserves for the drive. Two passages particularly stand out in this regard. First is a quotation from Rémi Chauvin. Chauvin says that animal instinct should not be understood like a donkey that needs to be whipped in order to go. It is not that an unlooked for object will suddenly activate it and do so automatically. Instinct should instead be understood as 'a horse always looking for barriers to leap'.[63] The analogy of the horse is not only the one Freud uses to speak of the energetic excess of the id which will be manifested in drive.[64] It goes all the way back to Plato's divisions of the soul in the *Phaedrus*: the two horse and chariot driver schema.[65] Ironically, Merleau-Ponty is closer to Freud's understanding of drive in discussing instinct here (where he does not cite Freud at all) than he is when he converts the Freudian unconscious into the phenomenological unconscious. Animal instinct is an interior tension that seeks release. This definition of instinct maintains the intrinsic heterogeneity between desire and its object contained in Freud's definition of drive as 'soldered' to an object where it finds a release of tension.

The second passage that illustrates how close Merleau-Ponty's reading of Lorenz is to Freud's concept of drive is a passage in which he analyses the animal's ability to separate the stimulus from the proper object, and which has as result 'a sort of fetishism of the object'.[66] A male butterfly will copulate with a stick covered with female secretion. The red-breast bird will 'enter into a (sexual) trance when it sees the colour red before it, as if it lost its head, even though its perception of forms is much more refined'.[67] Merleau-Ponty concludes that 'there is an oneiric, sacred and absolute character to instinct ... capable of making a world and attaching itself to whatever object of the world'. Again, this is the precise definition Freud gives his concept of drive in order to define it *against* animal instinct. The drive is soldered to its object artificially in contrast to instinct, which for Freud is the mechanical fulfilment of an end-directed desire. Both for the Freudian drive and Merleau-Ponty's reading of instinct through Lorenz, the desire is not intrinsically bonded to its 'proper object'. It is connected to a field of indirect associations.

These readings suggest that Freud's insights into human motivation were expanded into the animal world first by biologists and then philosophically by Merleau-Ponty. Merleau-Ponty uses this expansion of the Freudian explication of motivated action to describe more adequately the link between animality and humanity. A certain symbolism is now available to animals. His second series of lectures was the series that focused primarily on animality. This last section in the second *Nature* course on 'The study of instinct in Lorenz' and subtitled, 'The passage from instinct to symbolism', leads up to his discussion of the human body in the third *Nature* course. Because of the emptiness of its activity, an activity which is 'objectless', Merleau-Ponty suggests that 'instinct is going to be capable of going off course, or will pass from instinctive activity to symbolic activity'.[68] In other words, because Merleau-Ponty decoupled the concept of instinct from end-directed, mechanical action and located it in a virtual, interior and oneiric realm activated by fields rather than objects, animals can also be said to be operating on symbolic planes. Since even animal action is only sketched (*ébauché*) rather than accomplished and exhausted in its end, it 'easily becomes signification'.[69] Instinct has a direct link to symbolism because it concerns a schematic of the world that corresponds only partially to specific aspects of the correct 'object'. What Merleau-Ponty seems to mean by symbolism in this case is the oneiric dimension of instinct and its aim towards a field of associations rather than towards an object. Neither the 'real' nor the object is the aim of an instinct. The symbolic is thus characteristic of what lies between and before the instinctual desire and the thing it desires. The oneiric desire desires certain aspects or signs given by the exterior world that link it to the imagination of the dreamer and not to a particular thing in the world. Thus a whole ceremony and culture often envelops the sexual act among animals.[70] The ceremonial in the animal kingdom is not a mere embellishment to the act of copulation, nor is it merely a 'strategy' to get a mate. It is the sexual act itself unfolded into the ceremonial. The sexual is a whole texture of being, a field and milieu of sexuality, the creation of differentiated being within the context of the duplicity of sexed life. Such an analysis of instinct implies another critique of Freudian symbolism: sexuality is not sublimated into other activities that are 'really' about sex. These activities simply *are* sexuality itself.

7. The meaning of symbol in Merleau-Ponty's analysis of instinct

There is a direct connection to Schelling's understanding of symbol in this: Merleau-Ponty links the symbolic function of instinct to the fact that it is 'objectless'. Only because it is objectless does it create images. The desired one seduces, but the seduced also seduces himself. That the instinct is objectless means that it refers to its own inner tension. If instinct is a tension in the body searching for a place of release, then it is the symbolic as such that is under tension. And here the symbolic stands in stark contrast to Freudian symbolism where the symbol is the expression of the release of tension, not what is itself under tension. For Freud, the symbol is the product of a tension, not its source. We have seen that the Schellingian symbol is a Naturphilosophie concept in its capacity to repeat and to produce. Now we see that, as a Naturphilosophie concept, the symbol is a tension. This tension is what empowers it to be generative rather than a product that is generated.

In this light we can begin to see why Merleau-Ponty describes the human body as a symbolism, not merely something that produces symbols or sees (in) symbols. More than the introduction of the symbolic into animal life, it is its resolutely non-epistemological status that differentiates Merleau-Ponty's understanding of the symbolic from that of Cassirer. At the end of his analyses of Lorenz (the final paragraphs of the second *Nature* course), he poses the question concerning instinctual activity, whether instinct should be understood as 'of the order of things or of the order of consciousness or of a third order?'[71] He does not make clear whether this third order is in reference to Cassirer, who posed that the symbolic is a third order reserved for humans. We cannot doubt, however, that Merleau-Ponty has Cassirer in mind. He has already referred to Cassirer's work on symbol as early as the *Phenomenology* and will reference Cassirer again in the third lecture course. What von Uexküll describes as the receptor systems of animals could refer to 'the order of things' which Merleau-Ponty references here. It involves the movement from things to consciousness – the way a sentient being receives the world. Effector systems then would refer to 'the order of consciousness'. It involves the movement from consciousness to things – the actions of a sentient being on the world. The 'third order' that Merleau-Ponty alludes to at the end of this section (which, to remind ourselves, is entitled 'Passage from Instinct to Symbolism') – is an order that is not outside the receptor or effector systems, but between them. This is the symbolic order. But unlike Cassirer, Merleau-Ponty brings animality into symbolism. He thereby uses it as the key concept not of the human difference but of the passage from the animal to the human. Instinct is at least proto-symbolism if not a full-fledged symbolism. These analyses however make us wonder whether 'the passage from instinct to symbolism' is not the passage from the animal to the human but the passage from an old, mechanical formulation of animal behaviour to a newer model that understands all behaviour as essentially symbolic. There are several points to emphasise here.

First, the symbolic is not added over the top of receptor and effector systems, but sits between them, as a non-finalist and non-mechanistic middle. It is a force in tension that rises up. The symbolic expresses the fact that there is a certain ambiguous realm between desire and desire's objects. What is desirable in the objects belongs to fields and textures in which the desiring already takes part. If the desire can be made more complex, it is not because more parts can be added on like so many flourishes. Rather it is because the desire is towards the field which in its ambiguity allows for infinite new ceremonial folds and pleats. This ambiguous but not superfluous field is why 'we can validly speak of animal culture'.[72] It is this complex and complexifying milieu towards which the body tends (a 'thrust of symbolism')[73] and to which the body is connected in a non-finalist, non-mechanical way. This complexifying field is what Merleau-Ponty would call elsewhere the flesh of the world, but also the element of being – concrete but general, general but sensible, textured rather than formed into discrete objects. Its textures, folds and curves are its seductive ploys, but the seduction hides no essence.

Second, Merleau-Ponty arrives at animal symbolism by first expanding instinct to include the characteristics Freud reserves for drive. The energetic surplus, like the horse frenetically seeking obstacles to leap, does not result in a seizing of the object it searches for. Rather, the energetic surplus disassociates the desire from the object. The desire tends not towards singular objects but instead towards the general schema just as the horse would leap a fallen tree with the same muscle memory with which it would leap a stone wall. For the horse, the tree and the stone wall both fit into the general schema of 'jumpable obstacle'. Desire attaches to the schema by imagination. The oneiric essence of perception determines the field-directed motion of instinct. There is an essential non-equivalence between the instinct understood as an inner tension and the object through which it can expand this tension. Non-equivalence allows displacement from the 'proper object' and necessarily results in symbolic operations. We perceive symbolically. What we perceive is always a mixture of a general field and a sensible particular. What is other is nevertheless perceived as a symbol, bearing some generality, some resemblance. What signifies femininity for the masculine creates arousal. The real presence of the female is not necessary.

Third, the symbolic itself should be understood as a tension. This tension is what leads to Merleau-Ponty's understanding of the body as a symbolism. Even though there is no correspondence or adequation between desire and its object, it does not mean togetherness is not the starting point. It does not imply that the ontology of the flesh breaks down here. To the contrary, there are not two separated entities – separated as essences for example – that 'achieve' union as if the masculine would completely unite with the feminine so as to be identical or even to form a whole. In a note from his manuscript 'Notes sur le corps', Merleau-Ponty writes that the unconscious is 'this dimensional relation of being, with the other'.[74] Here he understands the unconscious specifically as libido as 'incorporation with the other which is a "primordial symbolization"'.[75] In the midst of all this talk about the unconscious as symbol, Merleau-Ponty refers specifically to Freudian operations like condensation and transference. He speaks of the need to understand these classic Freudian terms 'based on the topology of the body schema'.[76] It is for this reason that the body becomes not only the unconscious itself, but also a symbolism. If symbolism is no longer a mere expression of the unconscious, but *is* the unconscious, we begin to have a dynamic understanding of the symbol, something that expresses rather than something that is expressed. Symbol is the form that the power of *physis* takes. Body as symbol and as unconscious is necessarily a body open to the element of the flesh.

Symbolic desire is a penetration into the other – an enveloping and a being enveloped – without destroying the concreteness of the other. The symbol is completely within itself and yet is fragmentary, but the unity of the fragments cannot be achieved by identity or adequation. It is not a mechanical coupling like two pieces of a puzzle fitting together. Instead the unity is only achieved by creating a field of possibility between them. Symbolic fragments like the masculine and the feminine do not wholly fit together. We see this quite clearly in the fact that, while there may be a certain complementarity between the sexes, there are also irreconcilable differences. There are far more ways in which the sexes simply do not fit or even understand the desire of the other. For each, the other remains wild – incomprehensible by nature. And this is the essence of attraction. Likewise, the reason language does not correspond to the thing in itself is not because of a lack or imperfection in language. It is because language is just as concrete as the thing to which it refers. Participating in the same elemental milieu, language opens being rather than adequates to its objects.

Despite this 'passage from instinct to symbolism' within the animal world, Merleau-Ponty announces that his last lecture course is on the human body because only the body in its human form is the 'root of symbolism', that is to say, 'the junction of *physis* and of *logos*'.[77] We can only understand this consummation in the human if we are to understand the human *logos* as elemental non-being, as the mirroring element. This *logos* is what is most unconscious.

8. 'Symbol is the true unconscious': The irrational and the ambiguous

We began with the statement: 'perception is the true unconscious'. We have just analysed Merleau-Ponty's claim that symbol is the most true to perception – that perception is oneiric and that the concrete thing the perceiver perceives is embedded in a general field imbued with meaning. To conclude in syllogistic fashion, we can say: 'symbolism is the true unconscious'. Merleau-Ponty does not say so much in the form of a syllogism.

He arrives there inductively. When he begins to talk about the human body as a symbolism, we can start to see what this means. The unconscious understood *as* a symbolism implies a certain mediation between the Schellingian unconscious as the dynamic power of nature and the Freudian unconscious which Merleau-Ponty understands to be a 'restriction of the perceptual field' or a restriction of the body's possibilities, a certain configuration of the body schema. Following Schelling's notion of symbol as something that repeats or replicates itself, symbol is unconscious power. It is tautegorically inseparable from its concrete reality. Symbol is repressive unconscious because it restricts the field of perception to that which activates these instinctual tensions. It is therefore productive and repressive at the same time, unfolding into the field of possibilities it creates.

It is already an interesting development that he uses both the traditions of the productive unconscious and the repressive unconscious in a fruitful way. Yet there is something lost, I would argue, by interpreting Freud within a phenomenological context, where the repressive unconscious becomes what is unconsciously avoided within a perceptual field. This loss takes place in the transition from what in Freud remains 'irrational' to what Merleau-Ponty subsumes into 'ambiguity'. What Freud saw as the unconscious expressing its own wishes in dreams, slips and transferences, Merleau-Ponty saw as the discovery of 'what others have more accurately named *ambiguous perception*'.[78] As I have already hinted, there is a certain problem with doing away with Freud's hybrid system in which the drive is thought to be something beyond consciousness. Incorporating it into the dynamics of the body schema does not do full justice to what Freud showed us.

Above all, thinking the unconscious only as body schema risks reifying it into a structure. The Freudian unconscious allows slips, transference, sublimations only because of the dynamism between orders that cannot be reduced the one into the other. Mechanical uncontrollable drives are not lived thoughts and actions. Lived thoughts and actions cannot be reduced to the mechanical drives that undergird them. A part of this can be accounted for through the ambiguity of the object. A defence mechanism like transference, however, has at least as much to do with the uncontrollable energy of the drive. Ambiguity does not account for energy nor for the structure of mind that would enable it to displace a wish or desire from one object to another. As an excess of energy over any object, the drive emerges from a depth that cannot be accounted for in a world only populated by bodies. The drive must be understood as an infinite force, irreducible to the body it inhabits. Insofar as Merleau-Ponty is a thinker of the elemental, he is able to retain the insights of the Freudian drive, but insofar as he is a philosopher of the body, he risks flattening out the unconscious dismantling the apparatus on which its upward thrust depends. Flattening the unconscious to the body schema ignores the depth of the drive, the drive's essential incongruity with the object that bodies forth and the torsion that would be at the centre of the body. Incongruity is not ambiguity. This incongruity is precisely the incongruity between force, which is infinite, and body, which is finite.

As I see it, the difference concerns Freud's most essential insight: that mind is fundamentally restless and not fundamentally rational. Restlessness has more to do with energy than with the ambiguity of the chiasmic crossing. Mind as fundamentally restless suggests that rationality is not mind's only mode. Rationality is only one feature of mind. This is the case not only because the mind emerges in a body which is dark and material. The ambiguity of a chiaroscuro can indeed account for material darkness. But what Freud essentially proposes is that some of mind's very operations are *essentially and not accidentally irrational.* The Cartesian assumption that consciousness is transparent to itself maintains that the goal of philosophy and of psychotherapy is to bring things that were dark into the pure lucidity of consciousness. While Freud inherits this assumption, he also poses a new framework. What is at stake is not merely that things remain partially hidden or obscure, even when they become conscious. The question is whether the operation *coming-to-consciousness* is a *coming-to-reason* and further whether the operation itself *coming-to-consciousness* is in itself rational, governed by the principle of sufficient reason.

Jonathan Lear, for instance, sees Freud's fundamental insight as the systematisation of motivated *irrationality*. Psychoanalysis, he argues, is 'the first working out of a non-Socratic approach to human irrationality'.[79] Socrates posed the question: why do men sometimes choose to do something evil or to do the less good option of two options present before them?[80] To choose against the good seems like an irrational act. If the mind is rational, how do we choose a less good option when we know the better option, and even know that it is the better option? Socrates thinks that when we do an irrational act we must be deceived in some way. That the mind somehow tricks itself into thinking this option is the better option even though, ultimately, it knew that it was not. The basic assumption made by Socrates here is that the mind is rational, and that irrational behaviour can be explained rationally. Socrates presupposes that the mind is essentially rational and that it simply does not know the good or hides the good from itself. Most of Western philosophy has followed Socrates in this.[81]

Freudianism is a non-Socratic approach to the problem of irrational behaviour. It posits that mind has a built-in tendency to disrupt its own functioning. Irrational behaviour, in other words, is built into the healthy functioning of mind.[82] Irrational functioning is what allows for slips, transference, condensation, sublimation and symbolisation. In order for mind to be creative, it must sometimes be irrational. Mind makes meanings it doesn't itself understand. It both discovers and creates associations. While the ambiguity of the perceptual field – its disaccord with language – is one condition that makes such creativity possible, Freud posits that mind is essentially non-rational. As Jonathan Lear argues, restlessness is intrinsic to a mind that 'isn't just rigidly performing instinctual behaviors'.[83] Restlessness is more fundamental to mindedness than is rationality. Contrasting minded behaviour to instinctual behaviour helped Freud overcome the wedding cake understanding of the human mind: where reason sits atop and governs our baser animal instincts which lie as the lower layers of mind. Drive as a frontier concept between the psychic and the physical shows the way in which restlessness expresses itself all the way down to the most basic 'instinctual behaviors' like sex and eating, where previous accounts put rationality overtop, as what ought to rule and dominate the animality in a self-controlled person. The Freudian account of humans as minded rather than rational, makes mindedness something that goes all the way down and structures every behaviour. Rationality is one aspect of a mind that is not doubled between animal instinct and human reason. It is only one of the many functions of the restless mind.

Merleau-Ponty's achievement in revising the concept of the unconscious was to move beyond the Cartesian clear and distinct consciousness in which Schelling, Freud and Husserl were all caught up. He did this by speaking of perception as the true unconscious rather than equating the unconscious with the unperceived or the misperceived. Symbol is the essence of the perceptual unconscious which is ambiguous by right. Certain aspects of Freud can no doubt be better explained by Merleau-Ponty's reworking of the unconscious, and his synthesis of the Freudian unconscious with certain aspects of Schelling. But Freud's central insight on irrationality and the force of mind risks being entirely erased. One means of making up for this deficiency in Merleau-Ponty might be to retain the phenomenological unconscious and the psychological unconscious as two different forms of unconscious. Marc Richir opts for this approach. For Richir, the phenomenological unconscious is what inhabits a perceptual field without showing up within it. It curves perceptual space around it, as we have already seen. By contrast, what Richir calls the symbolic unconscious (for him, this is synonymous to the psychoanalytic unconscious) is characterised by its blind, mechanical character. It has no phenomenological foundation but operates next to the phenomenological unconscious. Richir's division is explicitly linked to Lacan. Richir describes the symbolic as a 'hole in being-in-the-world'.[84] The characteristic of symbolic meaning as opposed to phenomenological meaning, for Richir, is 'to not give itself, to escape into non-sense all the while making sense in another respect'.[85] Richir's approach seems to me to be unnecessarily obscurantist. What is interesting, however, is the way he retains two separate modes of unconsciousness that are not competing to be the 'right' one. Each says something different about the world and consciousness of it. Further, these two forms of unconscious cross over chiasmically. While the chiasmic structure of two forms of unconscious is Merleau-Pontian in inspiration, it is not what Merleau-Ponty himself does with the unconscious.

If we are asking essentially about the unconscious, Richir's seems to be the right approach. Who is to say that everything that is not conscious needs to be subsumed under the same thing: '*The Unconscious*' with a capital U? But if we are to turn from the question of the unconscious to the question of the symbolic, everything begins to look different. Is it more scandalous to put the symbolic side by side with phenomenology or to put the symbolic at phenomenology's very heart? Merleau-Ponty makes the latter move in his late work: 'It is only in the perceived world that we can understand all corporeity is already symbolism.'[86] If the symbolic is 'the most true to perception', isn't it nevertheless the most unfaithful to phenomenology? In this light, we might bring up a question first posed by Ed Casey: why does Merleau-Ponty focus on the pre-reflective body and Freud on the unconscious mind? Or 'for what good reason does Freud tie the unconscious domain so stringently to the mind? Why, for what good reason, does Merleau-Ponty link the prereflective realm so closely to the body?'[87] Casey suggests that these two thinkers recognise the terms body (*corps*, for Merleau-Ponty) and mind (*Geist*, for Freud) are 'modern philosophical abstractions'.[88] Freud replaces mind with psyche, that is, *Geist* with *Seele*, which is etymologically linked to the English word *soul*. Merleau-Ponty begins to privilege flesh over body. Both Freud and Merleau-Ponty see that meaning 'precedes the mind/body distinction and makes it possible'.[89] On Casey's reading, Freud and Merleau-Ponty chiasmically cross: Freud moves away from his psychological and neurological training towards a concept, *Seele*, that takes into account 'the life of a person in its full scope and sweep'. Merleau-Ponty distances himself from his Cartesian origins to speak of 'incarnate meaning'[90] and a 'flesh of the world', so that 'Merleau-Ponty can call for "a psychoanalysis of Nature," while Freud provides a phenomenology of the psyche in distress.'[91]

I want to take a different tack than that of Casey. This tack concerns the idea that Freud's hybrid method retains an insight about force that Merleau-Ponty largely suppresses. It may only be a question of accent, but in the accent, everything is at stake. While both Freud and Merleau-Ponty are concerned with the body in its relation to meaning, Freud doesn't do a very good job of making the body meaningful. His understanding of symbolism would not make room for the body *as* symbolism. And yet the accent he puts on mind (psyche) even above rationality or meaning is invaluable. For Freud, we might say that it is primarily a matter of the minded body. For Merleau-Ponty it is a question of the embodied mind. In Freud's turn to *Seele*, the question is fundamentally: 'What does it mean for the body to be minded?' In the concept of embodied mind, we cannot get away from the image of a mind entrapped in a body. But in the idea of a minded body is contained the idea of a body whose relation to the things of the world is upended by suddenly becoming minded. All at once instinct becomes drive, which is to say that the body now has a minded way of relating to the world. The world is full of bodies before there is any self-consciousness and certainly before there is drive-directed, minded consciousness. Being minded, as we have seen, affects the body and its consciousness all the way down to the most basic 'instincts'. But then suddenly the instincts are charged with symbolism. Suddenly desire is charged with so much force that it will spring from its 'natural' attachment to one object and become 'soldered' to another. The drive doubles the recoil of the body against the world.

Freud never critiques the understanding of consciousness as clear and distinct. There is, however, an implicit critique of an understanding of the world as made up of bodies and an understanding of forces as the 'equal and opposite reactions' of colliding bodies. In this sense, Freud is a follower of the one he calls 'the divine Plato'.[92] Like Plato, he imbues love and libido with fundamental reality.[93] He is closer to elemental philosophy than to Aristotelianism. Merleau-Ponty's focus on embodied mind brings him quite close to Aristotelian hylomorphism at times. In these moments, he is unable to think the force of the element which operates *through* bodies and fissures them rather than being contained by them. Elemental force, its destructive disequilibrium, results in an upward thrust. The negation of the indefinite moves upward. The limitations of the chiasmic structures of Merleau-Ponty's late thinking is here: every upward movement tends to be equalised by a downward one. Hence the flatness of the phenomenological unconscious when it is removed from the non-assimilable force. Reciprocal relations risk turning into a more sophisticated version of Newtonian physics – a physics of bodies – where every force is met with its equal and opposite force.

These field forces that the phenomenological unconscious describes do indeed exist. What we do not want to know curves our perceptual field around the unwanted object of knowledge in such a way that it remains unconscious. But in Merleau-Ponty's account there is no intrinsic force of mind that causes it to break with its rational functioning by means of excess of mind over reason, or an excess of force over body (schema). While Merleau-Ponty too shows that mind is intrinsically embodied, and that body and reason can never coincide, does he not fundamentally try to explain it in terms of the ambiguity of the body, the density of its mass, and not the buoyancy of its conflictual energies? Merleau-Ponty successfully brought the unconscious into phenomenology, but in doing so he suppressed the restless dimension of drive, which cannot just be understood as thickness, or even as resistance. It is something slippery that rises to the surface, an instability of relation, that only becomes stable because of an immense force, but which retains the possibility that the desire and its object might fall apart. Irrationality is not an exception within a fundamentally rational mind, nor is it merely the dark background. It constitutes mind as an energetic dynamic structure.

According to Lear, philosophical accounts of the irrational usually fail to account for the disruptiveness of the irrational. Drive reconfigures mentality as fundamentally nomadic. The mind is willing to set up its tent anywhere. To put it in Merleau-Pontian terms: not only is the relation of sensation a non-coinciding relation, but perceiving's relation to the perceived world involves an energetic surplus over the world it perceives, making the structure of mind particularly unstable. Our question then is precisely whether Merleau-Ponty's understanding of the 'ambiguous phenomenon' *necessarily* erases the insight to which the hybrid method led Freud, namely, the mind as fundamentally restless. Does Merleau-Ponty integrate the Freudian unconscious too well into phenomenology such that it loses its force? Merleau-Ponty's reference to wild being, which become in these late lectures more often than not 'wild mind' (*esprit sauvage*) at least tries to maintain this Freudian insight. Oftentimes, however, it seems to be a mere stand in that isn't doing any real work. I would argue that the reason for this is precisely the reduction of the psychoanalytic unconscious to a phenomenological unconscious. Merleau-Ponty's critique of Freud's unconscious (as another mind, a receptacle for non-present representations)[94] seems in this light a wilful misreading. His consequent repositioning of the unconscious *within* perception abolishes this irrational principle and thereby abolishes the force of mindedness. We do not have to take Merleau-Ponty's engagement of Freud, however, to be the last word of what he brings to psychoanalysis.

The way we can best understand this Freudian challenge to Merleau-Ponty would not be to look at what Merleau-Ponty says about Freud, but to use Merleau-Ponty to do away with Freud's essential blindspot, in other words to integrate Freudian mindedness into a Merleau-Pontian ontology and see how it holds up, that is to say, to rethink restlessness from the elemental bond. Our argument in Chapter 6, section 5 regarding Žižek,

Lacan and Schelling might suggest that the 'soldered' nature of drive could also be understood as an ontological first principle (of which the psychic drive is a microcosmic repetition) if we start from a philosophy of difference rather than of identity.

Merleau-Ponty rejects the idea of the unconscious as a depository that comes to the surface by a mechanical dynamic. By understanding the unconscious as the body schema, he eliminates certain aspects of Freudian drive and the essentially irrational nature of mind that Freud uncovered. While he uses Schelling's concept of the barbarian principle or wild being to speak about the irreducible remainder of what cannot come to consciousness, the term often becomes a mere cipher. The upward thrust of coming-to-consciousness is lost in the reversibility of chiasms. By expanding the notion of symbol, however, making it coterminous with the unconscious, Merleau-Ponty begins to introduce – if he never fully develops – a new way of thinking about force. The symbolic is essentially a centripetal force. As a fragment which is complementary to another concrete half, it is continually seeking a lost unity, it is driving, sometimes violently, towards its other. Homo symbolicus (Cassirer) is the incomplete being. It is a fragment of being 'abandoned to its individuation' (Fink). But in going into itself, in seeking its own centre, it drives towards the exteriority at its deepest interior. Hence the paradox of being a fragment through autonomy: the tautegorical opens out onto the other because of its own inner tension. It is the inner force of the symbol that most adequately replaces the mechanical force of the drive. It would be in the symbolic, even in the ground as element of being, that Merleau-Ponty's interpretation of Freudianism, his bringing it into contact with the Schellingian productive unconscious and the Husserlian phenomenological unconscious would provide the most adequate account of unconscious being: the unconscious as elemental milieu with its upward movement towards ever increasing individuation.

Notes

1. Merleau-Ponty's 'Preface to Hesnard's *L'Oeuvre de Freud*', trans. Alden Fisher in *Review of Existential Psychology and Psychiatry* 18.1–3 (1982–3), 71. Original French reprinted in P2, 283.
2. The history of the concept of unconscious is much more complex than that, but the division has its truths. See especially on this topic, Ffytche, *The Foundation of the Unconscious*. The introductory historiography of the unconscious (pp. 1–34) is particularly useful.
3. See McGrath, 'Schelling on the Unconscious', 85.
4. See Marcel Zentner, *Die Flucht ins Vergessen: die Anfänge der Psychoanalyse Freuds bei Schopenhauer* (Darmstadt: Wissenschaftlichen Buchgesellschaft, 1995).

5. Schelling, *System of Transcendental Idealism (1800)*, §1, 5. I have modified the translation of *Bewustlose* from 'nonconsious' to 'unconscious', for the sake of continuity of terms.
6. For a more thorough analysis, see Christian Kerslake, *Deleuze and the Unconscious* (London: Continuum, 2007), 105–10, which I am summarising in this paragraph and to whom I am indebted for the quotations.
7. Carl Gustav Jung, *The Collected Works*, vol. 15 (Princeton, NJ: Princeton University Press, 1966), 70.
8. Roland Dalbiez, *Psychoanalytic Method and the Doctrine of Freud*, trans. T. F. Lindsay (London: Longmans, Green & Co., 1941), 103.
9. Dalbiez, *Psychoanalytic Method and the Doctrine of Freud*, 101.
10. Carl Gustav Jung, *The Collected Works*, vol. 6 (Princeton, NJ: Princeton University Press, 1971), 474.
11. See Merleau-Ponty, *Causeries 1948*, ed. Stéphanie Ménasé (Paris: Seuil, 2002), 36.
12. Deleuze, 'From Sacher-Masoch to Masochism', trans. Christian Kerslake, *Angeleki* 9.1 (2004): 131.
13. B45. (Robinson translation).
14. P2, 281. Merleau-Ponty also refers to the soul of Heraclitus at NC, 152. On the connection of this passage to Husserl's deployment of the Heraclitean soul in the *Krisis*, see Stephen Noble, 'Entre le silence des choses et la parole philosophique: Merleau-Ponty, Fink, et les paradoxes du langage', *Chiasmi International 6: Entre Esthétique et psychanalyse* (2005), 116–17; and Annabelle Dufourcq, *Merleau-Ponty: une ontologie de l'imaginaire* (Dordrecht: Springer, 2012), 368–75.
15. Thomas Fuchs, 'Body Memory and the Unconscious', in *Founding Psychoanalysis Phenomenogically: Theory of Subjectivity and the Psychoanalytic Experience*, ed. Dieter Lohmar and Jagna Brudzinska (Dordrecht: Springer, 2012), 70.
16. Fuchs, 'Body Memory and the Unconscious'. Emmanuel Falque, *Ça n'a rien à voir: Lire Freud en philosophie* (Paris: Cerf, 2018).
17. Fuchs, 'Body Memory and the Unconscious', 70.
18. Fuchs, 'Body Memory and the Unconscious', 70. Husserl writes: 'What I do not "know", what does not stand over against me in my lived experiences, in my representing thinking and acting, as the represented, perceived, remembered, thought, etc., does not "determine" me as a spirit. And what is not intentionally included in my lived experiences, even if unattended or implicit, does not motivate me, even unconsciously.' *Ideas Pertaining to a Pure Phenomenology and to a Phenomenological Philosophy. Second Book: Studies in the Phenomenology of Constitution*, trans. Richard Rojcewicz and André Schuwer (Dordrecht: Kluwer, 1990), 243.
19. Fuchs, 'Body Memory and the Unconscious', 70. Here Fuchs is referring only to Freud and Husserl, but Schelling is within this Cartesian heritage as well.
20. Sigmund Freud, *The Ego and the Id* (New York: Norton, 1960), 7n4.
21. Freud, *The Ego and the Id*, 3.
22. Fuchs, 'Body Memory and the Unconscious', 71.
23. Freud, *Neue Folge der Vorlesungen zur Einführung in die Psychoanalyse* (Frankfurt: Fischer, 1940), 62; translated as *New Introductory Lectures on Psychoanalysis* (New York, Carlton House, 1933), 82.
24. Fuchs, 'Body Memory and the Unconscious', 72.
25. We are summarising from 'La spatialité du corps propre et la motricité', particularly PP, 171–83/158–70.
26. PP, 117/101.
27. Thomas Fuchs, 'The Cyclical Time of the Body and its Relation to Linear Time', *Journal of Consciousness Studies* 25 (2018): 53.
28. Fuchs, 'The Cyclical Time of the Body', 53. On the Bergsonian influence on Merleau-Ponty's understanding of body memory, see also Alia Al-Saji, '"A Past Which Has Never Been Present": Bergsonian Dimensions in Merleau-Ponty's Theory of the Prepersonal', *Research in Phenomenology* 38 (2008): 41–71.

29. Fuchs, 'Body Memory and the Unconscious', 73.
30. Fuchs, 'The Cyclical Time of the Body', 54.
31. R. D. Romanyshyn, 'Phenomenology and psychoanalysis', *Psychoanalytic Review* 64 (1977): 211–23.
32. See Fuchs, 'Body Memory and the Unconscious', 75–6.
33. 'L'homme et l'adversité', in S, 374.
34. PP, 112/96 (trans. mod.).
35. PP, 281/273.
36. EM3 [247]v(32) April or May 1960. I owe this quotation to Emmanuel de Saint Aubert, 'Merleau-Ponty's Conception of the Unconscious in the Late Manuscripts', in *Unconsciousness Between Phenomenology and Psychoanalysis*, ed. Dorothée Legrand and Dylan Trigg (Cham: Springer, 2017), 48. Saint Aubert here already makes the connection between this quotation and the quotation on the unconscious as 'perceptual links'.
37. Fuchs, 'Body Memory and the Unconscious', 80.
38. IP, 245/188.
39. IP, 247/246.
40. Cassirer summarises his general account and refers to this example drawn from von Uexküll in *An Essay on Man: An Introduction to a Philosophy of Human Culture* (New York: Doubleday, 1954), 41–4.
41. Although he did not have access to Merleau-Ponty's *Nature* courses, which were only on the verge of being published, Jacques Colette notes Merleau-Ponty's usage of Cassirer's three systems in an article written in 1994: 'La phénoménologie et l'être naturel. Après Schelling et Cassirer: Merleau-Ponty et les formes symbolique', in *Philosophies de la Nature*, ed. Olivier Bloch (Paris: Éditions de la Sorbonne, 2000).
42. N, 273.
43. N, 289.
44. N, 273.
45. N, 273.
46. PP, 281/273.
47. N, 281.
48. N, 290.
49. Johathan Lear, *Open Minded: Working Out the Logic of the Soul* (Cambridge, MA: Harvard University Press, 1998), 63. On Freud's psychological holism (which crucially includes the unconscious psyche), see *The Interpretation of Dreams*, in *The Standard Edition of the Complete Psychological Works of Sigmund Freud*, vols 4–5, trans. and ed. James E. Strachey (London: Hogarth Press, 1981), 97–100, 104–5, 179, 218–19, 280–4, 307–8, 330, 350–3, 652–3.
50. N, 274, 282, 290.
51. N, 290.
52. N, 274.
53. See SC 196–7. Also refer to Alain Beaulieu, 'Les Démêlés de Merleau-Ponty avec Freud: des pulsions à une psychanalyse de la Nature', *French Studies* 63.3 (2009): 298.
54. Freud, *Three Essays on the Theory of Sexuality*, in *The Standard Edition*, vol. 7, 147–8.
55. Freud, *Three Essays on the Theory of Sexuality*, in *The Standard Edition*, vol. 7, 168.
56. See Konrad Lorenz, *Studies in Animal and Human Behavior*, vol. 1 (Cambridge, MA: Harvard University Press, 1970).
57. N, 249.
58. N, 250.
59. N, 250.
60. N, 250.
61. N, 251.
62. N, 251.
63. N, 251.

64. Freud, *The Ego and the Id*.
65. *Phaedrus*, 246a–254e.
66. N, 252.
67. N, 252.
68. N, 254.
69. N, 254.
70. N, 256.
71. N, 258–9.
72. N, 258.
73. N, 258.
74. N-Corps [91]v. (Manuscript entitled, 'Notes sur le corps'.) For these quotes I am reliant on Emmanuel de Saint Aubert, 'Merleau-Ponty's Conception of the Unconscious in the Late Manuscripts', in *Unconsciousness Between Phenomenology and Psychoanalysis*, ed. Dorothée Legrand and Dylan Trigg (Cham: Springer, 2017), 49–51.
75. N-Corps [91].
76. N-Corps [91]v.
77. N, 259.
78. S, 374.
79. Lear, *Open Minded*, 89–90.
80. Plato, *Protagoras*, 358.
81. I would, however, contend the divided will in St Paul and St Augustine is one exception to this and is perhaps closer to what Freud in the end systematises than to Socrates.
82. For a longer exposition of this point, see Lear, *Open Minded*, 80–122.
83. Lear, *Open Minded*, 88.
84. Marc Richir, *Phénoménologie et institution symbolique* (Montbonnot-Saint-Martin: J. Millon, 1988), 36.
85. Richir, *Phenéménologie et institution symbolique*, 147.
86. N, 376.
87. Edward S. Casey, 'Unconscious Mind and Prereflective Body', in *Merleau-Ponty, Interiority and Exteriority, Psychic Life and the World*, ed. Dorothea Olkowski and James Morley (Albany: SUNY Press, 1999), 47.
88. Casey, 'Unconscious Mind and Prereflective Body', 51. Cf. PP, 204/192: 'the body expresses total existence, not because it is an external accompaniment to that existence, but because existence realizes itself in the body. This incarnate significance is the central phenomenon of which body and mind, sign and significance are abstract moments.'
89. Casey, 'Unconscious Mind and Prereflective Body', 51.
90. PP, 204/192.
91. Casey, 'Unconscious Mind and Prereflective Body', 53.
92. Preface to the fourth edition of *Three Essays on the Theory of Sexuality*, in *The Standard Edition*, vol. 7, 134: 'The enlarged sexuality of psychoanalysis coincides with the eros of the divine Plato.'
93. Jonathan Lear particularly emphasises the Platonic aspects of Freudian theory in several of his essays in *Open Minded: Working Out the Logic of the Soul*.
94. N-Corps [91]v and Natu3, p. 352/284. He claims that 'A philosophy of the flesh finds itself in opposition to any interpretation of the unconscious in terms of "unconscious representations," a tribute paid by Freud to the psychology of his day. The unconscious is sensing itself, since sensing is not the intellectual possession of "what" is sensed, but a dispossession of ourselves in favor of it, an opening toward that which we do not have to think in order that we may recognize it'. *Résumés de cours. Collège de France, 1952–1960* (Paris: Gallimard, 1968). Translated by John O'Neill as 'Themes from the Lectures at the Collège de France 1952–1960', in *In Praise of Philosophy and Other Essays* (Evanston, IL: Northwestern University Press, 1988), 178–9/198.

Conclusion

The Dream of Nature

The elemental turn is triggered, perhaps inevitably, at the moment that phenomenology recovers a logic of appearance. With Husserl's anti-Copernican revolution, we retrieve not only the sense of the earth as Earth. We also bring nature and appearance back together and thereby re-establish the Presocratic dynamism of *physis* and the prime element. Merleau-Ponty never rigorously distinguished between elemental imaginaries in the way I proposed in Chapter 4. He used the idea of the elemental to combat philosophies of reflection, like that of Sartre, and did not explicitly separate his conception from other elemental philosophies within phenomenology, whether that of Husserl, Heidegger or Levinas. In his 1959 lectures on Heidegger,[1] Merleau-Ponty does not distinguish his own elemental philosophy from Heidegger's horizonal thinking of earth and sky. Indeed, he often remains captive to the phenomenological horizon[2] as we saw at the end of the last chapter: the phenomenological unconscious as something that bends consciousness around what it does not want to know is a horizonal definition of the unconscious. His most radical late thinking, however, opens up an elemental operation that challenges the limits of the horizon imposes on phenomenality. Being breaches the surface of the aquatic element that withdraws from it. The upward thrust of this movement breaks away from the horizonal and the horizontal.

So long as the elemental imaginary is constrained to the logic of the horizon, perception is limited to the domain of knowing, for the union of earth and sky determine our field of vision. The horizon does not explain how we participate in that perceptual field. Nor can it account for the process of appearing, which is the very process of coming to be. Horizonal thinking keeps open the gap between the one who views the world and a world that is already individuated and fixed. By insisting on the originary togetherness of vision with the visible, Merleau-Ponty makes being perceptual all the way down and vision something that extends the visible. Perceptibility becomes an elemental power and ontologically basic. This can only be understood if we surpass horizonal thinking through the aquatic operation by which the visible becomes vision. The relationship between perceiving and the perceptual realm must be reconfigured along these lines. We now have the concepts to do it. The perceptual realm is the realm of *physis*, and perceiving is a symbolic repetition of the perceptual (and thus a second *physis*). No longer merely an act of knowing, perception unites being with making. Perception becomes ontologically basic to the degree that it takes part in the creativity of *physis*. It is the movement of the perceptual milieu into its future. This has led us to a formulation of being-as-symbol in the Schellingian sense. Only a natural symbolism expresses the inner tension of existence in its perpetual act of self-creation. Once we take on this Schellingian understanding of symbol, we cannot but link the operative non-being of the aquatic to the operation of a natural symbolism, for the symbol is just such a generation of being through a primordial negation of its barbarian source. The physis-element dyad is thus a symbolism par excellence.

Merleau-Ponty returns to an elemental ontology only so far as it reveals itself as a 'perceptual cosmogony' (see Introduction, section 6). Vision is a symbolic repetition of the visible milieu. Vision negates its own visibility, but rises upon the power of the visible, its mother. Philosophy likewise can now be grasped as a symbolic repetition of its own natal milieu – mythology. As phenomenology returns to a thinking of the indestructible togetherness of appearance and logos, it repeats the mythological dynamics by which primordial chthonic deities engender a world. No longer can we suppose that the first philosophers merely mimicked the structures of mythology when they spoke of the prime element and *physis*. No longer can we adhere to philosophy's self-congratulatory tale about its own overcoming of mythical superstition. In the aftermath of phenomenology, philosophy circles back from its self-assertion *against* the mythological modes of thinking that birthed it in order to rethink the very nature of that birthing. If it is not the case that philosophy merely mined the mythical for a hidden content, could we say instead that the mythical is what granted the gift of philosophy and did so precisely through its own withdrawal into the immemorial past, that is to say, through the operation of *physis* within it? We would need to conceive a more energetic relationship of the philosophic to the mythic, a relationship in which the mythic is understood as the unconscious of philosophy and philosophy as mythology's energetic discharge – its dream-symbol. *Physis* is both the term and the operation by which philosophy comes into existence. Philosophy, conversely, is the discourse that then gives us the concept of nature.

And nature still haunts the dream of the philosopher, for the philosopher is the one – perhaps the only one – who still dreams of a unifying principle. When Merleau-Ponty reunites ontology and perception, he brings philosophy back to its dream, which is the biggest possible dream, the dream of nature. But it is no longer clear who dreams first, for Merleau-Ponty's aquatic ontology leads to a radical reversal. Nature itself imagines. Nature itself dreams. Our images and concepts are but a participation in the symbolic formations which are nothing less than the wild imaginings of nature. And this is a starting point for understanding what Merleau-Ponty meant when he called for a 'psychoanalysis of Nature' as 'the flesh, the mother'.[3] If philosophy is indeed nature's dream-symbol and psychoanalysis begins in dream interpretation, wouldn't a psychoanalysis of nature start with a psychoanalysis of philosophy? Then we might finally recognise that it is not we who dream of nature, but nature who dreams in us.

Notes

1. 'La philosophie aujourd'hui', NC, 91–148. For a more detailed analysis of these lectures, please refer to Wayne Froman, 'Merleau-Ponty's 1959 Heidegger Lectures: The Task of Thinking and the Possibility of Philosophy Today', *Chiasmi International 5: Le réel et l'imaginaire* (2003): 29–40.
2. In the lectures on Heidegger, he particularly notes the connection of the horizon to the elemental without distinguishing it from his own conception: 'It is as milieu that the horizon itself is "element".' NC, 112. Refer back to Chapter 4, section 2 for my own exposition of this convergence of horizon with a concept of the elemental.
3. N, 315/267.

Works cited

Maurice Merleau-Ponty — Additional texts (non-abbreviated)

Causeries, 1948. Edited with notes by Stéphanie Ménasé. Paris: Seuil, 2002. [*The World of Perception*. Translated by Oliver Davis. London: Routledge, 2004.]
La Nature ou le monde du silence. Edited by Emmanuel de Saint Aubert. Paris: Hermann, 2008.
'Notes sur le corps'. Unpublished Manuscript, Bibliothèque Nationale Française, Paris. Merleau-Ponty collection, Volume XVII.
'Preface to Hesnard's *L'Oeuvre de Freud*'. Translated by Alden Fisher in *Review of Existential Psychology and Psychiatry* 18.1–3 (1982–3).
'Le primat de la perception et ses conséquences philosophique', *Bullétin de la société française de philosophie* 49 (1947).
Résumés de cours. Collège de France, 1952–1960. Paris: Gallimard, 1968. ['Themes from the Lectures at the Collège de France 1952–1960'. In *In Praise of Philosophy and Other Essays*. Translated by John O'Neill. Evanston, IL: Northwestern University Press, 1988.]

Other works cited

Alberti, Leon Battista. *On Painting*. Translated and introduction by John R. Spenser. New Haven, CT: Yale University Press, 1966.
Alloa, Emmanuel. *La résistance du sensible: Merleau-Ponty critique de la transparence*. Éditions Kimé: Paris, 2008.
Al-Saji, Alia. '"A Past Which Has Never Been Present": Bergsonian Dimensions in Merleau-Ponty's Theory of the Prepersonal', *Research in Phenomenology* 38 (2008): 41–71.
Aristotle, *The Complete Works*, 2 vols. Edited by Jonathan Barnes. Princeton, NJ: Princeton University Press, 1984.
Baas, Bernard. *De la chose à l'objet: Jacques Lacan et la traversée de la phénoménologie*. Leuven: Peeters, 1998.
Bachelard, Gaston. *L'activité rationaliste de la physique contemporaine*. Paris: PUF, 1951.
———. *L'eau et les rêves*. Paris: José Corti, 1942.
———. *La Terre et les reveries de la volunté: essai sur l'imagination de la matière*. Paris: Corti, 2003.

Badiou, Alain. *Deleuze: The Clamor of Being*. Minneapolis: University of Minnesota Press, 2000.
Barbaras, Renaud. *The Being of the Phenomenon: Merleau-Ponty's Ontology*. Bloomington: Indiana University Press, 2004.
———. *Le tournant de l'expérience. Recherches sur la philosophie de Merleau-Ponty*. Paris: Vrin, 1998.
Bataille, Georges. *Œuvres complètes*, vol 8. Paris: Gallimard, 1976.
———. *The Unfinished System of Nonknowledge*. Edited by Stuart Kendell. Minneapolis: University of Minnesota Press, 2001.
Beach, Edward Allen. *The Potencies of God(s): Schelling's Philosophy of Mythology*. Albany: SUNY Press, 1994.
Beaulieu, Alain. 'Les Démêlés de Merleau-Ponty avec Freud: des pulsions à une psychanalyse de la Nature', *French Studies* 63.3 (2009): 295–307.
Biancu, Stefano. 'Competing Paradigms: A Century of Humanism and *homo symbolicus*', *Munera* (2019): 111–27.
———. 'Le symbole donne (encore) à penser', *Revue de théologie et de philosophie* 148 (2016): 755–67.
Bishop, Jeffrey P. *The Anticipatory Corpse: Medicine, Power, and the Care of the Dying*. Notre Dame, IN: Notre Dame University Press, 2011.
Böhme, Jacob. *Concerning the Three Principles of Divine Essence*. Translated by John Sparrow. London: John M. Watkins, 1910.
Brisson, Luc. 'Les théogonies Orphiques et le papyrus de Derveni: notes critiques', *Revue de l'Histoire des Religions* 202 (1985): 389–420.
Brown, Robert F. *Schelling's Treatise on 'The Deities of Samothrace': A Translation and an Interpretation*. Missoula, MO: Scholars Press, 1977.
Capobianco, Richard. *Heidegger's Being: The Shimmering Unfolding*. Toronto: University of Toronto Press, 2022.
Carbone, Mauro. *La chair des images*. Paris: Vrin, 2011.
Cariou, Marie, et al., eds. *Merleau-Ponty aux frontières de l'invisible*. Milan: Associazione Culturale Mimesis, 2003.
Carlson, Thomas A. *The Indiscrete Image: Infinitude and Creation of the Human*. Chicago: Chicago University Press, 2008.
Casey, Edward S. *Getting Back into Place*. 2nd ed. Bloomington: Indiana University Press, 2009.
———. 'Unconscious Mind and Prereflective Body'. In *Merleau-Ponty, Interiority and Exteriority, Psychic Life and the World*. Edited by Dorothea Olkowski and James Morley. Albany: SUNY Press, 1999.
Cassirer, Ernst. *An Essay on Man: An Introduction to a Philosophy of Human Culture*. New York: Doubleday, 1954.
———. *Philosophy of Symbolic Forms II: Mythical Thought*. Translated by Ralph Manheim. New Haven, CT: Yale University Press, 1955.
Chrétien, Jean-Louis. *The Unforgettable and the Unhoped For*. Translated by Jeffrey Bloechl. New York: Fordham University Press, 2012.
Claudel, Paul. *Art Poétique*. Paris: Mercure de France, 1929.
Coleridge, Samuel Taylor. *Literary Remains*, vol 2. Edited by H. N. Coleridge. London: Pickering, 1839.
Colette, Jacques. 'La phénoménologie et l'être naturel. Après Schelling et Cassirer: Merleau-Ponty et les formes symbolique', 433–41. In *Philosophies de la Nature*. Edited by Olivier Bloch. Paris: Éditions de la Sorbonne, 2000.
Creuzer, Georg Friedrich. *Symbolik und Mythologie der alten Völker, besonders der Griechen: in Vorträgen und Entwürfen*. Leipzig and Darmstadt: Leske, 1810.
Curd, Patricia, ed. *A Presocratic Reader*. Indianapolis: Hackett Publishing, 2011.
Dalbiez, Roland. *Psychoanalytic Method and the Doctrine of Freud*. Translated by T. F. Lindsay. London: Longmans, Green & Co., 1941.

Dante Alighieri. *Inferno*. Translated by Mark Musa. New York: Penguin, 2003.
Deleuze, Gilles. *Desert Islands and Other Texts*. Los Angeles: Semiotexte, 2004.
———. *Difference and Repetition*. Translated by Paul Patton. New York: Columbia University Press, 1994.
———. 'From Sacher-Masoch to Masochism'. Translated by Christian Kerslake, *Angelaki* 9.1 (2004): 125–33.
———. 'Michel Tournier and World without others', *Economy and Society* 13.1 (1984): 52–71.
De Man, Paul. *Blindness and Insight: Essays in the Rhetoric of Contemporary Criticism*. 2nd ed. London: Methuen, 1983.
Derrida, Jacques. *Khora*. Paris: Galilée, 1993.
Descartes, René. *Œuvres philosophiques, Tome I: 1618–1637*. Edited by Ferdinand Alquié. Paris: Éditions Garnier, 1988.
———. *Œuvres philosophiques, Tome II: 1638–1642*. Edited by Ferdinand Alquié. Paris: Éditions Garnier, 1967.
Dillon, M. C. *Semiological Reductionism: A Critique of the Deconstructionist Movement in Postmodern Thought*. Albany: SUNY Press, 1995.
Dufour, Dany-Robert Dufour. 'Lacan et le miroir sophianique du Boehme'. Paris: Éditions et publications de l'École lacanienne, 1998.
Duportail, Guy Félix. 'Le Chiasme d'une amitié: Lacan et Merleau-Ponty', *Chiasmi International 6* (2005): 345–67.
Dufourcq, Annabelle. *Merleau-Ponty: une ontologie de l'imaginaire*. Dordrecht: Springer, 2012.
Eliade, Mircea. *Le mythe de l'éternel retour*. Paris: Gallimard, 1949.
Falque, Emmanuel. *Ça n'a rien à voir: Lire Freud en philosophie*. Paris: Cerf, 2018.
———. 'Éthique du corps épandu', *Revue d'éthique et de théologie morale* 288 (2016): 53–82.
———. *The Loving Struggle: Phenomenological and Theological Debates*. London: Rowman & Littlefield, 2018.
———. 'Principe barbare et il y a', *Revista Portuguesa de Filosofia* 78.3 (2022): 673–96.
———. *The Wedding Feast of the Lamb: Eros, the Body, and the Eucharist*. New York: Fordham University Press, 2016.
Ffytche, Matt. *The Foundation of the Unconscious: Schelling, Freud, and the Birth of the Modern Psyche*. Cambridge: Cambridge University Press, 2012.
Fink, Eugene. *Play as Symbol of the World and Other Writings*. Translated by Ian Alexander Moore and Christopher Turner. Bloomington: Indiana University Press, 2010.
Foucault, Michel. *Discipline and Punish*. Translated by Alan Sheridan. New York: Pantheon, 1977.
Franck, Didier Franck. *Chair et corps: Essai sur la phénoménologie de Husserl*. Paris: Minuit, 1981.
Freud, Sigmund. *The Ego and the Id: The Standard Edition*. New York: Norton, 1960.
———. *Neue Folge der Vorlesungen zur Einführung in die Psychoanalyse*. Frankfurt: Fischer, 1940.
———. *New Introductory Lectures on Psychoanalysis*. New York: Carlton House, 1933.
———. *The Standard Edition of the Complete Psychological Works of Sigmund Freud*. Edited by James E. Strachey. London: Hogarth Press, 1981.
Froman, Wayne. 'Merleau-Ponty's 1959 Heidegger Lectures: The Task of Thinking and the Possibility of Philosophy Today', *Chiasmi International 5: Le réel et l'imaginaire* (2003): 29–40.
Fuchs, Thomas. 'Body Memory and the Unconscious'. In *Founding Psychoanalysis Phenomenologically: Theory of Subjectivity and the Psychoanalytic Experience*. Edited by Dieter Lohmar and Jagna Brudzinska. Dordrecht: Springer, 2012.
———. 'The Cyclical Time of the Body and its Relation to Linear Time', *Journal of Consciousness Studies* 25 (2018): 47–65.

Gadamer, Hans-Georg and Karen Campbell, 'Heidegger and the History of Philosophy', *The Monist* 64.4 (1981): 440.
Galison, Peter. 'Descartes' Comparisons: From the Invisible to the Visible', *Isis* 17.2 (1984): 311–26.
Gasché, Rodolphe. *Of Minimal Things: Studies on the Notion of Relation*. Stanford, CA: Stanford University Press, 1999.
Goethe, Johann Wolfgang. 'Über die Gegenstände der bildenden Kunst'. In B. A. Sørensen, ed. *Allegorie und Symbol: Texte zur Theorie des dichterischen Bildes im 18. Und frühen 19. Jahrhundert*. Frankfurt am Main: Athenum, 1972.
Grant, Iain Hamilton. *Philosophies of Nature after Schelling*. London: Continuum, 2008.
———. 'The Remains of the World: Grounds and Powers in Schelling's Later Naturphilosophie', *Schelling Studien* 1 (2014): 3–24.
Guthrie, W. K. C. *Orpheus and Greek Religion*. London: Methuen & Co. Ltd, 1935.
Hadot, Pierre. *Le voile d'Isis: Essai sur l'histoire de l'idée de nature*. Paris: Gallimard, 2004.
Hamrick, William S. and Jan Van der Veken. *Nature and Logos: A Whiteheadian Key to Merleau-Ponty's Fundamental Thought*. Albany: SUNY Press, 2011.
Heckmann, Reinhard, Hermann Krings, and Rudolf W. Meyer, eds. *Natur und Subjektivität: zur Auseinandersetzung mit der Naturphilosophie des jungen Schelling*. Stuttgart-Bad Cannstatt: Fromann-Holzboog, 1985.
Heidegger, Martin. *Basic Questions of Philosophy*. Bloomington: Indiana University Press, 1994.
———. *Being and Time*. Translated by John Macquarrie and Edward Robinson. San Francisco: Harper, 1962.
———. *De l'origine de l'œuvre d'art. Première version (1935)*. Edited and translated by Emmanuel Martineau. Paris: Authentica, 1987.
———. *Gesamtausgabe 6.2 Nietzsche, II (1939–1946)*. Frankfurt: Klostermann, 1997.
———. *Poetry, Language, Thought*. Translated by Albert Hofstadter. New York: Harper & Row, 1971.
———. *The Principle of Reason*. Translated by R. Lilly. Bloomington: Indiana University Press, 1991.
———. *Questions I et II*. Translated into French by Axelos et al. Paris: Gallimard, 1990.
Henry, Michel. *Phénoménologie matérielle*. Paris: PUF, 1990.
Heraclitus, *Fragments*. Edited and translated by T. M. Robinson. Toronto: University of Toronto Press, 1987.
Herr, Lucien. 'Hegel', *Grande Encyclopedie*, vol. XIX (p. 99), reprinted in *Choix d'écrits*, vol. 2 (Paris: Rieder, 1932), 109–46.
Hesiod. *Theogony*. Translated by Glenn W. Most. Cambridge, MA: Harvard University Press, 2006.
Himanka, Juha. 'Husserl's Argumentation for the Pre-Copernican View of the Earth', *The Review of Metaphysics* 58.3 (2005): 621–44.
Homer. *The Iliad*. Translated by Peter Green. Oakland: University of California Press, 2015.
Hopkins, Gerard Manley. *The Major Works*. Oxford: Oxford University Press, 2009.
Husserl, Edmund. *L'Arche-originaire terre ne se meut pas*. Paris: Les Éditions de minuit, 1989.
———. *The Idea of Phenomenology*. Translated by William P. Alston and George Nakhnikian. Dordrecht: Kluwer Academic Publishers, 1964.
———. *Ideas Pertaining to a Pure Phenomenology and to a Phenomenological Philosophy – First Book: General Introduction to a Pure Phenomenology*. Translated by F. Kersten. The Hague: Kluwer Academic Publishers Group, 1983.
———. *Ideas Pertaining to a Pure Phenomenology and to a Phenomenological Philosophy. Second Book: Studies in the Phenomenology of Constitution*. Translated by Richard Rojcewicz and André Schuwer. Dordrecht: Kluwer, 1990.

———. *Logical Investigations*. 2nd ed. 2 vols. Edited by Dermot Moran. London: Routledge, 2001.
———. *Shorter Works*. Edited by Peter McCormick and Frederick A. Elliston. South Bend, IN: University of Notre Dame Press, 1981.
Janicaud, Dominique, ed. *Phenomenology and the 'Theological Turn': The French Debate*. Translated by Bernard Prusak. New York: Fordham University Press, 2000.
Jankélévitch, Vladimir. *L'odyssée de la conscience dans la dernière philosophie de Schelling*. Paris: F. Alquin, 1933.
Jaspers, Karl. *Schelling: Grosse und Verhängnis*. München: Piper Verlag, 1955.
Jeannière, Abel. *La pensée d'Héraclite d'Éphèse et la vision présocratique du monde*. Paris: Aubier, 1959.
Johnson, Galen A. 'The Problem of Origins: In the Timber Yard, Under the Sea'. *Chiasmi International 2: De la nature à l'ontologie* (2000): 249–57.
Jung, Carl Gustav. *The Collected Works of C. G. Jung*. Translated by R. F. C. Hull. Edited by Herbert Read, et al. Princeton, NJ: Princeton University Press, 1953–83.
Kearney, Richard. *Strangers, Gods, and Monsters: Interpreting Otherness*. London: Routledge, 2002.
Kelley, Andrew. 'Jankélévitch and Levinas on the "Wholly Other"', *Levinas Studies* 8.1 (2013): 23–43.
Kerslake, Christian. *Deleuze and the Unconscious*. London: Continuum, 2007.
Knight, Taylor. 'In a Mirror and an Enigma: Nicholas of Cusa's *De visione Dei* and the Milieu of Vision', *Sophia* 59 (2020).
Koyré, Alexandre. *La Philosophie de Jacob Böhme*. Paris: Vrin, 1929.
Krell, David Farrell. *Contagion: Sexuality, Disease, and Death in German Idealism and Romanticism*. Bloomington: Indiana University Press, 1998.
Lacan, Jacques. *Écrits: The First Complete Edition in English*. Translated by Bruce Fink. New York: W. W. Norton and Company, 2006.
———. *The Seminar of Jacques Lacan, Book XI: The Four Fundamental Concepts of Psychoanalysis, 1964*. Edited by Jacques-Alain Miller. Translated by Alan Sheridan. New York: W. W. Norton and Company, 1977.
Larison, Mariana. *L'Être en forme: Dialectique et phénoménologie dans la dernière philosophie de Merleau-Ponty*. Sesto S. Giovanni: Éditions Mimesis, 2016.
Lawlor, Leonard. *The Implications of Immanence: Toward a New Concept of Life*. New York: Fordham University Press, 2006.
———. *Thinking through French Philosophy: The Being of the Question*. Bloomington: Indiana University Press, 2003.
Lear, Jonathan, *Open Minded: Working Out the Logic of the Soul*. Cambridge, MA: Harvard University Press, 1998.
Legrand, Dorothée and Dylan Trigg. *Unconsciousness between Phenomenology and Psychoanalysis*. Cham: Springer, 2017.
Leibniz, Gottfried Wilhelm. *Philosophical Papers and Letters*. 2nd ed. Edited and translated by Leroy E. Loemker. Dordrecht: Kluwer Academic Publishers, 1989.
Levinas, Emmanuel. *De l'existence à l'existant*. Paris: Vrin, 2013.
———. *Totality and Infinity: An Essay on Exteriority*. Translated by Alphonso Lingis. Pittsburgh: Duquesne University Press, 1996.
Lorenz, Konrad. *Studies in Animal and Human Behavior*, vol. 1. Translated by Robert Martin. Cambridge, MA: Harvard University Press, 1970.
Löwith, Karl. *Nietzsche's Philosophy of the Eternal Recurrence of the Same*. Translated by J. Harvey Lomax. Berkeley: California University Press, 1997.
Macauley, David. *Elemental Philosophy: Earth, Air, Fire, and Water as Environmental Ideas*. Albany: SUNY Press, 2010.
McGrath, S. J. 'Schelling on the Unconscious', *Research in Phenomenology* 40 (2010): 72–91.
McIntyre, Ronald. 'Husserl and the Representational Theory of Mind', *Topoi* 5 (1986): 101–13.

Macke, Frank. 'Body, Liquidity and Flesh: Bachelard, Merleau-Ponty, and the Elements of Interpersonal Communication', *Philosophy Today* 51.4 (2007): 401–15.
Marion, Jean-Luc. *In Excess: Studies of Saturated Phenomena.* Translated by Robyn Horner and Vincent Berraud. New York: Fordham University Press, 2002.
———. *On the Ego and On God: Further Cartesian Questions.* Translated by Christina M. Gschwandtner. New York: Fordham University Press, 2007.
Matthews, Bruce. *Schelling's Organic Form of Philosophy.* Albany: SUNY, 2011.
Meillassoux, Quentin. *Après la finitude: Essai sur la nécessité de la contingence.* Paris: Éditions de Seuil, 2006.
Merleau-Ponty, Maurice, ed. *Les philosophes célèbres.* Paris: Éditions Mazenod, 1956.
———, ed. *Les philosophes de l'Antiquité au XXe siècle.* Revised and expanded by Jean-François Balaudé. Paris: Librairie générale française, 2006.
Mitchell, Andrew J. *The Fourfold: Reading the Late Heidegger.* Evanston, IL: Northwestern University Press, 2015.
Mulhall, Stephen. *On Being in the World: Wittgenstein and Heidegger on Seeing Aspects.* London: Routledge, 1990.
Neumann, Erich. *The Origin and History of Consciousness.* Translated by R. F. C. Hull. Princeton, NJ: Princeton University Press, 2014.
Noble, Stephen. 'Entre le silence des choses et la parole philosophique: Merleau-Ponty, Fink, et les paradoxes du langage', *Chiasmi International 6: Entre Esthétique et psychanalyse* (2005): 111–46.
Philipse, Hermann. 'Transcendental Idealism'. In *The Cambridge Companion to Husserl.* Edited by Barry Smith and David W. Smith. Cambridge: Cambridge University Press, 1995.
Plato. *Complete Works.* Edited by John M. Cooper. Indianapolis: Hackett, 1997.
Plotinus, *Ennead IV.* Translated by A. H. Armstrong. Cambridge, MA: Harvard University Press, 1984.
Renault, Alexandra. 'Merleau-Ponty et Lacan: un dialogue possible?' In Marie Cariou et al., eds. *Merleau-Ponty aux frontières de l'invisible.* Milan: Associazione Culturale Mimesis, 2003.
Renaut, Alain. 'La nature aime se cacher', *Revue de métaphysique et de morale* 81.1 (1976): 62–111.
Richir, *Phénoménologie et institution symbolique.* Montbonnot-Saint-Martin: J. Millon, 1988.
Romano, Claude. *Event and World.* Translated by Shane MacKinley. New York: Fordham University Press, 2009.
Romanyshyn, R. D. 'Phenomenology and psychoanalysis', *Psychoanalytic Review* 64 (1977): 211–23.
Rorty, Richard. *Philosophy and the Mirror of Nature.* Oxford: Blackwell, 1980.
Rudhardt, Jean. *Le thème de l'eau primordiale dans la mythologie grecque.* Berne: Éditions Franke, 1971.
Saint Aubert, Emmanuel de. *Du lien des êtres aux éléments de l'être. Merleau-Ponty au tournant des années 1945–1951.* Paris: Vrin, 2004.
———. *Être et Chair: Du corps au désir. L'habilitation ontologique de la chair.* Paris: Vrin, 2013.
———. *Le Scénario cartésien. Recherches sur la formation et la cohérence de l'intention philosophique de Merleau-Ponty.* Paris: Vrin, 2005.
———. *Vers une ontologie indirecte. Sources et enjeux critiques de l'appel à l'ontologie chez Merleau-Ponty.* Paris: Vrin, 2006.
Sallis, John. *The Return of Nature.* Indianapolis: Indiana University Press, 2016.
Sandars, N. K., trans. *Poems of Heaven and Hell from Ancient Mesopotamia.* Baltimore: Penguin, 1970.
Sartre, Jean-Paul. *L'être et le néant.* Paris : Gallimard, 1976.
Schelling, F. W. J. *Les Ages du monde.* Followed by *Les Divinités de Samothrace.* Translated by Samuel Jankélévitch. Paris: Aubier, 1949.

———. *The Ages of the World*. Translated by Jason Wirth. Albany: SUNY Press, 2000.
———. *Die Weltalter, Urfassungen*. Edited by Manfred Schröter. Munich: Biederstein/Leibniz, 1946.
———. *Essais*. Translated and edited by Samuel Jankélévitch. Paris: Aubier, 1946.
———. *First Outline of a System of the Philosophy of Nature*. Translated by Keith R. Peterson. Albany: SUNY Press, 2004.
———. *Grundelegung der Positiven Philosophie*. Torino: Bottega d'Erasmo, 1972.
———. *Historical-critical Introduction to the Philosophy of Mythology*. Translated by Mason Richey and Markus Zisselsberger. Albany: SUNY Press, 2007.
———. *Ideas for a Philosophy of Nature*. Translated by Errol E. Harris and Peter Heath. Cambridge: Cambridge University Press, 1988.
———. *Philosophical Inquiries into the Nature of Human Freedom*. Translated by James Gutmann. La Salle, IL: Open Court, 2003.
———. *Philosophy of Art*. Translated by D. W. Stott. Minneapolis: Minnesota University Press, 1989.
———. *Schellings Werke: Nach der Originalausgabe in neuer Anordnung*. Edited by Manfred Schröter. Munich: C. H. Beck, 1927.
———. *System of Transcendental Idealism (1800)*. Translated by Peter Heath. Charlottesville: University of Virginia Press, 1978.
———. 'Treatise Explicatory of the Idealism in the "Science of Knowledge"'. In Thomas Pfau, *Idealism and the Endgame of Theory*. Albany: SUNY Press, 1994.
Schulte-Sasse, Jochen, et al., eds. *Theory as Practice: A Critical Anthology of Early German Romantic Writings*. Minneapolis: University of Minnesota Press, 1997.
Scott, Robert, and Henry G. Liddell. *A Lexicon Abridged from Liddell and Scott's Greek-English Lexicon*. Oxford: the Clarendon Press, 1944.
Scott, Walter, trans. *Hermetica I*. Oxford: Clarendon Press, 1924.
Simondon, Gilbert. *L'Individuation à la lumière des notions de forme et d'information*. Grenoble: Millon, 2013.
Sperber, Dan. *Le symbolisme en général*. Hermann, Paris: 1974.
Struck, Peter T. *Birth of the Symbol: Ancient Readers at the Limits of their Texts*. Princeton, NJ: Princeton University Press, 2004.
Thoreau Henry David. 'Walking', *The Atlantic Monthly, A Magazine of Literature, Art, and Politics*. IX (LVI) (June 1862): 657–74.
Tilliette, Xavier. *Schelling: une philosophie en devenir*, vol. 2. Paris: Vrin, 1992.
Toadvine, Ted. 'The Chiasm'. In *The Routledge Companion to Phenomenology*, ed. Sebastian Luft and Søren Overgaard. London: Routledge, 2012.
Toadvine, Ted. "The Elemental Past." *Research in Phenomenology* 44 (2014): 262–279.
———. *Merleau-Ponty's Philosophy of Nature*. Evanston, IL: Northwestern University Press, 2016.
———. 'Natural Time and Immemorial Nature', *Philosophy Today* 53 (2009): 214–21.
Valéry, Paul. *Œuvres de Paul Valéry*. Paris: Éditions du Sagittaire, 1933.
Vasseleu, Cathryn. *Textures of Light: Vision and Touch in Irigaray, Levinas, and Merleau-Ponty*. London: Routledge, 1998.
Wahl, Jean. 'Sein, Wahrheit, Welt', *Revue de métaphysique et de morale* 65.2 (April–June 1960): 187–94.
West, M. L. *The Orphic Poems*. Oxford: Clarendon Press, 1983.
Westling, Louise. *The Logos of the Living World*. New York: Fordham University Press, 2013.
Whistler, Daniel. 'Naturalism and Symbolism', *Angelaki* 21.4 (2016): 91–109.
———. 'The New Literalism: Reading After Grant's Schelling', *Symposium* 19.1 (2015): 125–39.
———. 'The Schelling of religious existentialism', *International Journal of Philosophy and Theology*, 80.1–2 (2019): 178–95.
———. *Schelling's Theory of Symbolic Language: Forming the System of Identity*. Oxford: Oxford University Press, 2013.

Whitehead, Alfred North. *The Concept of Nature*. Cambridge: Cambridge University Press, 1920.
Wirth, Jason. 'The Reawakening of the Barbarian Principle'. In *The Barbarian Principle: Merleau-Ponty, Schelling and the Question of Nature*. Edited by Jason Wirth, Albany: SUNY Press, 2013.
Zachhuber, Johannes. 'Physis/Nature'. In *Routledge Companion to Early Christian Philosophy*, 2020.
Zentner, Marcel. *Die Flucht ins Vergessen: die Anfänge der Psychoanalyse Freuds bei Schopenhauer*. Darmstadt: Wissenschaftlichen Buchgesellschaft,1995.
Žižek, Slavoj. *How to Read Lacan*. London: Granta Publishing, 2006.
——. *The Indivisible Remainder: On Schelling and Related Matters*. London: Verson, 1996.

Index

act, 41, 47, 60–71, 74–6; *see also* energeia
air, 9, 29, 35, 73, 86, 98, 102, 167–8
aletheia, 16–17, 19, 26n, 106, 115
Alien (film by Ridley Scott), 174–5, 180
Anaximander, 13, 29, 56n, 98, 102, 108
Anaximenes, 29, 56n
apeiron, 13, 29, 92, 98, 108, 110, 122n, 130, 143–4
Apsu (Babylonian deity), 110
arché, 14–16, 127
Aristotle, 28, 40, 41, 46, 56, 60–76, 78, 81, 93, 98, 106, 113, 117, 138, 140, 142–3, 159, 180
atomism, 28, 76, 78–80, 83, 86–7, 93
axolotl, 42–3, 45–6, 50, 58n, 75, 112, 114

Bachelard, G., 8–9, 19, 35, 48, 51–3, 55, 68, 112, 113, 150–1
Barbaras, R., 4–6, 28–30, 32, 34, 60, 67, 91
barbarian principle, 124, 126–9, 137, 139, 144–5, 149, 154n, 157, 161, 172–4, 176, 179, 181, 192, 213, 218; *see also* être brut/être sauvage
Bataille, G., 163, 182n
Being-seen (*Être-vu*), 30, 47, 52, 54–5
Bergson, H., 18, 32, 35, 148, 193
body
  body memory, 192–5

body schema, 192, 197, 206–8, 213
  extended body, 180
  lived body, 43, 180, 193
  spread body, 180
Böhme, J., 19, 51, 150–1, 155n, 174, 184n
Brentano, F., 60, 189

Cartesianism, 60, 79, 95, 129, 191, 196, 208–10; *see also* Descartes
Casey, E., 10, 210
Cassirer, E., 14, 95, 197–8, 204
causa sui, 144
Cézanne, P., 116–17
chaos, 29, 30, 74–5, 84–5, 89–90, 92–3, 142, 149
Chauvin, R., 202
chiasm, 1, 3, 7, 53, 55, 68–9, 87, 91, 127, 132, 137, 156–69, 172, 174, 178–81, 190, 196, 208, 210–11, 213
Coghill, G., 42, 45
conatus, 165–8
consciousness, 4, 7, 21, 26n, 37, 49–51, 64, 66, 68, 71, 78, 80, 82–6, 88–95, 100–2, 117–18, 136–42, 145–7, 150–1, 154n, 156–61, 164–5, 168, 182n, 185–6, 188–96, 198, 200, 204, 207–11, 213, 217; *see also* mind

contradiction, 13, 47–48, 107, 141–4, 146, 147, 163, 181
contrariety, 142–4
Copernicus, 11–14, 72–3, 102, 217
corpuscularism, 81–3, 86, 92–4
correlationism, 7–8, 126, 136, 145, 158, 161
cosmogony, 15–16, 20–1, 29, 94–5, 98–103, 107–8, 110–12, 114, 116, 119–21, 162, 218
Creuzer, G. F., 130
Cusanus *see* Nicholas of Cusa

Dalbiez, R., 187
Dante, 109
Darwin, 42
de Saint Aubert, E., 60
Deleuze, G., 2, 5, 56, 186, 188
Derrida, J., 2, 4–5, 56
Descartes, R., 2, 71, 74, 76, 77n, 78, 79–81, 83–7, 89–92, 191; *see also* Cartesianism
Diana (Greek goddess), 34
drive, 147, 151, 172, 178–9, 185, 187, 189, 192, 199, 200–2, 205, 207–9, 211–13
Dubarle, R. P., 60
dynamis, 61–2

earth, 9, 11–17, 26n, 30, 33–4, 45, 95, 100–8, 110–11, 113–15, 118, 120, 136, 161–3, 168, 217
écart, 3, 5–7, 21–22, 68, 115, 168–9
Eckhart, M., 51
element *see* air; earth; fire; prime element; sky; water
Empedocles, 28, 56
energeia, 61–2, 70, 76; *see also* act
être brut or *être sauvage*, 76, 79, 92, 94, 112, 124, 191; *see also* barbarian principle
Eudemos, 108

Falque, E., 127–8, 180, 189
Fichte, J. G., 125–6, 138, 141, 146, 154n, 168
finality (final causality), 61, 65, 70–5, 144, 147–8
Fink, E., 169–70, 213
fire, 46, 73, 102, 119, 150, 155n, 174
flesh, 7–9, 14, 19–20, 22, 27n, 30–1, 39, 52–3, 55–6, 60–1, 65–6, 68, 70, 87, 93, 118, 120, 127, 156–8, 180, 205–6, 210, 216n, 219
force, 33, 49, 54, 74–5, 131, 136, 139–40, 143, 145–6, 148–50, 166, 178, 180–1, 186–7, 192, 200, 204, 207–13
form, 3–8, 20–2, 29–31, 33, 36–43, 50–2, 56, 64, 69–70, 74–5, 81, 87, 105, 108, 110, 113–14, 116–17, 120, 125, 128, 130–3, 136, 138, 141, 143–5, 158–9, 173, 186, 188
Foucault, M., 2, 5, 56
freedom, 33, 37, 43, 48, 114, 121, 126–7, 134, 136, 138–42, 144, 147–8, 154n, 168
Freud, S., 3, 7, 42, 185–203, 205, 207–13, 216n
Fuchs, T., 189–90, 192–3

Gaia (Greek deity), 100, 103, 107
Gestalt, 3, 23, 36–42, 56
Gilson, E., 71
Grant, I. H., 3, 125, 127, 139–40
ground, 11, 22, 38, 44, 49, 66–7, 75, 89–90, 92, 100–5, 109, 124, 127–8, 134, 137–51, 154n, 155n, 156, 169, 174, 190, 195–6, 213

Hadot, P., 33–4
Hamlet, 109–10
Hegel, G. W. F., 7, 24n, 71, 96n, 125–6, 131–5, 138, 151, 158

Heidegger, M., 6, 13, 16, 28, 32, 34–5, 46, 55, 82, 102–9, 111, 113–15, 120–1, 217
Heraclitus, 13, 33–6, 41, 44, 46–8, 51, 53–5, 102, 104, 159, 189
Hermes Trismegistus, 19, 118–19
Hesiod, 98, 101, 103, 107, 110
Homer, 103, 107, 110
horizon, 15–16, 103–11, 114–15, 121, 127, 178, 217, 219n
Husserl, Edmund, 1–2, 11–16, 32, 34–5, 64, 66, 68, 76, 78–9, 82–6, 88–94, 102, 111, 139, 182n, 185, 189–92, 209, 213, 214n, 217
hylomorphism, 44, 61, 113, 131, 158, 211

immanence (principle of), 83, 86, 89, 91, 93–4, 164
immemorial past, 18, 22, 136–8, 162–3, 218
individuation, 28, 40, 46, 55, 80–3, 93–4, 114–15, 121, 168, 177–9, 181, 213
instinct, 37, 109, 117, 175, 187, 193, 197–8, 200–9, 211
institution, 3, 68, 132, 156, 160–4
intentionality, 1–2, 60, 66, 68, 70, 74, 79, 82, 84, 89, 188–90, 198, 200
the invisible, 18, 53, 67, 112, 120, 138; *see also* the visible
Ionian philosophy, 9, 28–37, 39, 41, 56, 66, 98, 138
Isis (Egyptian goddess), 34

Jankélévitch, S., 124–5
Jankélévitch, V., 23n, 144–5, 154n, 156, 173
Jaspers, K., 124–5
Jeannière, A., 46–7, 54
Jung, K., 186–8, 191

Kant, I., 1, 3, 7–8, 24n, 82, 94, 126, 132, 135–6, 137, 138–9, 141, 148, 159, 168, 173, 190
khora, 4–5, 140, 156, 176
Klee, P., 116
Krell, D. F., 10, 177

Lacan, J., 173–8, 180, 184n, 209, 213
language, 5, 21, 33, 102, 127, 130–1, 135, 171, 197–9, 206, 209
Lawlor, L., 4–7, 10, 56
Leibniz, G. W., 96n, 132, 164–8
Levinas, E., 1–2, 13, 23n, 32, 102–3, 107–12, 127, 217
libido, 175–6, 178, 180–1, 205, 211
Lorenz, K., 197–204

Maine de Biron, 18, 193
Marchand, A., 116
Marion, J.-L., 153n, 171
matter, 8, 19–20, 22, 30, 41, 42, 44, 55–6, 73, 75, 80–1, 87, 93–4, 96n, 108, 113, 116–18, 120, 122n, 138, 140–3, 146–7, 157–8, 164–8, 173
Meillassoux, Q., 7
metastability, 36, 39–41, 65
mind, 8, 13, 22, 43, 50–1, 64, 65, 78, 80–5, 90–1, 102, 108, 126, 134–6, 138, 145, 147, 154n, 156, 158, 161–2, 164–8, 186, 192, 201, 207–13; *see also* consciousness
mythology, 14, 98–100, 124–5, 132, 134–5, 153n, 169, 218

Narcissus, 51–3, 55, 82n, 66
Naturphilosophie 6, 124–31, 136, 147, 172, 176, 203
negation, 9, 19–20, 42–53, 55, 94, 112, 114–5, 126, 130, 134, 140, 142–6, 151, 158, 172–3, 181, 186, 211, 218
Neoplatonism, 15, 18, 51, 96n, 98, 133–5, 175

INDEX | 231

Nicholas of Cusa, 51, 87
Nietzsche, F., 147
Noah, 14–15
non-being, 55, 58n, 75, 112–15, 121, 126, 134, 142, 175, 181, 206, 218, 17–20, 22, 30, 46–7, 49–50
non-contradiction, principle of, 47
nothingness, 9, 16, 30, 46, 48–51, 58n, 93, 115

Oceanos (Greek deity), 107, 110–11
ontogenesis, 3, 20, 111, 113–15
Orpheus, 98
Ouranos (Greek deity), 100, 103, 107

Parmenides, 6, 13, 28–31, 47, 56
physis, 3, 7, 9, 14, 28–36, 40–1, 44–6, 54–6, 75, 99, 102, 104, 106–7, 112, 114–15, 118, 130–3, 137, 144, 147–8, 164, 173, 181, 199, 206, 217–8
physis kryptesthai philei, 33–4, 36, 45–6, 54, 104, 112
Plato, 3–7, 15–18, 22, 28, 30, 38, 40–2, 47, 71, 111, 134, 139–40, 156, 159, 170, 175, 186, 202, 211
Plotinus, 17–19, 26n
possibility, 15, 18, 37, 41, 44, 56, 62, 72, 74, 75, 118, 120, 135, 140, 143, 206; *see also* dynamis; potency; power
potency, 30, 35, 41, 44, 50, 62–70, 72, 75, 88, 142, 169
power, 6–7, 9–10, 18–19, 26n, 31–2, 35–6, 41, 43–4, 46, 48, 51–2, 55, 56, 61–76, 78–9, 89–94, 98–9, 102, 106, 108, 110, 112, 114, 116, 118–20, 130, 133–5, 137–8, 140–51, 155n, 157–8, 171, 179, 185, 192, 206–7, 218
prime element, 9, 13–14, 28–32, 35, 41, 56, 70, 98–100, 102, 106, 217, 218
Proteus, 29

realism, 7, 34, 69, 90, 91, 117, 126, 158, 162–3, 190
Richir, M., 209–10
Romano, C., 171
Rousseau, J.-J., 173
Rudhardt, J., 110

Sartre, J.-P., 2, 8–9, 16, 48–9, 53, 68, 93, 125, 217
Schelling, 3, 7, 18–20, 31–2, 35, 51, 124–51, 154n, 156, 164, 167–8, 173, 175–80, 185–92, 199, 209, 213, 214n
Schlegel, A. W., 130
Schopenhauer, A., 147, 186
sexuality, 174–81, 188, 201–3, 216n
sign, 24n, 127–32, 157, 169–72, 180, 187
Simondon, G., 28–9, 32, 36, 39–41
sky, 13–15, 95, 100–1, 103–8, 111, 114–15, 96n, 99
Socrates, 4, 208, 216n
soul, 12–13, 17, 19, 26n, 55, 60–5, 71, 173, 188–9, 202, 210
space, 6, 11–12, 15, 29, 67, 69, 71–3, 104, 108–10, 116, 118–20, 146, 163–8, 190, 209
structuralism, 3–7, 131
symbol, 3, 20, 29, 95, 119, 126–33, 137, 144–51, 156–59, 164–81, 187–91, 197–200, 203–13, 218–19
symbolism, 22–3, 127, 137, 167, 171, 181, 185, 188, 191, 198–200, 202–11, 218

tautegory, 127–9, 132, 137, 149, 152n, 158, 169–70, 172, 179
tehom, 110
telos, 65, 70–1, 73–5, 140
Tethys (Greek deity), 107, 110, 121n, 122n

Thales, 13, 29, 55, 56n, 98, 102
Tiamat (Babylonian deity), 110
time, 8, 11, 17, 26n, 54, 57n, 67, 69, 74, 84, 87, 89–90, 115, 117, 137, 154n, 158, 160–4, 166–8, 178, 193
Toadvine, T., 4, 7, 160–3

the unconscious, 7, 102, 132, 134, 136, 141, 147, 185–99, 205–10, 212–13, 215n, 216n, 217–8

Valéry, P., 102, 159
the visible, 16, 18, 53, 55, 66–7, 76, 87, 90, 93, 119–20, 137, 158, 162, 179, 218
vitalism, 37, 148
von Uexküll, J. J., 36, 197, 204

water, 9, 15–22, 27n, 29–30, 35, 45, 50–3, 55, 73, 86, 98, 100–3, 105, 107, 110–21, 150, 162, 168
Whistler, D., 3, 129, 131
Wittgenstein, 83
world egg, 15, 175, 178–9

Žižek, Slavoj, 173–6

EU Authorised Representative:
Easy Access System Europe Mustamäe tee 50, 10621 Tallinn, Estonia
gpsr.requests@easproject.com

Printed and bound by CPI Group (UK) Ltd, Croydon, CR0 4YY
05/03/2026
02065149-0002